INSIDE MARKETING

A Selection of Readings from BUSINESS WEEK

Charles Futrell

Texas A&M University

McGraw-Hill Book Company

New York   St. Louis   San Francisco   Auckland   Bogotá   Hamburg   Johannesburg
London   Madrid   Mexico   Milan   Montreal   New Delhi   Panama
Paris   São Paulo   Singapore   Sydney   Tokyo   Toronto

INSIDE MARKETING
A Selection of Readings from
BUSINESS WEEK

1 2 3 4 5 6 7 8 9 0   D O C D O C   8 9 2 1 0 9 8 7

ISBN   0-07-060951-9

This book was set in Times Roman.
The editors were Sam Costanzo, Elisa Adams and Joseph F. Murphy;
the production supervisor was Joe Campanella.
The designer was Caliber Design Planning, Inc.
R.R. Donnelley & Sons Company was printer and binder.

Library of Congress Catalog Card Number: 87-60241

INSIDE MARKETING

A Selection of Readings from
BUSINESS WEEK

Contents

Preface

As we approach the end of the 1980s, it is increasingly clear that marketing is the name of the game in both business and nonbusiness organizations. Moreover, as we prepare for the 1990s and look forward to the next century, marketing will continue to be where the action is.

Today companies want employees with marketing experience—who understand such concepts as target markets, product life cycles, and market segmentation. These companies are seeking a renewal of the risk-taking, dynamic, entrepreneurial spirit they need if they are to grow and be successful.

In a business firm, marketing generates the revenues that are managed by the financial people and used by the production people in creating products and services. The challenge of marketing is to generate those revenues by satisfying customers' wants at a profit and in a socially responsible manner.

But marketing is not limited to business. Whenever you try to persuade somebody to do something—donate to the Salvation Army, fasten a seat belt, lower a stereo's volume during study hours in the dorm, vote for your candidate, accept a date with you (or maybe even marry you)—you are engaging in a marketing activity. So-called nonbusiness organizations—they really are in business but don't think of themselves as business people—also engage in marketing. Their "product" may be a vacation place they want you to visit, a social cause or an idea they want you to support, a person they are thrusting into the spotlight, or a cultural institution they want you to attend. Whatever the product is, the organization is engaging in marketing.

As you may gather, and as you will read in your text, marketing is a very broad-based activity, and, consequently, it calls for a broad definition. The essence of marketing is a transaction—an exchange—intended to satisfy human needs and wants. That is, marketing occurs anytime one social unit (person or organization) strives to exchange something of value with another social unit. Thus, marketing consists of all activities designed to generate and facilitate any exchange intended to satisfy human needs or wants.

In order to provide you with current, up-to-date information and examples of the many businesses using marketing today, *Business Week* was asked to help. *Business Week* is an authoritative source, capable of providing articles that capture the essence of American marketing practices.

Over the years, *Business Week* articles have been invaluable in helping students to appreciate the reasons for obtaining a background in marketing. The articles help them to see the practical benefits they can derive from the course. What students read helps reinforce the course's material. Students quickly realize that their course is "real-world." It covers what is happening today.

To be selected, articles had to be timely, varied, interesting, thought-provoking, and challenging. And each article had to relate to one or more chapters contained in the various marketing textbooks that might be used by a student.

It is a privilege to have a small part in helping with your course.

Charles Futrell

INSIDE MARKETING

A Selection of Readings from
BUSINESS WEEK

PART 1

MARKETING, ENVIRONMENT, STRATEGY, AND DECISION INFORMATION SYSTEMS

What better way to start a course than to talk about "money"? Annual compensation of America's executives in 1985 was led by Victor Posner ($12,739,000), Lee Iacocca ($11,426,000), and T. Boone Pickens, Jr. ($8,431,000). If you look at the most recent first May issue of *Business Week*, chances are salaries have continued to rise. In 1985 top executives' average salary was $679,000.

Not bad for executives who change their ideas concerning managing so often that their management philosophies have been referred to as "fads." Yet Peters and Waters reported on 43 "excellent" companies whose successes have been based upon eight attributes of "excellence," the second attribute being to learn the customers' preferences and cater to them. This is what marketing is all about.

But some of these 43 companies have fallen on hard times in recent years. Why? There is simply not enough space in this book to expain the reasons for these organizations' drop from stardom. However, all companies today agree that marketing must be a top priority.

More than any time in the history of America, the environment we do business in is influencing the way we produce and market our goods and services, both in the United States and in other countries around the world. Counterfeit products, federal regulations, computers, and our movement from a manufacturing to a service economy continue to emphasize the need for careful analysis of environmental changes and influences on our marketing program.

To compete in the 1980s and to prepare for the 1990s, companies did things in the mid-1980s never done before. Strategic thinking became the "buzz" word. Top executives, such as Lee Iacocca, became "business celebrities" by going directly to consumers and asking for their business via television and print advertisements. And consumers wondered if they got paid for it. Isn't $12 million a year enough for Lee? Only in America.

Even firms like AT&T, Coca-Cola, General Mills, IBM, and Johnson & Johnson, and little Fanny Farmer, have adapted their corporate and marketing strategies to the changing world of business. It appears that big and small firms are increasing their level of customer service in response to the growing intensity of competition. It's about time—don't you think?

To compete in today's ultracompetitive marketplace requires the collection of huge amounts of information. Millions of dollars are now being spent by American corporations to develop state-of-the-art marketing information systems run by computers. Computers are changing the way we do business—whether it's in a supermarket or a bank. High-tech marketing methods are here to stay.

Articles in this section touch on all these things: money, environment, strategy, and information systems. All are necessary to manage an American business. The articles help introduce you to the wonderful world of marketing. Before reading the articles, you may wish to study the article synopses that follow. They provide a capsule overview of the major thrust of each article, plus clues to the underlying principles that can be explored.

PART 1 ARTICLE SYNOPSES

THE FIELD OF MARKETING

EXECUTIVE PAY: HOW THE BOSS DID IN '85	*Business Week*'s 36th annual compensation survey, compiled with Sibson & Co., the Princeton (N.J.) consultants, provides the first comprehensive look at 1985 executive pay. There are several surprises. To begin with, top pay numbers aren't nearly as big as those in years past, when a few entrepreneurs were pulling in $40 million or more. In all, 258 companies listed in the Executive Compensation Scoreboard raised their top executives' salaries and bonuses an average of 9 percent, to $679,000, in 1985. This allowed executives to outstrip easily the year's inflation rate of 3.8 percent.
BUSINESS FADS: WHAT'S IN—AND OUT	American executives these days seem eager to latch onto almost any new concept that promises a quick fix for their problems. There's nothing inherently wrong with this idea. What's wrong is

that too many companies use these business fads to evade their problems and/or challenges.

WHO'S EXCELLENT NOW? According to studies by *Business Week*, management consultants McKinsey & Co., and Standard & Poor's Compustat Services, at least 14 of the 43 "excellent" companies highlighted by Peters and coauthor Robert A. Waterman, Jr., in their book just two years ago have lost their luster.

MARKETING: THE NEW PRIORITY Vast economic and social changes have made better marketing an imperative. Realization of that fact has set off a near free-for-all in recruiting circles for successful marketers, now hotter prospects for high-level jobs than executives with financial experience. Everybody wants a president with marketing experience.

THE MARKETING ENVIRONMENT

THE COUNTERFEIT TRADE Counterfeit trade is perhaps the world's fastest-growing and most profitable business; it involves big dollars and, all too often, the possibility of quiet death. Products now routinely counterfeited include chemicals, computers, drugs, fertilizers, pesticides, medical devices, military hardware, and food, as well as parts for airplanes and automobiles.

THE HOLLOW CORPORATION The United States faces a serious loss of manufacturing productivity as the industrial economy increasingly becomes a service economy, and as more and more manufacturers become marketers for foreign producers. Supporters of the service economy development overlook the need for a continuously growing industrial base to buttress those very services, for example, in high-tech.

STRATEGIC MARKETING PLANNING

BUSINESS CELEBRITIES Many executives are no longer content with making themselves known only on Wall Street and in Washington. The day may soon come when their popularity rivals that of athletes and entertainers. There is evidence of this trend already on television and in magazines.

WHY AT&T ISN'T CLICKING Though AT&T's long-distance operation and equipment sales to phone companies are doing well, these traditional enterprises are not offsetting the operating losses caused by sales of computers and phone systems to businesses and consumers. Observers say that the new CEO, James Olson, will have to make hard decisions in areas of cost cutting, corporate self-understanding, and strategic planning.

GENERAL MILLS STILL NEEDS ITS WHEATIES

In an effort to add vitality to a sales growth well below industry average and a disheartening profit decline, General Mills adopted a strategy of shedding its fashion and toy lines and concentrating on a more traditional line: Big G cereals and the profitable chain of Red Lobster restaurants. Such moves might avert an otherwise tempting takeover deal.

THE NEW BREED OF STRATEGIC PLANNER

This article presents an argument favoring a shift of many strategic planning responsibilities from a formal planning staff to line managers. Perhaps best stated, the intent is to enable managers at all corporate levels who are responsible for the implementation of various parts of a strategic plan to have a heightened role in its development.

THE FUTURE CATCHES UP WITH A STRATEGIC PLANNER

Boston Consulting Group, Inc., or BCG, built a powerhouse reputation as a strategic planning consultant, coining such concepts as "experience curve." But corporate managers, faced with ever more competitive conditions, demand not only brilliant strategies but also ways to implement such ideas through an integrated system of management processes. Strategic analysis has thus come of age, requiring that BCG and other consulting firms adopt a customer-oriented, back-to-basics approach to planning.

UP FROM $4.95 FUDGE: FANNY FARMER TRIES TO BE A *CHOCOLATIER*

Fanny Farmer is upscaling its chocolate to try to ease its chronic losses. Americans are eating chocolate again. However, the company will have a hard time changing its image when faced with big-name competitors.

MARKETING INFORMATION SYSTEMS

INFORMATION POWER

Computers are increasingly being used for more than number crunching. Computers and telecommunication equipment are collecting, interpreting, and distributing information. The personal com-

	puter has had a major impact. The role of the data processing manager has changed.
AT TODAY'S SUPERMARKETS, THE COMPUTER IS DOING IT ALL	Computers are changing the way supermarkets do business. Automation has reduced the workload of managers while increasing the information available.
BANK OF AMERICA RUSHES INTO THE INFORMATION AGE	Until recently, Bank of America had no way of correlating customer information between product lines. Now it is investing heavily in information systems to deal with the marketing and control problems caused by its previous lack of technology.

EXECUTIVE PAY: HOW THE BOSS DID IN '85

THE AVERAGE CORPORATE CHIEF TOOK HOME A HEFTY $1.2 MILLION

MAY 5, 1986, PP. 48-52, 56, 58

The reporter patiently sat through the Apr. 22 press conference in a packed room in the Washington Convention Center. She was waiting for the chance to pop *the* question to the man in the double-breasted, pinstripe suit. Finally, it came: "Mr. Iacocca," she said, "don't you think your compensation . . . is out of line?"

"I'm not a socialist," retorted Chrysler Corp. Chairman Lee A. Iacocca, who was among the highest-paid executives in 1985. "I believe in the American system." In the best theatric style, he waved at his Chrysler colleagues in the front row, many of whom he recruited when the company was on the brink of bankruptcy in 1980. "I had nothing to offer them but stock options," he says. "Our salaries were two-thirds the going rate. Their wives said you can paper a room with them. They lived through this for five to six years. Now they're cashing in. What the hell is wrong with that?"

LEAN YEAR. It's that time of year again—when corporate voyeurs and shareholders peek into densely written proxy statements to find out how much the boss made. The big winners in 1985 are decidedly a mixed lot, from corporate raiders such as Victor Posner and T. Boone Pickens to big business chieftains such as Exxon Corp.'s Clifton C. Garvin Jr. and Rockwell International Corp.'s Robert Anderson.

BUSINESS WEEK's 36th annual compensation survey, compiled with Sibson & Co., the Princeton (N. J.) consultants, provides the first comprehensive look at 1985 executive pay. There are several surprises. To begin with, top pay numbers aren't nearly as big as those in years past, when a few entrepreneurs were pulling in $40 million or more.

Victor Posner, the reclusive Miami Beach financier, leads the list on the basis of his pay from one of his many intertwined companies, *DWG* Corp. But Posner's total compensation of $12.7 million is a mere half of what the 1984 leader pulled down. The top money-maker in last year's survey was Mesa Petroleum Co.'s T. Boone Pickens Jr. He comes in third in the new rankings, right behind Iacocca, who received $11.4 million in total compensation.

In a sophisticated analysis linking recent pay with performance, *BUSINESS WEEK* and Sibson also found that Ethyl Corp. Chairman Floyd D. Gottwald Jr. gave his shareholders the biggest bang for the buck during the past three years. In contrast, Posner delivered the least as chairman of *DWG*, a holding company that includes Royal Crown Cos.

For corporate executives, 1985 was generally a bullish year. Rising stock prices made it a tempting time to exercise stock options, many of which had been accumulated over long careers. Last year, 146 executives entered the Million Dollar Club by earning total compensation of $1 million or more. Five years ago only four executives made that much.

A 37% rise in compensation from long-term incentive plans helped drive up many of these numbers. In fact, pay tied to stock market performance accounted for more than half of the total compensation of the 25 highest-paid executives. All this boosted the average chief executive's pay to $1.2 million.

In all, the 258 companies listed in the Executive Compensation Scoreboard raised their top executives' salaries and bonuses an average of 9%, to $679,000, last year. Although that ended two consecutive years of double-digit raises, it allowed executives to outstrip easily 1985's inflation rate of 3.8%. Those pay increases also looked healthy compared with the meager gains of 5.1% for white-collar workers and 4% for union officials. "We're seeing more moderate increases in pay as a result of increasing sensitivity and criticism of executive pay," says Jude T. Rich, president of Sibson. "A lot of companies have moved toward long-term stock-based plans because they can stand up and more easily defend them. There's no better link between pay and performance than the stock option."

RIDING THE BOOM. Executives who work on Wall Street enjoyed some of the heftiest gains. Of the top 25 earners, in fact, one in five works at an investment banking firm. Among the well-paid financial titans: Phibro-Salomon Inc. Chairman John H. Gutfreund, whose salary and bonus rose by more than a third, to $3.1 million, and First Boston Corp. Chairman Alvin V. Shoemaker, whose pay jumped by 64%, to $2.3 million.

With the market continuing to break records, some of the biggest winnings in executive pay are still to come. Iacocca has been one of the biggest beneficiaries of the bull market. About $9.8 million of his total 1985 pay of $11.4 million was in long-term incentive income. And he is virtually assured of landing on 1986's best-paid list, too.

The man who once worked as Chrysler's chief for a token $1 for 12 months was also promised 300,000 shares of stock, worth some $12.4 million, just to stick around a little longer. Iacocca will collect 225,000 shares by staying until Nov. 2, and he will get the rest if he remains at Chrysler until Dec. 8, 1987. That's not all. He's holding options on an additional 522,000 shares—worth at least $10.9 million—that must be exercised within the next 60 days.

The booming stock market had another important side effect on executive compensation: It allowed companies to activate dozens of golden parachutes for top executives. The winner in that category is Michel C. Bergerac, who left Revlon Inc. last November. The former chairman had a $35 million severance package, making him the executive who collected the most money from a company in 1985 (page 14). If all executives with golden parachutes were included in the highest-paid list, they would dominate it, replacing 5 of the top 10 and 8 of the top 25.

Legislative efforts to rein in some of these big parachute numbers with penalty taxes have had little effect on their popularity. Bergerac's largesse escapes the legislated penalties because it was drawn up seven months before Congress acted in 1984. Some other companies, such as Borg-Warner Corp., have sidestepped the issue by agreeing to reimburse their executives for any additional taxes they end up paying.

So parachutes that provide for generous severance and benefits payouts to key executives whose companies have been acquired are continuing to spread. One recent study found that 21 of the top 100 industrial corporations now report such agreements in their proxy statements, up from a dozen two years ago.

Judging from the compensation figures, some executives are probably wishing that they could have taken the money and run. With corporate profits down last year by 17%, roughly one third of the scoreboard's executives suffered pay cuts. At Wang Laboratories Inc., where net income fell to its lowest level since 1978, Chairman An Wang saw his pay snipped by a third to $405,000. And Monsanto Co., suffering net losses of $98 million last year, cut Chairman Richard J. Mahoney's salary and bonus by 29%, to $500,000.

GOLDEN MISTAKES. Pay cuts, however, didn't always follow lackluster company results. At *AMP* Inc., where net income fell by 46%, Chairman Walter F. Raab more than doubled his salary and bonus last year, to $956,000. *UAL* Inc., racking up

---

> Pay often doesn't make sense. Coke's officers got millions after the most publicized flop of the year

---

losses of $48.7 million, doubled Chairman Richard J. Ferris' pay, to $883,000.

A few fortunate executives were even rewarded for strategic mistakes. Coca-Cola Co. is a case in point. The company's compensation committee granted "performance units" to Chairman Ro-

ETHYL'S GOTTWALD DELIVERS THE MOST FOR HIS MONEY

Unlike his colleagues at other chemical companies, Floyd D. Gottwald Jr., chairman of Ethyl Corp., doesn't earn a gargantuan salary. Nor does he get huge stock option packages or large annual increases. The 63-year-old Southern gentleman doesn't even travel in a company limo.

His austerity apparently has paid off. In the past three years, shareholders of the Richmond (Va.) company have seen their stock more than triple in value, while Gottwald himself has collected just $1.7 million in salary and bonus. That makes him a bargain for shareholders, according to *BUSINESS WEEK*'s pay-performance analysis (page 11).

'CHICKEN FEED.' Gottwald is no pauper among corporate chiefs, however. As the holder of 5.6 million Ethyl shares, which broke the $40 barrier for the first time Apr. 22, he is one of the richest men in America. His Ethyl stock alone is worth $230 million, and last year he pocketed an extra $3.2 million in Ethyl dividends.

When directors of the $1.5 billion company determine Gottwald's pay, they consider his stock profits. Says Lawrence E. Blanchard Jr., an Ethyl director and former vice-chairman: "What the hell's wrong with a little chicken-feed salary if the stock is doing well? So many executives cry poverty and take a 400% pay increase if the company performed well one year. They should get the same percentage raises as the rest of the company."

Gottwald, a 6-ft. jogger and fisherman who rarely grants interviews, abides by that belief, a common one at family-run companies. His is a company dominated by family and longtime employees. In 1943, Gottwald joined his father at Ethyl's predecessor, Albemarle Paper Mfg. Co., a blotting paper maker. The elder Gottwald bought Ethyl in a leveraged buyout in 1962, and his son moved into his chair in 1968. Now two of Floyd Jr.'s three sons work for Ethyl. The Gottwald clan—including Floyd's brother Bruce C. Gottwald, Ethyl's president—controls 17.8% of the 62.9 million outstanding shares. Directors and employees control an additional 15% of the stock.

DEFT MOVES. Thanks to the family's involvement, management has pressed ahead at times when a dispassionate leadership might have given up. Since its inception, the company has deftly maneuvered into new products and out of antiquated ones. The elder Gottwald ditched the original blotting paper business in 1962 and moved into antiknock lead for gasoline. But long-standing regulatory battles over that product forced the company to diversify into plastics for garden hoses, chemicals for computer chips, insurance, and the pain reliever ibuprofen.

Family management—combined with Ethyl's ability to keep earnings growing through diversification—has attracted investors. "They treat the company like it's their own, and it is," says Louis E. Hannen, senior vice-president for research at Wheat, First Securities Inc. in Richmond. "So many hired guns run other companies, and they don't have the equity interest."

But Ethyl hasn't had all smooth sailing. Just last year earnings dipped by 11%, to $117 million, largely because of the sale of the company's antiknock lead plant in Baton Rouge, La. Still, with a return on equity of 15.8%, Ethyl managed to outperform most of its competitors in the chemical industry. As long as Gottwald keeps turning in that kind of performance, he won't have to worry much about a little chicken-feed paycheck.

By Laurie Baum in New York

---

berto C. Goizueta and President Donald R. Keough potentially worth millions of dollars last year. The reason: their "courage, wisdom, and commitment" in introducing new Coke, the most publicized new-product flop of the year.

Goizueta, 54, won't be able to savor any of these benefits until at least 1991 and Keough, 59, not until he retires. On paper, however, they already are worth $6.4 million and $3.5 million, respectively. That's a considerable pop for a product that has fizzled so far. How could Coke's board justify such a generous new benefit?

"They had the courage to put their jobs on the line, and that's rarely done today at major American companies," says Herbert A. Allen, president of Allen & Co. and chairman of Coke's compensation committee. Allen, whose company received nearly $3 million in investment banking fees from Coke subsidiaries in 1985, proposed the award, which was unanimously approved by the board. "It's not controversial at all," adds James B. Wil-

liams, vice-chairman of SunTrust Banks Inc. and a Coke director. "It was a unanimous, happy decision. We've got more market share than we would've had with one [Coke]."

True, Coke increased its U. S. market share by two full percentage points, to 39%, the company's net income was up 15%, and its return on equity, at 23.5%, was the highest in 15 years. Yet the performance units are a totally new benefit on top of existing incentive plans that with salary and bonus allowed Goizueta and Keough to earn $2.2

THE 25 HIGHEST-PAID EXECUTIVES

	Company	1985 salary and bonus	Long-term compensation	Total pay
			Thousands of Dollars	
1. **VICTOR POSNER,** Chmn.	DWG	$12,739		**$12,739**
2. **LEE A. IACOCCA,** Chmn.	Chrysler	1,617	$9,809	**11,426**
3. **T. BOONE PICKENS JR.,** Chmn.	Mesa Petroleum	4,203	4,228	**8,431**
4. **DREW LEWIS,** Chmn.†	Warner Amex	1,000	5,000	**6,000**
5. **ROBERT L. MITCHELL,** Vice-chmn.†	Celanese	700	4,056	**4,756**
6. **SIDNEY J. SHEINBERG,** Pres.	MCA	509	3,975	**4,484**
7. **ROBERT ANDERSON,** Chmn.	Rockwell	1,326	2,310	**3,636**
8. **CLIFTON C. GARVIN JR.,** Chmn.	Exxon	1,454	2,107	**3,561**
9. **DAVID S. LEWIS,** Chmn.	General Dynamics	1,062	2,289	**3,351**
10. **JOHN H. GUTFREUND,** Chmn.	Phibro-Salomon	3,066	140	**3,206**
11. **GEORGE B. BEITZEL,** Sr. v-p†	IBM	608	2,409	**3,017**
12. **ROY A. ANDERSON,** Chmn.	Lockheed	916	2,060	**2,976**
13. **JOSEPH B. FLAVIN,** Chmn.	Singer	660	2,312	**2,972**
14. **PETER A. COHEN,** Chmn.†	Shearson Lehman Brothers	1,704	1,207	**2,911**
15. **MICHAEL D. ROSE,** Chmn.	Holiday	549	2,360	**2,909**
16. **FRANK PRICE,** V-p†	MCA	509	2,385	**2,894**
17. **RICHARD J. SCHMEELK,** Exec. v-p†	Phibro-Salomon	2,640	199	**2,839**
18. **STEVEN J. ROSS,** Chmn.†	Warner Communications	2,800		**2,800**
19. **GERALD GREENWALD,** Vice-chmn.	Chrysler	1,167	1,613	**2,780**
20. **DAVID R. BANKS,** Pres.†	Beverly Enterprises	423	2,355	**2,778**
21. **RICHARD M. FURLAUD,** Chmn.	Squibb	1,050	1,710	**2,760**
22. **HENRY KAUFMAN,** Vice-chmn.	Phibro-Salomon	2,640	120	**2,760**
23. **HAROLD K. SPERLICH,** Pres.†	Chrysler	1,085	1,675	**2,760**
24. **SPENCER SCOTT,** Chmn.†	Citadel Holding	356	2,291	**2,647**
25. **PETER T. BUCHANAN,** Pres.	First Boston	2,300	233	**2,533**

THE 10 BIGGEST GOLDEN PARACHUTES

	Company	What led to payment	Total package* thousands of dollars
1. **MICHEL C. BERGERAC,** Chmn.	Revlon	Pantry Pride takeover	**$35,000**
2. **WILLIAM W. GRANGER JR.,** CEO	Beatrice	leveraged buyout	**6,400**
3. **DAVID E. LIPSON,** CFO	Beatrice	leveraged buyout	**4,270**
4. **LEONARD H. GOLDENSON,** Chmn.	ABC	Capital Cities takeover	**3,820** **
5. **FREDERICK S. PIERCE,** Pres.	ABC	Capital Cities takeover	**3,820** **
6. **JAMES L. DUTT,** CEO	Beatrice	termination	**3,800**
7. **JOHN E. MCCONNAUGHY JR.,** Chmn.	Peabody International	Pullman takeover	**3,700** **
8. **FRANK E. GRZELECKI,** Exec. v-p	Beatrice	leveraged buyout	**2,570** ***
9. **MICHAEL SAYRES,** Sr. v-p	Revlon	Pantry Pride takeover	**2,320** **
10. **SAMUEL I. SIMMONS,** Sr. v-p	Revlon	Pantry Pride takeover	**2,320** **

†Excluded from the Compensation Scoreboard because data were unavailable or because not one of company's two top officers collected—along with parachute payment ** Granted in 1985 but exercised this year *** Partially paid in 1985 * Includes final salary, bonus, and long-term compensation

DATA: SIBSON & CO. AND BUSINESS WEEK

THE 10 CHIEF EXECUTIVES WHO GAVE SHAREHOLDERS THE MOST FOR THEIR PAY . . .

		1983-1985		
		3 years pay* (thousands of dollars)	Total** shareholder return	Pay performance index
1. FLOYD D. GOTTWALD JR.	Ethyl	$1685	288.7%	38
2. JOSEPH L. JONES	Armstrong World Inds.	1151	94.6	42
3. C. EDWARD ACKER	Pan Am	1425	113.8	43
4. WILLIAM J. MCCUNE JR.	Polaroid	1131	83.2	43
5. PHILIP KRAMER	Amerada Hess	1410	14.7	43
6. LEW R. WASSERMAN	MCA	1409	116.0	45
7. EDWARD J. NOHA	CNA Financial	1719	271.2	47
8. R. GORDON MCGOVERN	Campbell Soup	1879	19.6	52
9. FREDERICK W. SMITH	Federal Express	1249	63.3	52
10. PHILIP E. LIPPINCOTT	Scott Paper	1954	166.4	53

. . . AND THE 10 WHO GAVE SHAREHOLDERS THE LEAST

1. VICTOR POSNER	DWG	12,739	−4.3	820
2. T. BOONE PICKENS JR.	Mesa Petroleum	31,729	+ 40.2	645
3. EDSON D. DE CASTRO	Data General	9,999	+ 128.3	353
4. AN WANG	Wang Laboratories	5,340	−32.1	317
5. JOHN SCULLEY	Apple Computer	5,223	−26.4	317
6. LEE A. IACOCCA	Chrysler	17,585	+ 173.1	302
7. JAMES F. BERE	Borg-Warner	7,108	+ 43.6	271
8. CHARLES R. PALMER	Rowan	2,057	−21.5	271
9. WILLIAM S. COOK	Union Pacific	7,141	+ 26.1	259
10. JOHN G. BREEN	Sherwin-Williams	7,163	+ 111.5	238

Note: In calculating superior pay performance, companies with three-year total returns less than the inflation rate are excluded

*Total salary, bonus, and long-term compensation for three years

**Stock price at the end of 1985 fiscal year plus dividends divided by original stock price for three-year period.

DATA: SIBSON & CO, AND STANDARD & POOR'S COMPUSTAT SERVICES INC.

million and $1.2 million, respectively, in total pay last year.

Executive compensation, of course, doesn't always have to make sense. Troubled American Motors Corp., which piled up $125.3 million in losses in 1985, substantially boosted by at least 23% the pay of each of its three top executives. Meantime, Japan's Mazda Motor Corp. and Nissan Motor Corp., concerned about declining profits as a result of the strengthening yen, trimmed top executive pay by 15% and 10%, respectively.

The difference between Japanese and U. S. managers? *AMC* officials maintain that despite the red ink, they made progress toward the company's goal of returning to profitability. Critical to that plan is a new Canadian plant that will produce midsize cars. "Given the choices they had, I think they've done a great job," says Andrew G. C. Sage

II, chairman of *AMC*'s compensation committee and managing director of Shearson Lehman Brothers Inc. "If three years from now we find our Canadian product lays an egg, we won't be talking about how small the raises are, we'll be out looking for new people."

Tough talk. And many experts claim that new programs designed to tie pay more closely to ability are working. Two widely publicized 1984 studies done by business professors at the University of Rochester, in fact, show a link between what executives make and how well shareholders fare.

Some leading compensation experts, however, now suspect that the Rochester data are flawed. One is David Larcker, a well-known compensation guru at the University of Pennsylvania's Wharton School, who studied pay data for 400 companies over a 15-year period. He found a link

POSNER'S SPECTACULAR HAUL— AND DUBIOUS SUCCESS

It was not one of Victor Posner's better years. His Evans Products Co., chafing under a debt of $540 million, filed for Chapter 11. His Sharon Steel Corp., dragged down by $209 million in losses in the past two years, has been scrambling to restructure its debt to avert a similar fate. Short on cash, Posner abandoned raids on National Can Corp. and City Investing Co. And if that weren't enough, he spent the year awaiting trial for a 1982 federal tax-evasion charge.

Yet all the trouble in his empire hasn't hit the wallet of the reclusive dean of corporate raiders. Posner extracted total compensation of $12.7 million last year from *DWG* Corp.—a holding company that earned a slim $5.6 million on $989 million in revenues. Some $4.6 million was an outright cash grant for his "extraordinary achievements." The millions not only made Posner America's highest-paid executive. He was also the *CEO* who returned the least to shareholders for the money, according to *BUSINESS WEEK*'s pay-performance index (table, page 11).

NO APOLOGIES. *DWG* shareholders must be wondering why Posner deserved the money. In the first nine months of fiscal 1986, *DWG* lost $5.9 million. The company's shares have tumbled to a paltry 1⅝, from 3¾ in 1984.

Posner makes no apologies. "I don't think he needs to justify his pay," says Donald J. Glazer, a *DWG* spokesman. Glazer maintains that *DWG*'s bottom line doesn't tell the whole story of what Posner is worth. Dozens of corporate entities fall under *DWG*'s umbrella, he notes, including Royal Crown Cos., acquired in 1984. Each has Posner as chairman, chief executive, and president, and each compensates him separately. "There are problems,

between executive pay and a company's earnings but little evidence of a strong correlation between what the shareholder earns and what a chief executive makes. "There isn't much of a correlation between stock prices and salary and bonus," he says.

A Sibson study of chief-executive pay over five years at the nation's 50 largest companies reveals widespread anomalies in pay and performance. Take two well-known executives of major industrial-products corporations: Lewis W. Lehr, 3M's chieftain, and Harry J. Gray, United Technologies' chairman. Lehr drew an annual salary and bonus of $829,000 last year, 24.5% less than Gray's $1.1 million. And that doesn't account for another $449,000 that Gray picked up in 1985 in long-term compensation.

SHAREHOLDERS' LAMENT. Yet Lehr has returned $1,486 in stock appreciation and dividends to shareholders for every dollar that he has earned since 1981. Gray returned only $85 for every dollar of pay. Put another way, Lehr earned a mere 0.07% of what he gave to shareholders; Gray got 1.17%.

Or consider John M. Richman, chairman of Dart & Kraft, and Donald M. Kendall, chairman of PepsiCo. For every buck Richman has received in the past five years, his shareholders lost $154. For every dollar Kendall got, his shareholders gained $876.

For the third consecutive year, *BUSINESS WEEK* and Sibson compared executives' total pay over three years with the shareholder returns of the companies that employ them. By relating the pay of executives and the performance of companies in similar industries, these figures yield a performance index that shows whether pay is commensurate with shareholder returns. When the index number is low, it suggests that shareholders are getting a bargain for their money. When it's high, the index suggests that a chief executive may be overpaid. Eight of the 10 chief executives who made this year's list of those who returned the least to shareholders relative to their pay are there partly because they exercised sizable stock options. And 4 of the 10—Mesa Petroleum's T. Boone Pickens, Data General's Edson D. de-Castro, Wang Laboratories' An Wang, and Borg-

but there are profits, too," says Glazer. "You have all these companies that Posner manages on a daily basis, and they have improved with time and effort."

Plenty of creditors and former executives of Posner companies beg to differ. Once-profitable conglomerates such as *NVF*, *DWG*, and Pennsylvania Engineering—the heart of his empire—have been skidding into red ink and staggering debt since 1982—in direct contrast with Posner's skyrocketing pay. In 1984, Posner pocketed a tidy $7.6 million from *NVF*, while the company lost $146.5 million. "Look at his salary, look at his performance, and draw your own conclusions," fumes an *NVF* investor. Creditors are demanding that Posner limit his Sharon Steel salary to $1 million as a condition for restructuring the company's debt.

'BEING BLED.' Posner has acquired a reputation as an asset stripper. After *DWG* gobbled up Graniteville Co., an ailing textile maker, in 1983, he promised: "We're builders, not liquidators." But he then shuttered several mills, slashed the work force, and dismissed top executives. He even cut off police and garbage service in Graniteville, S. C., one of the country's last company towns. Glazer says Graniteville Co. will soon be profitable as a result of "substantial investments" in new machinery, but sources familiar with the company say otherwise. "Posner's capital outlay has been next to nothing," says one lender. "There is every indication the company is being bled."

Royal Crown is now making a profit, Glazer claims, although it lost $12.6 million in the first nine months of 1985. The company has boosted sales of *RC* Cola for the first time in seven years. But analysts don't give Posner much of the credit. They attribute the gains to savvy marketing by Jim Harralson, *RC*'s new chief operating officer, who must send all purchase orders and checks for more than $500 to Posner's Miami Beach office for clearance. Otherwise, Posner has honored a pledge to stay out of management. "He kept his word," says Harralson. "He has left me strictly alone."

By Pete Engardio in Atlanta

Warner's James F. Beré—made the list for the second straight year.

Iacocca, the Chrysler miracle worker, turns up on this list as well. Is he worth all the money he has received? Few shareholders are complaining. After all, they have seen him rescue their company from near-bankruptcy, and they have enjoyed returns of 173% from stock and dividends in the past three years. Iacocca's total compensation over the same period: a tidy $17.6 million.

Options provided more than half of the $7.1 million Beré earned in the past three years. But he received the options as far back as 1974. From that time through 1983, the company says, shareholder returns grew at an annual compound rate of 35%.

Data General Chairman de Castro's second appearance still reflects his exercise of $7.5 million in stock options in 1984. With profits off by 71% last year, de Castro took no bonus and only $375,000 in salary. "A poor year wasn't a year top executives should be rewarded," he says. Still, de Castro has more than doubled his shareholders' returns since 1983.

Shareholders of Sherwin-Williams Co. aren't apt to grouse about Chairman John G. Breen's pay, either. In the past three years he has returned 111.5% to them. However, Breen's total compensation package of $7.2 million isn't peanuts.

Neither is the $31.7 million T. Boone Pickens has earned since 1983. For that money, the corporate raider has returned 40.2% to Mesa Petroleum's shareholders. Pickens last year pocketed $4.2 million as his share of the $41 million after-tax profit Mesa made from its raid on Phillips Petroleum Co., in addition to the $4.2 million he received in both salary and bonus.

BIGGEST BANG. Supporters argue that Pickens is worth it. Many small oil companies similar to Mesa have disappeared through mergers during the past three years. But Mesa has grown to be the nation's largest independent oil company, while paying down its debt with takeover gains.

Few could possibly dispute the role Chairman Floyd D. Gottwald Jr. has played in making Ethyl Corp., a diversified industrial-chemical producer in Richmond, Va., a stellar performer.

BERGERAC'S GOLDEN PARACHUTE: THE BIGGEST EVER

Michel C. Bergerac riding in a commercial airliner is a bit like a deposed king taking a bus. As chairman of Revlon Inc., the giant health and beauty company, Bergerac shuttled around the world for the last decade on a Boeing 727 corporate jet comfortably outfitted with couches, plush carpeting, and a bedroom. But more recently, as Michel Bergerac, private citizen, he's been reduced to flying with common folk.

The transition has been a crash course in reality. "I found a whole new world," he says. "There are no longer porters in airports. . . . And then you look at the suitcases, and they all have wheels. . . . And I discovered nobody uses leather luggage any more."

Bergerac converted to vinyl baggage. But he could easily afford leather. The 54-year-old executive took away a $35 million prize—including the largest golden parachute severance payment ever made—after little-known takeover artist Ronald O. Perelman, chairman of Pantry Pride Inc., wrested control of Revlon last November.

SOFT LANDINGS. While Bergerac pulled the rip cord on a parachute more than twice as big as the next largest one last year, many of his counterparts also had some pretty soft landings (chart, page 10). After Beatrice Cos. agreed to sell out to Kohlberg Kravis Roberts & Co. last November, William W. Granger Jr., chief executive of the giant food company, took home $6.4 million. The *KKR* deal came three months after Granger was named *CEO*. And should he leave Baxter Travenol Laboratories Inc., Karl D. Bays, who headed American Hospital Supply Corp. before Baxter took it over, will get $8.2 million. Handsome golden parachutes were also awarded to executives in the Allied-Signal, *GE-RCA*, and R. J. Reynolds-Nabisco mergers, but they have yet to be exercised.

Bergerac's severance package breaks down like this: five years of salary and bonus, valued at

---

Companies constantly seek better ways to link pay and performance

Gottwald's total compensation package of $1.7 million since 1983 and Ethyl's 288.7% return to shareholders easily gives him the distinction of delivering the most bang for the buck (page 9).

Dresser Industries Inc. Chairman John J. Murphy is another bargain for shareholders—but not on the basis of investor returns. Since 1983, Dresser shareholders have failed even to match the rate of inflation on their investment, and Murphy has received a mere $847,000 in total compensation over the past three years. He has, in effect, been penalized for Dresser's lackluster performance in an exceedingly tough industry. "Murphy made peanuts," declares Rich of Sibson, "and that's an indication that Dresser's pay programs work."

EYING THE COMPETITION. Corporate compensation committees are continuing to devise plans that will relate pay and performance much more effectively, and some currently view such incentives as a crucial part of corporate planning. Ford Motor Co., for example, has overhauled its compensation plans this year to align executive pay more closely with strategic goals.

The Ford plan is expected to reduce the use of short-term cash bonuses and place greater emphasis on long-term incentive stock grants as a reward for meeting specific five-year performance targets. The goals include financial measurements such as return-on-equity, but they are also based on product quality, customer satisfaction, and employee involvement.

The targets, what's more, are pegged to how Ford fares against its competitors. "If our quality

nearly $7 million; stock options and accelerated payment of restricted stock worth $13 million; and a $15 million golden parachute. The first two items were part of Bergerac's original contract in 1974, when Revlon founder Charles Revson hired him away from *ITT* Corp. The Revlon board added his and other golden parachutes in late 1983 to prevent its executives, potentially worried about losing their jobs in a takeover, from passing up a good deal.

Bergerac had taken Revlon from a beauty company with $500 million in sales to a diversified health care concern with revenues of more than $2 billion. Yet after Bergerac's expansion drive, Revlon's profits declined sharply—along with its cosmetics market share. Last year, earnings approached $125 million, well below the 1980 peak of $192 million. So his severance arrangement has prompted cries of foul. "No one is worth that much money unless they walk on water," says a former Revlon senior executive.

UPPING THE ANTE. Revlon directors say Bergerac helped the company grow, and they wanted him to stay—at any cost. "Michel diversified the company at a time when the cosmetics industry was in a decline. It would have been worse without him," says Lewis L. Glucksman, former Lehman Brothers Kuhn Loeb chairman and a former director of Revlon's compensation committee. Aileen Mehle, a *New York Post* gossip columnist and another compensation-committee member, also defended the sum. "We wanted Michel to feel he was wanted so he would hang in there," says Mehle, who uses the byline Suzy Knickerbocker. "But if a buyer came along, we wanted him to do what was best for stockholders."

Ultimately, Bergerac argues, he did just that. Pantry Pride originally offered $1.9 billion for Revlon shares but eventually upped the ante to $2.7 billion. "In the end, the shareholders got some $800 million more than they would have gotten," Bergerac points out. With 260,000 shares of Revlon stock in his golden parachute, Bergerac also benefited from the increased offer. Does he think his compensation was fair? "Clearly, it's an enormous amount of money. Whether it should be less or more, how do you judge those things? I don't know," he says. Nonetheless, he is "delighted to abide by the wisdom of the board."

By Amy Dunkin and Laurie Baum in New York

improves 20% and the competition improves 40%, the board isn't going to be very happy because our relative position will have slipped," explains Robert F. Tanner, Ford's manager of executive compensation.

Not everyone thinks stock and option-based compensation plans offer such potential. Warren E. Buffett, the chairman of Berkshire Hathaway Inc. and one of the nation's savviest investors, believes these incentives are a shareholder ripoff. "Rhetoric about options frequently describes them as desirable because they put managers and owners in the same financial boat," he says. "In reality, the boats are far different. No owner has ever escaped the burden of capital costs, whereas a holder of a fixed-price option bears no capital costs at all. An owner must weigh upside potential against downside risk. An option holder has no downside."

Buffett, however, holds a minority view. Today, numerous companies are moving to moderate cash payments and to link executive compensation to some broad measure of corporate success. That means stock options are likely to play an increasing role in the future of executive pay.

By John A. Byrne in New York, with bureau reports

BUSINESS FADS: WHAT'S IN—AND OUT

EXECUTIVES LATCH ON TO ANY MANAGEMENT IDEA THAT LOOKS LIKE A QUICK FIX

JANUARY 20, 1986, PP. 52-55, 58, 60, 61

Allan A. Kennedy had just delivered his $5,000, 90-minute pep talk on corporate culture to a select group of top executives of an industrial-service corporation.

The show was slick. Kennedy, a former McKinsey & Co. consultant and co-author of *Corporate Cultures*, had run through his chat on company rituals some 200 times. "By now I've got an act that could play on Broadway," he says.

Yet even Kennedy was taken aback by the audience's enthusiasm when the curtain came down. "This corporate culture stuff is great," the chairman raved at dinner following the talk. Then, turning to his president, he demanded, "I want a culture by Monday."

Astonishing as it may seem, the executive was serious. There is, of course, merit in Kennedy's belief that a corporation's culture—its shared values, beliefs and rituals—strongly influence its success or failure. But it would seem obvious to most executives that a culture must be built over years, not ordained overnight.

Or would it? Like Kennedy's client, a lot of American executives these days seem eager to latch on to almost any new concept that promises a quick fix for their problems.

Having trouble developing new products? Try "intrapreneurship," the process for getting entrepreneurial juices flowing in a big company.

Having a tough time competing against the Japanese? Try "quality circles," the managerial export from Japan that has U. S. workers and managers sitting around tables finding ways to increase productivity and ensure quality.

Having problems with employee productivity? Try "wellness," the new buzzword for fitness programs that encourage managers to exercise, eat healthy foods, and stop smoking.

Facing the threat of a hostile takeover? Restructure your company by writing off a mature business and taking on a mountain of debt. Wall Street will almost surely respond by jacking up your stock price, and that should keep the raider at bay.

HOLLOW SYMBOLS. There's nothing inherently wrong with any of these ideas. What's wrong is that too many companies use them as gimmicks to evade the basic challenges they face. Unless such solutions are well thought out and supported by a sincere commitment from top management, they are doomed to fail. They quickly become meaningless buzzwords, hollow symbols, mere fads.

Even more disturbing is how these fads change, often by 180°. In the 1960s it seemed everyone wanted to diversify, to become a conglomerate. Today, an opposite trend has emerged under the fancy rubric of "asset redeployment." It's the term for conceding that a past diversification spree was a mistake, for spinning off businesses and getting back to the basics.

Or take strategic planning. In the late 1970s it was all the rage. Following the lead of General Electric Co., many companies hired planners at corporate headquarters to chart the future plans of their businesses. Today corporate planning staffs have been substantially reduced or eliminated, because it makes more sense for line managers, closer to the business, to plot strategy.

Business fads are something of a necessary evil and have always been with us. What's different—and alarming—today is the sudden rise and fall of so many conflicting fads and how they influence the modern manager.

What's hot right now? "Touchy-feely" managers who are "demassing." Translation: Nice-guy bosses are laying off still more workers. Other companies are forming "strategic alliances"—launching a joint venture with their No. 1 competitor, perhaps, to plug a product or technology void. The thoroughly modern corporation wants to turn its managers into "leaders" and "intrapreneurs" through "pay for performance." Those same managers flock to Outward Bound expeditions to learn survival skills.

On the other hand, autocratic bosses are out. So are the corporate planners and economists who not long ago pontificated on "reindustrialization," "synergy," and "management by objectives." On the way out: the hostile takeover wave that has dominated business for the past two years, the raiders who used junk bonds, and the golden parachutes that managers devised to protect themselves from the raiders.

And so it goes, to the consternation of those whose task it is to run a business. "Last year it was quality circles," says Harvey Gittler, a Borg-Warner Corp. manager in Elyria, Ohio. "This year it is zero inventories. The truth is, one more panacea and we will all go nuts."

He is not alone in this feeling. A marketing manager with a big Midwest equipment maker feels whipsawed. "In the past 18 months, we have heard that profit is more important than revenue, that quality is more important than profit, that people are more important than profit, that customers are more important than our people, that big customers are more important than small customers, and that growth is the key to our success," he recounts. "No wonder our performance is inconsistent."

One new fad seems to be an attempt to clear up some of this confusion. Some large companies, including General Motors Corp. and Ford Motor Co., have issued managers glossy, pocket-sized cards to remind them of their companies' guiding principles—a key ingredient of their changing corporate cultures. Ford's mission statement—handed out last March—was two years in the making, involved hundreds of employees, and was O.K.'d by its board of directors. Some *GM* managers have been issued as many as three reminders, each adorned with a mug shot or two of the top brass. Call it Management by Card.

Why the proliferation of business fads? And why have they become more ephemeral than ever? Perhaps it's because many managers are frustrated by their inability to compete in a world marketplace. Or perhaps it's because they are under intense pressure from Wall Street to perform short-term miracles. The result is a mad, almost aimless scramble for instant solutions. "We're all looking for magic," explains Thomas R. Horton,

president of the American Management Assn. "If you tell me I can avoid a cold by taking half a pound of Vitamin C, I'll want to believe you even if it only gives me indigestion."

The search has fueled an industry of instant management gurus, new-idea consultants, and an endless stream of books promising the latest quick fix. Indeed, when it came time for Ralph H. Kilmann, a University of Pittsburgh business professor, to concoct a title for his new management book, he settled on *Beyond the Quick Fix*, in itself a reflection of how faddishness has come to dominate management thinking.

The book's point will probably be lost on many managers, however. A major corporation recently asked Kilmann if he could give its top 50 officers a seminar on his new book in only 15 minutes. "You mean you want me to do *Beyond the Quick Fix* quickly," he responded. The author declined the invitation.

TANGLED WEBS. It is not clear how big a threat this rash of palliative trends poses. Business fads have waxed and waned through the decades, yet corporations survive. Faddish ideas began to influence U.S. executives in a major way with the emergence of the professional manager in America after World War II. Seat-of-the-pants management was becoming old hat. Instead it became popular to follow the principles of Frederick Winslow Taylor, the inventor of time-and-motion studies 50 years earlier. He contended that running a company should be more a science than an art.

'This corporate culture
stuff is great.
I want a culture by Monday'

Managers rushed to try scientific methods, such as observation, experimentation, and reasoning. They immersed themselves in quantitative analysis. "Operations research" became the rallying cry. By itself, not a bad idea. But the success of operations research begat a series of unintelligible acronyms and buzzwords and an avalanche of charts, curves, and diagrams.

Remember *PERT*? Program Evaluation & Review Technique charts were spiderweb-like diagrams to ensure that projects would be completed on time. "We all did them," recalls Donald N. Frey, chief executive of Bell & Howell Co. "But it took so much effort to get the charts done, you might as well have spent the time getting the job done."

Frey, then a young manager at Ford, had a rude awakening about *PERT*'s pitfalls. "We went to Wright Patterson Air Force base, where they had *PERT* charting down to a science. They had more guys working on *PERT* charts than they had doing the job. It was an enormous overhead cost just to allow the generals to show visitors their *PERT* charts."

Executives also found that management by objectives, another 1950s invention, often tangled them in paper. "We got so balled up in the details that we spent more time on paperwork than the whole damn thing was worth," says George W. Baur, president of Hughes Tool Co.'s tool division.

MAINFRAME MONKEYS. When the mainframe computer came along in the 1950s, it contributed to the mounting pile of paper. Many companies installed computers in rooms with huge display windows to show them off. "A lot of people got computers because *GE* got them," says Ian Wilson, a 26-year *GE* veteran now with the Stanford Research Institute. "It was monkey see, monkey do."

When *GE* decentralized its operations in 1950, scores of companies followed, thinking that this was the antidote for corporate bureaucracies. Similar moves became so fashionable that almost no executive could be heard advocating centralized management. That is, until some companies discovered that decentralizing led to more vice-presidents who built up their own cumbersome fiefdoms and gave line managers even less autonomy.

Centralized companies decentralized, and then some decentralized corporations centralized. "It depended on which consultant you hired," remembers Donald P. Jacobs, dean of Northwestern's Kellogg School of Management.

In the 1960s a wave of "people-oriented" management thinkers gained prominence. Many of the fads they promoted mirrored social trends. T-Groups, group encounter sessions for executives, came into vogue as the Beatles and Bob Dylan sang to a new, less bridled generation. Their popularity heralded the start of the touchy-feely approach to business; "sensitive," participative managers started sharing the spotlight with the management-by-numbers conglomerateurs who dominated the times. The new managers espoused Theory Y, a model for participative management created by a Massachusetts Institute of Technology management professor, Douglas McGregor, in the 1950s. It was the beginning of the end for Theory X, an authoritarian form of governance that grew out of managers' World War II military experiences.

Oh, how the times had changed. John Clemens, then a young, freshly scrubbed manager for Pillsbury and now a Hartwick College professor, remembers it well. Along with 20 or so colleagues, he was summoned to a country-club meeting room to face a bearded, rather hip, psychiatrist. The T-Group trainer, Clemens recalls, instructed them to take off their ties, shoes, and name tags. Then the lights went out.

"We began crawling on the floor in the dark when I bumped into our president," he says. "It was atrocious. We would have done better figuring out how to sell more brownie mix."

Tens of thousands of managers from such companies as *IBM*, *TRW*, Union Carbide, and Weyerhaeuser trekked to T-Group sessions in search of self-awareness and sensitivity. The concept, popularized by National Training Laboratories, was simple: Mix a dozen or more people together in a room without a leader or an agenda and see what happens. Often, delegates would hurl personal insults across a room. The resulting "feedback," it was hoped, would make Theory X managers less bossy and more participative.

PLOTTING PEOPLE. As the decade came to an end, T-Groups gave way to Grid-Groups. And T-Grouped managers such as Clemens became G-Grouped quickly enough. Launched by Robert R. Blake and Jane S. Mouton's *The Managerial Grid* in 1964, the grid rated managers on two characteristics—concern for people vs. concern for production. "The beauty of it is that you could plot people all over the place," adds Clemens. "If you scored a high concern for people and a low concern for production, people would say, 'This guy's a wimp. He's a 1-9.' If you had a high concern for production (9-1), you were a dictator."

In the decade of the *MBA*, the 1970s, it was perhaps inevitable that the numbers-oriented students turned out by the B-schools would help to make strategic planning *de rigueur*. Another approach pioneered by *GE*, it caught the fancy of many executives. "After we put in our strategic planning system in 1970, we were deluged with people from around the world wanting to talk to us about it," recalls *GE* alumnus Walker.

Some of these visitors failed to distinguish between form and substance. They became engrossed in the mechanics of setting up a planning system rather than focusing on finding the answers, says Harvard business school's Michael E. Porter. "Too often it became a function of shuffling papers with no underlying value."

DOG STARS. Porter was one of the many consultants who helped make strategic planning a buzzword. Consultants have always had a role in launching fads. They sold managers on psychological tools such as the Thematic Apperception Test in the 1950s. (Executives were told to conjure up stories based on series of pictures.) They also peddled sensitivity training in the 1960s. But consultants have been working overtime to roll out new fads since the 1970s.

One of the most rapidly spreading and widely used theories ever to emerge was the gospel according to Bruce D. Henderson's Boston Consulting Group Inc. Henderson put cows, dogs, stars, and question marks on matrix charts in hundreds of executive suites. Businesses were put into such categories as cash cows (mature companies that could be milked) and dogs (marginal performers in a market with poor prospects).

Fads multiplied in the 1980s as U. S. executives grappled for ways to contend with foreign competition—so much so that management by best-seller came into vogue. William Ouchi's *Theory Z* and Richard Pascale and Anthony Athos' *The Art of Japanese Management* were the first such best-sellers when published in 1981. Both books pushed U. S. companies to adopt such Japanese management techniques as quality circles and job enrichment.

Some wags wondered if U. S. managers would soon be issued kimonos and be required to eat with chopsticks. "There wasn't an American manager who wasn't talking about it four years ago," says James J. O'Toole, a management professor at the University of Southern California. But when O'Toole's *New Management* magazine recently asked readers to name the most influential management books in recent years, not a single reader mentioned *Theory Z*.

Theory Z is still having an impact, however. Quality circles, an updated version of the employee suggestion programs and labor-management councils of the 1950s, are still in. In 1979, the International Association of Quality Circles had only 200 members. Now membership is almost 8,000.

IMMORTALITY. Why such mass popularity? Edward E. Lawler III, director of the University of Southern California's Center for Effective Organizations, says that *QC*s are partly a fad. "In a number of cases we studied," says Lawler, "the *CEO* of the company had seen a *TV* program or read a magazine article on *QC*s and decided to give them a try. Circles were simply something the top told the middle to do to the bottom."

Quality circles may be helping some companies improve productivity, though they have received mixed reviews. Koppers Co. installed *QC*s in 1981 at a plant in Follansbee, W. Va. They flopped when Koppers axed half the work force. Now it's trying a program called *PITCH*—for People Involved in Totally Changing History. The jury is still out on *PITCH*, but outsiders wonder how seriously employees will take a program that seems to promise immortality for working at a plant that makes creosote roofing tar.

Taking the best-seller even further were consultants Thomas J. Peters and Robert H. Waterman Jr. Their *In Search of Excellence*, published in 1982, added Skunk Works, Management By Walking Around, and Stick to Your Knitting to the manager's vocabulary.

One *Excellence*-type slogan caught on more

widely than any other: "People are our most important asset." But how seriously did executives take it? One major property and casualty insurer adopted this motto two years ago, promoting it in its annual report and in management memos. Yet as one divisional manager grouses, there was no real commitment. "Since the introduction of that campaign, our training budget has been cut in half and our employee profit-sharing plan has been eliminated," he says. "We've laid off 1,000 staff members. Our tuition reimbursement program has been dissolved, and the athletic center has been closed. A lot of those important assets are looking for new jobs."

PIES AND SALADS. Some of the folks who promote new management ideas will even call a fad a fad. Take wellness, fitness programs that attempt to get employees to eat salads instead of hamburgers. "We feel it probably has a two- to three-year life cycle," figures Robert G. Cox, president of *PA* Executive Search Group. Cox's consulting outfit tells potential clients that managers who smoke cost them $4,000 annually in lower productivity and higher absenteeism.

On a recent engagement, *PA*'s consultants stood duty in a corporation's cafeteria. "We noticed they picked up a lot of desserts when they went through the cafeteria line," relates Cox. "We also noticed that the lemon meringue pie was at the beginning of the line and the salads were in the back." The consultants' solution: switching the pies and the salads.

In many cases, a fad lasts as long as the boss is interested. "Our *CEO* got very excited about wellness two years ago," confides a personnel manager for a major transportation company. "We all went through stress-management programs, got rewarded for stopping smoking, and had to read *Fit or Fat.* But last year wasn't profitable, and now all of that has stopped."

And today there is intense competition for the executive's attention. A slew of instant gurus have emerged to spread the differing gospels, each with a proprietary lexicon of his own. Gifford Pinchot talks of intrapreneurship. Allan Kennedy talks of corporate culture. Ichak Adizes, a self-styled "organizational therapist" based in Santa Monica, Calif., advocates consensus-building meetings and brainstorming sessions.

DIRTY HANDS. Adizes has the ear of BankAmerica President Samuel H. Armacost. The banker was introduced to the Yugoslavia-born consultant by board director Charles R. Schwab in 1983 via cassette tape. Armacost, says Adizes, listened to his "Adizes Method Audio Series" until 2 a.m. one night and was so impressed that he arranged a retreat with the consulting whiz for top management at the posh Silverado Country Club in Napa County.

The upshot? The Adizes method cost BofA an estimated $3 million. Top managers, figures one BofA officer, spent much of their time trying to build consensus under the method. "Several senior guys were spending half their time in these meetings for months on end," says one insider. Adds a consultant who worked with the bank: "The real fix would have been to fire five levels of management so the top guys could get their hands dirty." A bank spokesman says Adizes helped reorganize the bank into two divisions.

The impact goes well beyond the waste of time and resources. Companies risk losing the support and confidence of their people. "The people below are often laughing at the senior management," says consultant Kilmann. "They are saying, 'How stupid can you be?'"

A little faddishness may be helpful because it makes managers think about new ways to do their jobs better. In earlier decades, fads appear to have had that effect. They tended to be in fashion for years, if not decades, and did less harm. They seemed less goofy, too.

Today, the bewildering array of fads pose far more serious diversions and distractions from the complex task of running a company. Too many modern managers are like compulsive dieters: trying the latest craze for a few days, then moving restlessly on.

By John A. Byrne in New York,
with bureau reports

WHO'S EXCELLENT NOW?

SOME OF THE BEST-SELLER'S PICKS HAVEN'T BEEN DOING SO WELL LATELY

NOVEMBER 5, 1984, PP. 76-79, 83, 86

Not long after *In Search of Excellence* zoomed to the top of the best-seller list, co-author Thomas J. Peters gave a speech to a division of Hewlett-Packard Co., one of the star companies in the book. After the speech, as Peters recalls, the division's manager told him: " 'What we should do is call you in to give a speech once a quarter. So we can remember what it was that we were when we were really a great company. And to remind us how damned hard it is to maintain some of those traits once you get big.' "

Judging from Hewlett-Packard's current difficulties, the manager knew what he was talking about. The turmoil and product-development problems plaguing *HP*—the third-largest computer maker after International Business Machines Corp. and Digital Equipment Corp.—hardly make it look like one of America's most innovative, best-run companies. Although its earnings are still strong, *HP* has stumbled badly in the critical microcomputer and superminicomputer markets.

DISENCHANTMENT. To regain its stride, *HP* is being forced to abandon attributes of excellence for which it was praised. Its technology-driven, engineering-oriented culture, in which decentralization and innovation were a religion and entrepreneurs were the gods, is giving way to a marketing culture and growing centralization. The continuing exodus of disenchanted managers—12 have left in just the last six months—tells the story. "The time spent in coordinating meetings has increased by an order of magnitude in the last four years," sighs André Schwager, a former *HP* general manager who left in September. "It's clear that the culture is beginning to change."

Hewlett-Packard is not the only "excellent company" that is not looking so excellent these days. According to studies by *BUSINESS WEEK*, management consultants McKinsey & Co., and Standard & Poor's Compustat Services Inc., at least 14 of the 43 "excellent" companies highlighted by Peters and co-author Robert H. Waterman Jr. in

their book just two years ago have lost their luster (table, page 23).

If judged on their performance during the last decade, Delta Air Lines, Walt Disney Productions, Eastman Kodak, and Texas Instruments would not pass the financial tests for excellence laid down in the book. In more recent years, nine others—Atari, Avon, Caterpillar Tractor, Chesebrough-Pond's, *DEC*, Fluor, Levi Strauss, Revlon, and Dart & Kraft's Tupperware International—have suffered significant earnings declines that stem from serious business problems, management problems, or both. While most outsiders still view them as well-managed and in robust financial health, other members of the elite have been humbled by blunders: Johnson & Johnson in high-technology medical equipment, Dana in financial services, and 3M in office automation.

It is far too early to determine whether these troubles are only temporary. For example, Delta Air Lines Inc., which has had to contend with deregulation, and Texas Instruments Inc., which sustained a staggering loss in 1983 because of its foray into home computers, are reporting strong earnings this year.

Even so, it comes as a shock that so many companies have fallen from grace so quickly—and it also raises some questions. Were these companies so excellent in the first place? Are the eight attributes of excellence the only eight attributes of excellence? Does adhering to them make a difference?

NEW LESSONS? Not surprisingly, critics question whether there was any new lesson to be learned from the book in the first place. Management writer Peter F. Drucker, for one, dismisses *In Search of Excellence* as "a book for juveniles" and as nothing more than a reaction to the last recession, when "a great many American managers [became] convinced that if things become too complicated, you can't run them."

In their own defense, Peters and Waterman argue that their intent was to address those quali-

THE EIGHT ATTRIBUTES OF EXCELLENCE

1. BIAS FOR ACTION: A preference for doing something—anything—rather than sending an idea through endless cycles of analyses and committee reports

2. STAYING CLOSE TO THE CUSTOMER: Learning his preferences and catering to them

3. AUTONOMY AND ENTREPRENEURSHIP: Breaking the corporation into small companies and encouraging them to think independently and competitively

4. PRODUCTIVITY THROUGH PEOPLE: Creating in all employees the awareness that their best efforts are essential and that they will share in the rewards of the company's success

5. HANDS-ON, VALUE-DRIVEN: Insisting that executives keep in touch with the firm's essential business and promote a strong corporate culture

6. STICK TO THE KNITTING: Remaining with the businesses the company knows best

7. SIMPLE FORM, LEAN STAFF: Few administrative layers, few people at the upper levels.

8. SIMULTANEOUS LOOSE-TIGHT PROPERTIES: Fostering a climate where there is dedication to the central values of the company combined with tolerance for all employees who accept those values

THE 'EXCELLENT COMPANIES' CITED BY PETERS AND WATERMAN

Allen-Bradley	International Business Machines
Amdahl	Johnson & Johnson
Atari	K mart
Avon Products	Levi Strauss
Bechtel Group	Marriott
Boeing	M&M Mars
Bristol-Myers	Maytag
Caterpillar Tractor	McDonald's
Chesebrough-Pond's	Merck
Dana	National Semiconductor
Data General	Procter & Gamble
Delta Air Lines	Raychem
Digital Equipment	Revlon
Dow Chemical	Schlumberger
Du Pont	Standard Oil (Indiana)
Eastman Kodak	Texas Instruments
Emerson Electric	3M
Fluor	Tupperware International
Frito-Lay	Wal-Mart Stores
Hewlett-Packard	Walt Disney Productions
Hughes Aircraft	Wang Laboratories
Intel	

DATA: *IN SEARCH OF EXCELLENCE*

ties of good management that too many managers had ignored. That *Excellence* has so far sold nearly 2.8 million copies in the U. S.—and hundreds of thousands of copies abroad—proves that it struck a responsive nerve in U. S. and even foreign managers. Indeed, it is important to recall the context in which the book appeared: Japan was conquering many of the markets that U. S. companies had dominated. And it was becoming increasingly evident that there was too much analysis-paralysis, too much bureaucracy, too little innovation, and too little attention being paid to customers and employees at too many American companies.

The book's basic message was that U. S. companies could regain their competitive edge by paying more attention to people—customers and employees—and by sticking to the skills and values they know best. And when virtually all eyes were turned to Japan for the answer, the book showed there were worthy models of management in our own backyard.

Then why have so many of the excellent companies fallen? "There's no real reason to have ever expected that all of these companies would have done well forever and ever," says Peters. Adds Waterman: "If you're big, you've got the seeds of your own destruction in there." The excellent companies, Peters and Waterman contend, just seemed to be big corporations that were "losing less fast."

Clearly, several of the 43 companies, including Revlon Inc. and Atari Inc., should never have made anyone's list of well-managed companies. Charles Revson, the late founder of Revlon, was an entrepreneurial and marketing genius. But even those who still worship him admit he was no great manager.

LOVE OF NUMBERS. Atari, the company that rose and fell with the video-game boom and collapse—and stuck Warner Communications Inc. with hundreds of millions of dollars in losses—managed to break almost all of the eight commandments of excellence. Out-of-control management and bloated fiefdoms—not autonomy, entrepreneurship, and a simple and lean form—were hallmarks at that company, whose payroll zoomed from a few hundred to 7,000 and back to a few

WHY SOME OF THE 'EXCELLENT' COMPANIES HAVE STUMBLED
The commandments of excellence they broke

	BIAS FOR ACTION	STAYING CLOSE TO THE CUSTOMER	AUTONOMY AND ENTREPRENEUR-SHIP	PRODUCTIVITY THROUGH PEOPLE	HANDS-ON, VALUE-DRIVEN	STICK TO THE KNITTING	SIMPLE FORM, LEAN STAFF	SIMULTANEOUS LOOSE-TIGHT PROPERTIES
ATARI (b)(c)	✔	✔	✔	✔	✔		✔	✔
AVON PRODUCTS (c)		✔		✔		✔		
CATERPILLAR TRACTOR (c)	✔						✔	
CHESEBROUGH-POND'S (c)	✔				✔	✔		
DELTA AIR LINES (a)(c)		✔						
DIGITAL EQUIPMENT (c)	✔		✔				✔	
DISNEY PRODUCTIONS (a)(c)		✔	✔					
EASTMAN KODAK (a)			✔				✔	
FLUOR (c)						✔		
HEWLETT-PACKARD (c)								
LEVI STRAUSS (c)		✔					✔	
REVLON (c)	✔	✔	✔	✔	✔	✔		
TUPPERWARE (b)(c)		✔		✔				
TEXAS INSTRUMENTS	✔	✔	✔			✔	✔	✔

(a) Did not pass Peters' and Waterman's financial-criteria hurdle in 1974-83   (b) Not tested against financial criteria because they were not included in Compustat's data base
(c) Difficulty adapting to fundamental change in market

DATA: BW, STANDARD & POOR'S COMPUSTAT SERVICES INC., McKINSEY & CO.

---

hundred in just seven years. Atari was so out of touch with its market that it failed to realize its customers were losing interest in video-game players and switching to home computers—a fatal oversight.

At several companies, a love for product, customers, and entrepreneurship gave way to a love for numbers. This helps explain why Chesebrough-Pond's Inc. stalled in 1981, when sales in its core health and beauty businesses slowed and some of its vaunted acquisitions—notably Bass shoes and Prince tennis rackets—ran into trouble. This was also the case at Revlon under Michel C. Bergerac. The *ITT* Corp. alumnus installed some of the so-called modern management techniques that Revlon needed. But former executives and industry experts say an overemphasis on numbers has dulled much of Revlon's marketing pizzazz.

Peters argues that it is virtually impossible to score a perfect 10 on all eight attributes of excellence. Several excellent companies that fell by the wayside overstressed some attributes and ignored others. Disney Productions' employees were so devoted to the clean-taste values established by its founder that it lost its creative flair and failed to respond to changes in moviegoers' tastes. Employees were so wedded to the legacy that many protested the making of *Splash*, one of the company's first efforts in recent years to make a truly contemporary film—and one that turned out to be a hit.

In most instances, the transgressors ran amok by walking away from the principles that had been key to their earlier successes. A slew of companies—*TI*, Revlon, Fluor, Avon, Johnson & Johnson, Dana, and 3M—did not "stick to their knitting" and are paying the price. Fluor Corp. made the mistake of paying a staggering $2.3 billion for St. Joe Minerals Corp. in 1981—right before metals prices collapsed. Instead of helping Fluor ride out the rough times in its mainstay engineering-construction business, St. Joe has added to Fluor's financial woes. Its earnings plummeted to $27.7 million last year from $158.9 million in 1981. Its stock, which was trading at 71 right before its acquisition, is now hovering around 18.

WHEN STRICTNESS HURTS. In the *Harvard Business Review*, consultant Daniel T. Carroll attacked *Excellence* for ignoring the importance of such

LEVI'S: THE JEANS GIANT SLIPPED AS THE MARKET SHIFTED

Levi Strauss & Co. developed and built its jeans business by operating as close to its customers as the pockets on a pair of its 501 button-fly jeans. So close, in fact, that a former company president, on returning from a camping trip, ordered that a rivet be removed from the basic jeans line because he and fellow campers had discovered that the tiny fastener burned them as they crouched around the fire.

Unfortunately for Levi's, that kind of sensitivity to customers was lost in the midst of the jeans industry's heady growth in the 1970s. *In Search of Excellence* lauds Levi's as one of the excellent few that are "pushed around by their customers, and they love it." But that analysis now proves to have been sadly out of date. By the early 1980s, Levi's was grappling with diversification, marketing, and fashion dilemmas. Its confusion translated into disappointing performance and retrenchment for the nation's largest garment maker.

INWARD FOCUS. A family-run business for all of its 134 years, Levi's built its reputation on two basic principles: adherence to quality and a one-big-happy-family corporate culture. As the company grew, its managers concentrated on manufacturing enough jeans to supply a seemingly insatiable market. But that inward focus left Levi's unequipped to deal with a slowdown in jeans sales growth and the market's shift toward more fashionable apparel. "For so long, we were [always] sold out. Our time was prioritized on getting more product, new factories, more raw materials. We were internally oriented," notes one executive. The main casualty of Levi's inward focus was the customer. "We let that relationship with our retailers fall into a sad state of disrepair," admits one Levi's insider. As the jeans industry grew 15% annually for most of the past 20 years, retailers could sell every pair of jeans they received from Levi's. That "created tensions in the relationship and unfortunate habits on the part of some of our people," admits President Robert D. Haas, the great-great-grandnephew of founder Levi Strauss.

Retailers saw Levi's as aloof and inflexible. The company spent little on joint local advertising campaigns and did not support in-store promotions. When jeans demand slackened, Levi's lacked a loyal retail customer base from which to launch new products and stave off competitors who were providing better service, such as *VF Corp.* with its Lee brand and Blue Bell Inc. and its Wrangler line.

In losing touch with its customers, Levi's also distanced itself from the fashion trends of the 1980s and failed to anticipate the consumer shift away from basic goods. Says Robert L. Pugmire, general manager of Seattle-based Bernie's Menswear Inc., a 40-store chain that carries Levi's products: "In fashion, if you have to change your entire business overnight, you do it. Levi's can't react that fast. That's why it's important to have relationships with people who can see the changes coming."

Levi's suffered several false starts when it belatedly tried to broaden its product base. In 1979 the company positioned its David Hunter line against famous designer labels such as Ralph Lauren's Polo brand. But Levi's advertising program failed to convince customers that clothing with the Levi's label was comparable to the designer lines. For the same reason, its Activewear line of sports clothing has failed to challenge the likes of Nike Inc. and Adidas-Sportschuhfabriken. And one attempt to penetrate the European market with lighter-weight jeans failed because consumers wanted the heavy-duty American variety after all.

After a three-year earnings slide beginning in 1980, Levi's rebounded with the economy in 1983, with earnings rising 54% on sales of $2.7 billion. Most of that rise, however, was a result of retailers' restocking barren inventories and Levi's filling the pipeline for Sears, Roebuck & Co. and J. C. Penney Co.'s stores, two new customers. Some retailers, angry that Levi's had turned to such mass merchandisers, dropped the Levi's line entirely. And consumers suddenly decided they wanted more fashionable sportswear, turning away from such old-time favorites as blue jeans.

The result: Levi's sales for the first nine months of 1984 slipped 6%, and earnings plummeted 72%.

In response, Haas, who took over as president in April, is moving to end the paralysis that caused Levi's to lose touch with customers. He has expanded Levi's local advertising budget and its participation in special promotions. Levi's co-sponsored a local track meet with Seattle's Bernie's—a marketing gambit that would have been unheard-of a few years ago, says retailer Pugmire.

MORE RESPONSIVE. Levi's is also offering retailers volume discounts for the first time. And the company will exchange unsold goods for other products. In the past, retailers were stuck with anything they could not sell. These changes seem to be having an impact. A merchandise manager for Robinson's Department Stores in Los Angeles now calls Levi's one of his most responsive vendors.

Levi's efforts to improve its rapport with customers are crucial to what insiders see as its most significant management challenge: responding more quickly to shifts in the apparel market. Because the hot market today is higher-priced fashions made in relatively small quantities, "sticking to its knitting" as a jeansmaker is unlikely to serve as a cure for what ails Levi's. But Haas says the basic jeans and corduroy lines—which make up almost two-thirds of sales—will continue as the company's mainstays throughout the 1990s. Levi's, in fact, will spend $36 million advertising its basic 501 button-fly jeans this year.

The big question is: Can Levi's successfully pursue both the basic jeans and higher-fashion markets—something it has failed to achieve in the past? To do so will require a fundamental change. Asserts Alan L. Stein, director of corporate finance at Montgomery Securities and a Levi's director: "Levi's needs to become more a marketing company and less of a production company."

FEWER LAYERS. A critical test will be Haas's current effort to move into high-growth leisure and fashion goods. To facilitate that effort, Haas is creating autonomous units under the new Battery Street Enterprises (*BSE*) operating division. The division, which will make a push into fashion apparel, is so independent that employees' paychecks do not even bear the Levi's name. One indication of how much importance Haas is placing on such enterprises is the man he picked to be the *BSE* Fashion Group champion: James A. McDermott. McDermott, who formerly served as Levi's senior vice-president for marketing, is credited with developing a niche market for Levi's women's wear.

To respond quickly to fashion shifts, *BSE* has fewer layers of middle management than the jeanswear divisions. And McDermott boasts that his managers "are spending much more time with the retailer than in the past. We're going out with the salesmen and sitting with them . . . and we're listening, not just giving lip service."

Haas seems determined to make his jeanswear divisions more market-oriented and flexible, too. Sources say the company is searching extensively for top marketing talent to join a management dominated by operations men.

A simple form and lean staff are also company-wide goals. In 1982, Levi's violated its proud tradition of lifetime employment and trimmed 2,400 people—including middle managers—from its payroll. And this year, Levi's cut its 38,000-member work force by an additional 12% and closed 19 plants. But in an attempt to preserve its legendary employee loyalty, Levi's offered generous severance and retraining benefits.

All this prompts McDermott, for one, to claim that Levi's has climbed back on the path toward excellence. "We've seen the error of our ways," he says.

---

factors as proprietary technology, government policy, and national culture. The *BUSINESS WEEK* and McKinsey studies suggest that the criticism is well-founded. Of the 14 excellent companies that had stumbled, 12 were inept in adapting to a fundamental change in their markets. Their experiences show that strict adherence to the eight commandments—which do not emphasize reacting to broad economic and business trends—may actually hurt a company.

For example, Delta Air Lines, which had flourished by maintaining a low debt and exploiting a

TI: SHOT FULL OF HOLES AND TRYING TO RECOVER

Even at the time *In Search of Excellence* was written, its authors realized there were cracks in Texas Instruments Inc.'s armor. But because of the Dallas company's reputation for innovation and its 20-year financial record, they felt they had no choice but to include *TI*. Given the company's more recent record, however, co-author Thomas J. Peters acknowledges that today "we wouldn't have written about *TI*."

One could argue that the company has been breaking so many of the "eight commandments" of excellence for so long that even when the book was published in 1982, *TI* was not one of America's best-managed companies. The most dramatic evidence came last year, when *TI* folded its home computer business and accepted a $660 million operating loss and write-down. In 1983, *TI* suffered its first annual loss—$145.5 million on sales of $4.6 billion—in its 54-year history. But *TI*'s home computer fiasco was only the most glaring symptom of a host of fundamental management problems that had taken root:

□ Its engineers, accustomed to industrial customers, lacked expertise in consumer markets. *TI*'s foray into home computers—not to mention its earlier digital watch disaster—amply illustrates this. *TI* cut prices to create demand for its home computer. But the tactic, borrowed from its industrial chip markets, failed to generate a lasting interest. What *TI* thought was a revolution turned out to be only the hot Christmas gift of 1982.

□ The company believed it could dictate to its customers rather than listen to them. Indeed, the home computer sprang from management's desire to find a mass market for its newest microprocessor. Even when it became clear that the microprocessor was too costly for the market, *TI* refused to buy cheaper microprocessors from outsiders.

□ An overly complex management system—including matrix management and numbers-dominated strategic planning—tended to smother entrepreneurship. *TI*'s confusing reporting structures, for instance, delayed the design and production of key new products like large-scale computer memory chips. And headquarters' demand that operations project such factors as floor space and manpower needs made *TI*'s planning process more of a liability than a weapon.

□ The domineering styles of Chairman Mark Shepherd Jr. and President J. Fred Bucy often intimidated product managers, who told them what they wanted to hear—not what was really going on. For example, neither learned of the home computer problems until the company was drowning in inventory.

The *TI* of Shepherd and Bucy is remarkably different from the *TI* of Shepherd's legendary predecessor, Patrick E. Haggerty, who headed the company from 1945 to 1976. This was *TI*'s golden age, during which decentralization gave rise to a flood of innovations. Under Haggerty, the company that started in oil-field seismology blossomed into the largest manufacturer of integrated circuits, a huge defense contractor, and a major power in minicomputers.

It was Haggerty who introduced strict financial controls and strategic planning to control *TI*'s rapid growth and increasingly complex business mix. But Haggerty also championed *TI*'s stable of

close-knit culture to keep costs low, failed to see that deregulation had changed its world. The Atlanta-based carrier was slow in recognizing the importance of computers to keep tabs on ticket prices in different markets. Consequently, Delta

first failed to meet competitors' lower prices. Then it overreacted. The result: an $86.7 million loss in its fiscal year ended June, 1983, and a brand-new computer system.

Staying close to the customer can backfire on a

entrepreneurs, understanding that people, not rigid systems, produce innovation.

Shepherd and Bucy had to learn that lesson the hard way. In 1982 they scrapped *TI*'s matrix management system and returned control of products to their managers. Before then, semiconductor product managers had marketing responsibilities but lacked control over the labs that developed chips and the plants that made them. Now, memory chip manager and Senior Vice-President Timothy B. Smith, for instance, is responsible for research and development, manufacturing, and marketing. The result: *TI*'s memory devices grabbed a leading market share and also command the industry's highest average price.

MORE PRAGMATIC. Efforts to rein in strategic planners' demands for ever more data also appear to be paying off. The 15 variables that product managers had to project out 10 years have been reduced to four. This helps explain *TI*'s dramatic rebound in innovation: In the past 18 months the company introduced more new products than in any similar period in its history.

There are also signs that the not-invented-here syndrome that was fatal in home computers is giving way to pragmatism. *TI* recently initiated semiconductor ventures with Fujitsu Ltd. and National Semiconductor Corp. The company is even using archenemy Intel Corp.'s chips in its Professional Computer.

Moreover, Shepherd, 61, and Bucy, 56, are loosening their grip. They have expanded the membership and scope of *TI*'s executive committee: It now includes more senior operating managers. Another significant move was the appointment of Bucy, who is considered a better delegator than Shepherd, to *CEO* in 1984. Shepherd, still chairman, now oversees only long-term strategy.

While *TI*'s leaders have atoned for some of their sins, they are not totally repentant: They still cling to their strategy of applying their technological muscle to three key areas: semiconductors, computers, and consumer electronics. And they bristle at suggestions that *TI*'s engineering culture and consumer markets do not mix. But *TI*'s travails in personal computers tell a different story. Although the company has been successful in selling its Professional Computer through its own sales force to commercial markets, its effort to sell it through computer stores is foundering.

When *TI* launched the computer in 1983, it chose a design that could exchange data with International Business Machines Corp.'s Personal Computer but required customized software. The intent: to position the Professional as a high-performance computer. While that might be sensible for competing over the long haul against *IBM* and its de facto standard, retailers deem it a bad strategy for the here and now. "[The Professional] is a fantastic product," says William E. Ladin, chairman of the 55-store ComputerCraft Inc. "But it has to have all different software and a separate inventory. It kills us."

Ladin has dropped the product—and he is not alone. Future Computing Inc., a market research firm, estimates that only 13% of the nation's retail computer stores now carry the Professional—down from 20% in January. And, it adds, computer-store sales of the product have slipped from 1,500 per month to 650.

Nonetheless, Shepherd and Bucy have begun reviving *TI*'s entrepreneurial drive. A reinvigorated semiconductor group paced the company's record first-half profits of $165.7 million. The recovery and big defense budgets also helped.

"We're not [now] a paragon of excellence," admits R. Michael Lockerd, *TI*'s vice-president for strategic planning, "but I wouldn't send us to the minors." As Lockerd, Shepherd, and Bucy know only too well, it will be *TI*'s performance over the long run that determines whether the company once again deserves to be picked as an all-star.

company when a market shifts dramatically, leaving the company close to the wrong customer. This is what happened to Avon Products Inc. and to Dart & Kraft's Tupperware unit when the housewives to whom they catered began to pursue careers. Similarly, *DEC* and *HP*—companies run by engineers for customers who are engineers—have stumbled in trying to sell to customers without a technical background.

FRUSTRATION. Hewlett-Packard's famed innova-

DEC: BOGGED DOWN BY BLOATED MANAGEMENT

The most popular name around the offices of Digital Equipment Corp. these days is Venus—the company's brand new supermini-computer, which packs twice the punch of its previous top-of-the-line model. Venus is expected to be a huge success with *DEC*'s existing customers and should help revive the 27-year-old Maynard (Mass.) company's profit margin, which has plummeted to 7%, less than half of the 1981 level.

But Venus, scheduled for introduction on Oct. 31, may fail to work much magic in the broader marketplace because its unveiling is two years late. An addition to *DEC*'s *VAX* family of computers, Venus is more powerful than the comparable machines of such key competitors as *IBM*, Data General, and Prime Computer. Its bang for the buck, however, hardly comes close to the superminis of such startups as Elxsi, a $30 million San Jose (Calif.) company that claims to have stolen half its customers from *DEC*. Says one industry expert: "Will Venus get *DEC* any new customers? I doubt it."

It is ironic that *DEC* looked to antiquity for the supermini's code name. In many ways, *DEC*'s recent failure to measure up as an excellent company is the result of founder and President Kenneth H. Olsen's seeming preoccupation with an illustrious past. The company that pioneered the development of the minicomputer now seems incapable of adjusting to another new age in computers—one increasingly dominated by microcomputers and larger superminis.

Since 1980, the second-largest computer maker has had to contend with a dual challenge: fending off colossus International Business Machines Corp. and a host of startups in its key scientific and engineering markets and reorienting itself to go after new high-growth fields ranging from office automation to computer-aided design and manufacturing. It has done a poor job on both fronts. *DEC* is not a major player in the market for work stations, the powerful desktop machines that are increasingly replacing cabinet-sized minis for engineering and scientific applications. And its sales of text-editing equipment totaled only $97 million in 1983, says Dataquest Inc.

DEC's struggles show how hard it can be for a company whose culture and skills are sharply honed for a specific market to adapt to a fundamental change in its world. Until just a few years ago, *DEC* thrived by building extraordinary ties with its customers: sophisticated data processing managers, scientists, engineers, and original-equipment manufacturers who customized its minis for end-users. *DEC* counted on these customers to find new applications for its minis. Instead of striving to be first in the market with new technology, *DEC*'s primary emphasis was making highly reliable products.

NEW GAME. As underscored by a spectacular 31% average earnings growth from 1977 to 1982, *DEC*'s approach worked splendidly when the name of the game was technological evolution and nurturing an existing customer base. But when the game changed to one of technological revolution and a need for a different customer base, *DEC*'s playbook was ineffective. The result: After earning a record $417 million in the fiscal year that ended June 30, 1982, *DEC*'s earnings plunged to $284 million in fiscal 1983 and totaled only $329 million in 1984.

DEC failed to foresee the advent of desktop work stations and personal computers. And once *DEC* did wake up to the threat, it could not marshal its forces to respond. What was described as a fluid, unbureaucratic management structure in *In Search of Excellence* was really a top-heavy, chaotic, and politicized organization. The most important thing to many managers was expanding the power of their own fiefdoms—not getting new products out the door.

Chief Executive Olsen, 58, launched a massive reorganization of his company in early 1983. It was an all-out attempt to streamline a bloated headquarters staff and replace *DEC*'s celebrated "rampant chaos"—as *Excellence*'s authors describe it—with a marketing-oriented, team spirit. Since 1982, 11 of 34 vice-presidents have left the company.

Olsen succeeded in trimming *DEC*'s minicomputer product line and in gearing up efforts to peddle *VAX* superminis. But there are few signs that the reorganization has accomplished another major purpose: speeding up product development. Indeed, the introduction of *DEC*'s long-awaited 32-bit work station—originally scheduled for this year—has now been rolled back until next March.

Olsen's team seems torn between its loyalty to the traditional minicomputer business and the need to sell such products as personal computers and work stations. Accustomed to selling to data processing and technical professionals, *DEC* also is still struggling to learn how to sell to nontechnical businesspeople.

DEC had hoped to use personal computers to penetrate the fast-growing commercial and small-business markets. But it has tried three marketing strategies in the past 18 months with little success. In that period, the number of retailers carrying *DEC* personal computers plunged to 500 from 900. And *DEC*'s total personal computer sales—virtually all of them to its existing 250,000 customers—totaled only $325 million in 1983.

Olsen's ambivalence about personal computers and work stations reflects the essence of *DEC*'s problem. Long a believer that if you had a good product customers would beat down your doors, Olsen, an engineer trained at Massachusetts Institute of Technology, refused to allow aggressive marketing of personal computers. For instance, *DEC*'s outlays for television advertising have been only a tiny fraction of those of *IBM* and Apple Computer Inc.

Now, Olsen insists that *DEC* was "sticking to its knitting" in minicomputers and never intended to be a major player in the personal computer game. "We had six *PC*s in-house that we could have launched in the late '70s. But we were selling so many [*VAX* minicomputers], it would have been immoral to chase a new market. [*PC*s and work stations are] the kind of high-growth business we're trying to get out of," he says.

HOMEGROWN. These comments contradict what Olsen has told *BUSINESS WEEK* for four years. They could be interpreted as an attempt to downplay *DEC*'s humiliation in personal computers and its difficulty in getting its new work station out the door. But they also reflect Olsen's seeming reluctance to accept that the minicomputer market is maturing. That attitude would explain why *DEC* reportedly designed its personal computer so that it could not run powerful new software programs, speculates Michael Goldstein, a vice-president at Macmillan Inc.'s publishing group. Mac-Pub, for instance, just introduced a program that transforms a $5,000 personal computer into a laboratory terminal able to tackle jobs that used to require a $35,000 *DEC* mini. Says Goldstein: "I think they wanted to protect their minis."

Unlike his counterparts at such other computer companies as Data General, Burroughs, and Apple, Olsen does not appear to see the need to recruit top-level managers from other companies to help *DEC* adjust to the demands of the new marketplace. His reliance on homegrown managers is part of a pattern of management that has tended to increase *DEC*'s dependence on its existing customers. As a result, he has put *DEC* in a defensive posture that could ultimately relegate the company to an also-ran status in the industry.

tive culture and decentralization spawned such enormously successful products as its 3000 minicomputer, the handheld scientific calculator, and the new ThinkJet nonimpact printer. But when a new climate required its fiercely autonomous divisions to cooperate in product development and marketing, *HP*'s passionate devotion to the "autonomy and entrepreneurship" that Peters and Waterman advocate became a hindrance.

To its astonishment, *HP* found itself frustrated in trying to move into such new high-growth, high-tech markets as superminicomputers, engineering work stations, personal computers, and office automation. Two years after its rollout, the *HP* 9000 work station that was developed in a $100 million crash effort still lacks competitive software, and *HP* has been outstripped by a crowd of startups. *HP*'s response: centralizing.

One major lesson from all this is that the excellent companies of today will not necessarily be the excellent companies of tomorrow. But the more important lesson is that good management requires much more than following any one set of rules. *In Search of Excellence* was a response to an era when management put too much emphasis on number-crunching. But companies can also get into trouble by overemphasizing Peters' and Waterman's principles. Says Waterman: "The book has been so popular that people have taken it as a formula for success rather than what it was intended to be. We were writing about the art, not the science of management."

MARKETING: THE NEW PRIORITY

A SPLINTERED MASS MARKET FORCES COMPANIES TO TARGET THEIR PRODUCTS
NOVEMBER 20, 1983, PP. 96-99, 102-104, 106

Question: What do John Sculley and James J. Morgan have in common? Answer: Each is an experienced, highly regarded consumer goods marketer who has recently moved to a top job at a large corporation. Sculley, an alumnus of PepsiCo Inc., is now president of Apple Computer Inc. Morgan, who came from Philip Morris Inc., is chairman of Atari Inc. In the past, Apple and Atari had concentrated more on developing new technologies than on understanding the dynamics of the marketplace—and suffered because of it. The recruitment of Sculley and Morgan is one of the more visible signs that marketing has become the new corporate priority.

Vast economic and social changes have made better marketing an imperative. Realization of that fact has set off a near free-for-all in recruiting circles for successful marketers, now hotter prospects for high-level jobs than executives with financial experience. Companies of every stripe are looking for managers, presidents, or chief executive officers who can not only develop long-term product strategies but also instill an entrepreneurial spirit into corporations that, more often than not, practice risk-avoidance.

NO BEAN COUNTERS. Says Gerard R. Roche, chairman of Heidrick & Struggles, a top recruiting firm: "Nobody wants bean counters now. Everybody wants a president with marketing experience—someone who knows about product life cycles and developing product strategies." James R. McManus, chairman of Marketing Corp. of America, a consulting firm, agrees: "Today, companies realize that their raw material, labor, and physicial-resource costs are all screwed down and that the only option for dramatic improvement will come from doing a better marketing job."

As companies define marketing more clearly, they no longer confuse it with advertising, which uses media to let consumers know that a certain product or service is available. In essence, marketing means moving goods from the producer to the consumer. It starts with finding out what consumers want or need, and

---

'Everybody wants a president with marketing experience—someone who knows about developing product strategies'

---

then assessing whether the product can be made and sold at a profit. Such decisions require conducting preliminary research, market identification, and product development; testing consumer reaction to both product and price; working out production capacities and costs; determining distribution; and then deciding on advertising and promotion strategies.

Simple as those steps may sound, many of them were all but forgotten in the 1970s, when inflation kept sales pacing upward and marketing was of secondary importance. Corporate strategies emphasized acquisitions, cash management, or the pursuit of overseas markets. Then came the recession, with its stranglehold on consumer spending, and companies were forced into trying to understand what made the domestic marketplace tick. They soon discovered that demographic and lifestyle changes had delivered a death blow to mass marketing and brand loyalty. A nation that once shared homogeneous buying tastes had splintered into many different consumer groups—each with special needs and interests.

The emergence of this fragmented consumer population, together with an array of economic factors—intense international competition, the impact of rapid technological change, the maturing or stagnation of certain markets, and deregulation—has altered the shape of competition. "If you have to change how to compete, then all of a sudden marketing is a very important function," says Robert D. Buzzell, a Harvard University School of Business Administration professor who specializes in strategic market planning.

RALLYING CRY. Robert L. Barney, chairman and CEO of Wendy's International Inc., understands this all too well. "The main thrust today is taking business away from the competition, and that fact, more than any other, is modifying our business," he explains. To pick up market share, the fast-food and hamburger chain is trying to build up its breakfast and dinner business, to achieve greater store efficiencies, and to introduce a slew of new products that will attract a broader spectrum of consumers. Wendy's has not only raised its ad budget by 45% but also increased its marketing staff to 70, from 10 five years ago. "You have to out-execute the competition, and that's why marketing is more important than ever before," asserts Barney.

The realization that marketing will provide the cutting edge in the 1980s not only has hit well-known packaged goods marketers—such as Procter & Gamble, Coca-Cola, and General Foods—but is affecting industries that used to be protected from the vagaries of consumer selling by regulatory statutes. Airlines, banks, and financial-services groups are looking for ways to grow and prosper in an environment of product proliferation, advertising clutter, escalating marketing costs, and—despite advances in research and testing—a dauntingly high rate of new-product failures.

With marketing the new priority, market research is the rallying cry. Companies are trying frantically to get their hands on information that identifies and explains the needs of the powerful new consumer segments now being formed. Kroger Co., for example, holds more than 250,000 consumer interviews a year to define consumer wants more precisely. Some companies are pinning their futures to product innovations, others are rejuvenating timeworn but proven brands, and still others are doing both.

Unquestionably, the companies that emerge successfully from this marketing morass will be those that understand the new consumer environment. In years past, the typical American family consisted of a working dad, a homemaker mom, and two kids. But the 1980 census revealed that only 7% of the 82 million households then surveyed fit that description. Of those families that reported children under the age of 17, 54% of the mothers worked full- or part-time outside their homes. Smaller households now predominate: More than 50% of all households comprise only one or two persons.

MEN ALONE. Even more startling, and most overlooked, is the fact that 24% of all households are now headed by singles. This fastest-growing segment of all—up some 80% over the previous decade—expanded mainly because the number of men living alone increased. Some 20% of households include persons 65 or older, a group that will grow rapidly. Already, almost one out of six Americans is over age 55.

These statistics are significant to marketers. "It means that the mass market has splintered and that companies can't sell their products the way they used to," says Laurel Cutler, executive vice-president for market planning at Leber Katz Partners, an advertising agency that specializes in new products. "The largest number of households may fall into the two-wage-earner grouping, but that includes everyone from a manicurist to a Wall Street type—and that's really too diverse in lifestyle and income to qualify as a mass market." Cutler foresees "every market breaking into smaller and smaller units, with unique products aimed at defined segments."

Even the auto makers agree. "We've treated the car market as a mass one, but now I'm convinced that concept is dead," says Lloyd E. Reuss, general manager of General Motors Corp.'s Buick Motor Div. Reuss now believes in target marketing: specific products and ads aimed at selected groups.

CANNED HEALTH. Despite this segmentation, there is enormous common interest in convenience, service, health, cost, and quality. Some companies have already translated these desires into successful products. Makers of soft drinks sell caffeine- and sugar-free products to health- and calorie-conscious consumers. Diet and low-salt foods have found a small but growing number of takers, and so too have high-quality frozen entrées. Robert A. Fox, the first marketing-oriented CEO in Del Monte Corp.'s 65-year history, has wasted little time getting this company into fancy frozen-food products. And he has repositioned its existing line of canned vegetables and fruits as low-salt and low-sugar items.

Philadelphia's ARA Services Inc. offers the patrons of its workplace cafeterias the option of picking up full dinners for consumption at home. It has also acquired a day-care operation and expanded the number of centers from 40, in 1980, to more than 150. "Changing demographics have a tremendous influence on the services we provide," affirms Joseph Neubauer, ARA's CEO. He says the changes have given marketing "one of the key roles—if not the key one—in corporate strategy."

As families and dwellings grow smaller, the need for more compact products and packages grows more pressing. General Electric Co. downsized its microwave oven and then modeled it to hang beneath kitchen cabinets, thereby freeing valuable counter space. The result: GE went from an also-ran in this category to a strong No. 2.

HOW-TO DATA. Yet many new consumer segments are not being mined. Men, for instance, are probably the most ignored of all buying groups—especially for household items. A recent study by Langer Associates Inc. found that men living alone were indeed interested in furniture, cooking, and cleaning and resented their "domestic dummy" stereotype. What they wanted, and what they were not getting, was straightforward how-to information from peer figures.

> 'We've treated the car market as a mass one, but now I'm convinced that concept is dead'

Teenagers, too, have become a much larger shopping force. A Yankelovich, Skelly & White Inc. poll, undertaken with *Seventeen* magazine, found that nearly 75% of teenage girls with working mothers now regularly shop for groceries. Yet few companies try to reach this group to sell anything but games, records, and clothes.

Many companies still gear their products and ads to 18-to-34-year-olds, who dominated the marketplace of the 1970s but have been supplanted in power and size by the 25-to-45-year-olds. "Youth reflected everything we did as a culture for a long time, but that's not where the bulge is today," says Paula Drillman, executive vice-president and director of research at McCann-Erickson Inc.

This means that companies must sell to an older, better-educated consumer who regards the marketplace with a jaundiced eye. Drillman, for one, believes that this skepticism accounts for the slow growth of brands in such industries as liquor. "The shopper is saying, 'Why should I pay so much more for Smirnoff when all I do is put it in a glass and mix it with something? Vodka is vodka is vodka.'"

This indifference to brands is partly the result of the massive proliferation of consumer goods. In an attempt to fire up sales, companies have been swamping the market with new products and line extensions backed by ads, coupons, giveaways, and sweepstakes. For instance, of the 261 varieties of cigarettes for sale today, about half are 10 years old or less.

ME, TOO. This huge influx of products has shifted the balance of power from manufacturers to retailers. Lawrence C. Burns, a partner with the Cambridge Group, a Chicago firm of marketing consultants, finds that "stores are eliminating slow movers and won't take on any new products unless they are assured of good inventory turns and margins. They want proof that a product really is a success, and the only way companies can provide that is through more regional roll-outs and more test marketing."

But achieving those affirmative results is more difficult because so many of the offerings are basically parity items. Says Robert E. Jacoby, chairman and CEO of Ted Bates Worldwide Inc. "We seem to be experiencing a never-ending flow of me-too products or line extensions, which makes it difficult to make a unique claim about the product." Roy Grace, chairman and executive creative director of Doyle Dane Bernbach Inc., seconds that view. He comments, "If a new technology appears, most companies can quickly copy it or acquire it. So it's really hard to gain a competitive advantage."

Examples of this difficulty abound. Aseptic packag-

SAFEWAY JILTS 'THE FAMILY OF FOUR' TO WOO 'THE JOGGING GENERATION'

Two years ago, Safeway Stores Inc. was in a sorry way. The Oakland (Calif.) supermarket chain had built a $16 billion, 150,000-employee business on the concept of look-alike stores that kept the same hours and carried the same goods. But while the 2,500 Safeway units remained the same, their customers had changed.

"Our customers used to be the family of four, and 85% of the shopping was done by women early on Saturday morning," says John H. Prinster, senior vice-president and marketing director for Safeway. With the trend toward smaller families and two-income households, Safeway began losing customers. In Los Angeles alone, its market share was halved, to about 7%, from 1975 to 1980. As a result, operating income fell 34%, to $184 million.

At that juncture, Peter A. Magowan, who had taken over as chairman and chief executive officer from William S. Mitchell in 1980, began emphasizing marketing. Magowan, whose father had overseen Safeway's fast growth from 1955 to 1969, had a retail background and felt that under Mitchell—an accountant by training—financial and legal considerations had overshadowed merchandising.

Magowan's first move was to create Prinster's job. Until then, marketing had been left up to each of the 18 divisions. Prinster hired seven new executives to run national marketing programs in the grocery, meat, variety, deli, dairy, and bakery departments, as well as a new one—natural foods.

Outside help was also sought. Doody Co., best known for department-store layouts, designed a new kind of supermarket. The prototypes have a high-tech emphasis: Safeway's square, box-style store has been scrapped in favor of a hub-and-spoke unit, with beams and wiring in full view.

'FRESH AND FULL.' The new design is only part of an effort to diversify each store to keep up with what Prinster terms "the jogging generation"—those aged 25 to 44. Stores are staying open longer, and new departments, such as bakeries, delis, and pharmacies, have been created to appeal to consumers who have eclectic tastes and little shopping time. The store's new motto is "Fresh and Full at 5."

Safeway has also placed automated teller machines in 200 stores and is experimenting with computer sales. It is selling hardware, software, and books in a Seattle unit. The chain houses 1,800 video games and is testing warehouse sales of 40 bulk items, such as sugar, flour, and nuts. Produce sections that carried 60 items now bulge with 180 different offerings—including 13 kinds of melons.

To reach its target customers, Safeway is using upscale magazines, drive-time radio, and prime-time TV. Newspapers have become a secondary buy; the chain's studies indicate that only 40% of its customers read a daily.

Under Magowan, Safeway is trying hard to become an innovator. "We used to watch what the other guy was doing, then test the hell out of the idea and bring it out late," says Prinster. The new "try it" philosophy has backfired on occasion—an attempt to introduce home-repair centers in its stores was a failure—but other efforts have fared better. When the TV mini-serial *Shogun* was attracting huge network audiences, Safeway pounced on a major display and ad program for the book and sold 400,000 copies—or one-quarter of all paperback sales.

In addition, the food chain is using its scanner equipment to test the results of price or display changes and to help figure out shelf space allocations. "Right now we're monitoring the customer, but more and more we're going to try to predict the consumer," explains Prinster. Indeed, Safeway is giving check-cashing privileges and discounts to customers who fill in questionnaires on a regular basis. "Marketing is now our prime focus," declares Prinster. "In the past, we ran our business by giving the consumers what we thought they wanted. Now we've got to find out what they want and then develop the products."

CAMPBELL SOUP: COOKING UP A SEPARATE DISH FOR EACH CONSUMER GROUP

Ever since R. Gordon McGovern took the helm at Campbell Soup Co. in 1980, the old-line food processor, known best for its soups and its Pepperidge Farm, Swanson, Franco-American, and Godiva products, has been undergoing a rapid and remarkable transformation. The 56-year-old McGovern has been working feverishly to shift the company's emphasis from production to marketing.

McGovern started by reorganizing Campbell's four divisions into about 50 business groups and making group managers responsible for the marketing, manufacturing, and profit and loss of their units. He believes this structure fosters entrepeneurship and brings "the managers much closer to the market."

RAISING EYEBROWS. "There's a tremendous feeling of urgency because an overseas company could come in here with innovative packaging and technology and just take us to the cleaners on basic lines we've taken for granted for years," McGovern says, pointing to the success of Japanese companies selling *ramen* noodles in the dry-soup category. "They've made a penetration at the low end of the American food market just as they did with cheap cars, and they are going to smash into a lot of other things," he worries.

To keep that from happening to Campbell, the push is on to target the consumer and improve quality. "I think we've had some serious problems in losing touch with our markets," says McGovern. Last year he raised industry—and company—eyebrows when he publicly labeled the Swanson TV-dinner line "junk food." McGovern insists: "It was great in 1950, but in today's world it didn't go into the microwave; it didn't represent a variety or a good eating experience to my palate." Campbell has set up Project Fix to improve the quality of its old standbys, and the Swanson line has been bolstered by the new, high-priced Le Menu entrées.

McGovern's goal for Campbell is "to be positioned with consumers as somebody who is looking after their well-being." Last fall the company set up a health and fitness business unit, and in May it bought a small maker of fitness and sports medicine products. Campbell is also emphasizing segments such as frozen foods, fish (it acquired Mrs. Paul's Kitchens Inc. in 1982), juices (a new Pepperidge Farm apple juice hit the market recently), and produce (Campbell now sells fresh mushrooms).

The program is working. For the last two fiscal years, average tonnage rose 6.5%—exceeding the 5% goal and an improvement over the previous two years,

ing, a technology for putting food and drinks in specially prepared foil or cardboard pouches that require no refrigeration has been embraced by nearly all juice makers during the past 18 months. And after the Food & Drug Administration ruled last summer that aspartame, a natural sweetener, could be used in soft drinks, all the major manufacturers raced to reformulate their diet brands to include it. Even Procter & Gamble Co. is easing up on its age-old philosophy of testing a product for years and bringing it to market only when convinced that some claim of superiority can be made. P&G has rushed its Citrus Hill brand into the spurting orange-juice category, even though it admits it cannot make any unique claims for the juice.

The result is a vicious cycle. With the plethora of new choices, products have much shorter life spans,

so a steady flow of new items is needed to keep sales curving upward. "The number of entrants in a given category has increased, and the implication is that there is greater market segmentation and shorter product life cycles," points out Derwyn F. Phillips, executive vice-president at Gillette North America. "And we find ourselves really working hard at projecting a given brand's life cycle—when the bell curve is likely to peak and the point at which it is no longer intelligent to support a given brand."

Phillips says that Gillette is now trying to speed up new-product development to prevent its combined market share in a category from shrinking. Half of the company's $2.2 billion revenues last year came from products that did not exist five years ago.

Despite advances in the technology of testing, the

which showed an average decline of 2%. "Our share of market is holding and in some cases building," McGovern says. Mrs. Paul's, for example, reversed a market share decline, going from 24% to 27% in a year.

Much of the new strategy hinges on targeting the consumer. "My 83-year-old mother doesn't eat like my son," McGovern observes. "And my daughters eat differently than their parents, and we eat differently from the people around the corner." So Campbell will gear particular products and ads to specific groups and even do regional marketing. For instance, it will sell its new, spicy Ranchero Beans only in the South and Southwest.

But Campbell also wants new products that will have national appeal. Its Prego spaghetti sauce has been a big winner and a breakthrough product for Campbell. For the fiscal year ended Aug. 1, Prego ran up sales of around $100 million, even though it was not in national distribution for the full year. It is now the No. 2 sauce behind Ragu, grabbing a 22% share.

' LINE EXTENSIONS. ' Prego almost did not get made. The former Campbell policy was that a new product had to show a profit within a year, and the payout on Prego was expected to be three years. Herbert M. Baum, vice-president for marketing, notes that in the 10 years before Prego, Campbell had only two major new-product successes—Chunky Soups and Hungry Man dinners—"and both were nothing more than glorified line extensions." But because the policy held back product development, then-Chief Executive Officer Harold A. Shaub changed it, and Prego, which

was started in 1978, went national in September, 1982. Campbell has recouped its investment in Prego. In all, there are now 20 to 30 new U.S. products in various test-market stages. One of these is Juice Works, a line of fruit-juice blends without added sugar, aimed at children. Research on the line included 6,000 evaluations by kids.

Advertising strategy is also being rethought. Campbell used to cut ad spending at the end of a quarter to boost earnings. Besides hurting the brands, "it gave us a terrible reputation among the media," says Baum. Spending is now up—and continuous. Ad expenditures for fiscal 1983 rose 39% over the previous year, to $144 million. This year's budget will be $175 million. And the message focuses on the nutritional benefits of its products. "Soup is good food" is an example. Previously, Campbell had relied on the sing-and-sell approach: "M-m-m good" was its slogan for years.

McGovern, who rose through the ranks at Pepperidge Farm, sees his role as one of leader and goader. He voices strong opinions on Campbell products. He calls the new Pepperidge Farm Star Wars cookies "a travesty," saying they do not fit the brand's high-quality, upscale adult image and are faddish. Plus, at $1.39 a bag, "it's a lousy value," says McGovern. But he didn't veto them because, he concedes, "I could be wrong."

Clearly, McGovern is challenging managers to do better, to respond to the market faster, and to develop products "that consumers perceive to be in their best interest." He seems to be getting his message across.

---

level of new-product casualties remains astonishingly high. Two out of three new entries still fail—the same proportion as in the 1960s—while the cost of introducing a new item has skyrocketed. An outlay of some $50 million is needed to launch a national brand in a major category. P&G is said to be spending almost $100 million to roll out Citrus Hill orange juice.

ANALYSIS PARALYSIS. At those odds and prices, companies are understandably wary about committing themselves to high-risk endeavors. They are demanding more research, more strategic planning, and more "review" committees to weed out problems. More often than not, however, the result of all these checks is total confusion and inactivity. Ellen I. Metcalf, a senior consultant with Arthur D. Little Inc., reports: "In some companies, you can spend six weeks going

through psychographics, trend-line analysis, quarterly consumer reports, scanner data from grocery products—rooms just full of data. Then you ask, 'How do you use this information?' And they say they don't know what to do with it."

Ad agencies, in particular, resent the analysis-paralysis climate. "There are more and more people

---

Advertising should aim at new consumer groups: Men, teenagers, singles, and older shoppers

[at a company] who can say no and very few who can say yes," laments Barry Loughrane, president and CEO of Doyle Dane. This risk-avoidance atmosphere worries Allen G. Rosenshine, chairman and CEO of ad agency Batten Barton Durstine & Osborn Inc. "Everyone has developed a corporate timidity." That, along with the B-school mentality—quantify everything, take few chances—is threatening the entrepreneurialism that companies need if they are to grow, he feels.

But the outlook may not be altogether bleak. Enlightened companies have recognized the challenge and are radically overhauling their operations to put more emphasis on marketing, seeking top marketing executives, and changing the nature and scope of their jobs. Lester B. Korn, chairman of Korn/Ferry International, says he recently filled the top marketing slot at a major consumer goods company—a $350,000-a-year post that typifies the trend to give marketing more clout. "Companies want marketing executives to be responsible for total business results—they're putting the profit-and-loss in with the job—and that's a big step forward from the past, when they had only been responsible for volume and share growth," he says. Companies hope to create a culture that encourages more risk-taking, accepts some failures, and rewards success.

The hottest companies to recruit from are P&G, Johnson & Johnson, Philip Morris, General Foods, and Thomas J. Lipton—large, disciplined consumer product marketers with broad product lines. "These companies teach their people how to create profitable product lines in brutally competitive industries, and their consistency is what makes them so attractive," says J. Gerald Simmons, president of Handy Associates Inc.

SUPPORT SYSTEMS. Some executive-search specialists express reservations, however, about placing a P&Ger. "Their support system is just so strong that they end up working for the system rather than being creative," says David S. Joys, executive vice-president of Russell Reynolds Associates Inc. "Many clients prefer that a P&G executive go to another company first, and then they'll go after him."

Today, most companies believe that their brightest chances for success in coming years will hinge on the development of innovative products aimed at specific consumer niches. But because of the risks, they are trying to direct development efforts toward producing

CHRYSLER TRIES TO SHARPEN ITS BRAND IDENTITY

For decades, Detroit believed not only that sales and marketing were synonymous but also that they were less important than finance, engineering, and manufacturing. But fuel crises, imports, recession, and quality-conscious consumers shook those beliefs. "If there's a growing respect for the market, it's because we've learned that disrespecting it cost us an arm and a leg," says Bennett E. Bidwell, executive vice-president for sales and marketing at Chrysler Corp.

Indeed, the increased emphasis on marketing is most pronounced at Chrysler, which from 1979 to 1982 hovered near bankruptcy. In 1979, Chairman Lee Iacocca created Chrysler's first executive position aimed at long-term market planning. Joseph A. Campana, a 15-year sales and marketing executive with Ford Motor Co., became Chrysler's director for marketing plans and started studying variables such as family size, fuel prices, and psychological factors that might affect sales five years down the line. Last July, Chrysler set up an office of the chairman consisting of Iacocca, Bidwell—who had joined the company a month earlier—and two executives responsible for finance and manufacturing. Bidwell notes that the new arrangement "bakes in marketing organizationally."

related items in order to achieve economies of scale and a greater overall market share. "You have to go into areas where you have some right to be in that category," says McManus of Marketing Corp. "Companies that go with a product in search of a market or one that has no fit with their existing businesses are doomed to a bloody nose."

Hershey Foods Corp. learned that very lesson when it tried to get into the canned-frosting business. Hershey's problem: It did not have a cake mix to support its frosting, unlike its chief competitors, General Mills, P&G, and Pillsbury. These rivals discounted the frosting and made up the difference on the cake batter. Her-

DECISION TIME. Chrysler is now carving out a long-term product strategy: Should it emphasize low-, middle-, or high-end vehicles? Should it opt for independence or joint ventures? A decision is expected in the next few months. Basically, though, Chrysler views itself as a mass producer with niche opportunities—it launched the boomlet in convertible sales—and thinks it can beat General Motors Corp. at such a game because it is smaller and can react faster.

But its size and lingering doubts about its financial health mean that Chrysler must do a better marketing job than its rivals. One key feature of its game plan is a five-year, 50,000-mi. warranty that addresses consumers' concerns about durability and quality. For pickup trucks, Chrysler offers a five-year, 100,000-mi. warranty on rust. Both programs are free and are unique among Detroit car producers.

The company is also trying to target markets. For example, pickup drivers are concentrated in Texas and Louisiana and like to listen to country-and-Western music. Chrysler now buys radio time on C&W stations to promote its trucks. "It's like a rifle taking aim at a direct target vs. a shotgun that's fired in a 360° arc," says Campana, now vice-president for marketing.

Campana oversees a marketing group that has doubled in size to 125 since last November. At that time, Chrysler set up separate marketing staffs and hired different ad agencies to handle its two divisions—Chrysler-Plymouth and Dodge. The purpose is to give each division stronger identities. Research indicated that Dodge had almost no market identity, while Plymouth had upscale demographics but no matching image.

To carve out an identity for Dodge, the division is using the theme "Dodge, an American Revolution." The commercials and print ads consistently use the same basic format and boldly feature the division rather than the particular vehicle being shown.

By contrast, ads for the Chrysler-Plymouth Div. are all different. The Chrysler line already has a strong market image—relatively upscale and luxurious—and the ads reinforce that. For instance, spots for a new front-wheel-drive sports car, the Laser, compare it with the Porsche 944. Plymouth ads stress the product's value and warranty program with a "match it if you can" slogan.

SLAYING THE DRAGON. But Chrysler has not quite slain the marketing dragon. It says it wants to solidify the images of each division, yet on its line of imported cars (from Mitsubishi Corp.), the nameplates will be the same, no matter which division or dealer organization sells them. Last year, for example, one Mitsubishi car was sold as either the Plymouth Champ or the Dodge Colt. This year the same car is called the Colt by both divisions.

There is also confusion about one of Chrysler's domestic lines. In 1982 the Chrysler New Yorker was a rear-drive model. In the 1983 model year, the new front-wheel-drive version was called the New Yorker and the rear-drive became the New Yorker Fifth Avenue. For the 1984 year, the front-drive version is called the New Yorker, and the other, the Fifth Avenue. Clear? Bidwell acknowledges the confusion and vows to "rationalize" Chrysler's line. "Marketing has to grow up and go for product rationality and simplicity," he says.

---

shey, with no companion product to fall back on, had to discount its product to stay in the market. "The competition was suicidal, and while we could have stayed in the market, it wouldn't have been prudent," says Jack Dowd, Hershey Chocolate Co.'s vice-president for new-product development. "But you've got to have the right to fail."

The company has recouped with its new Hershey's chocolate milk, packaged in a rich brown container that makes chocoholics drool in anticipation. Hershey had planned to have the chocolate milk in four markets by the end of the year, but strong demand has already put it in 12 cities, and the figure is growing.

HANG WITH IT. To minimize the risk of failure with new products, experts make several recommendations. "Companies need to have a high-level executive who will champion the new creation—hang with it—and move fast," says Cutler of Leber Katz, which since 1969 has helped clients develop 10 major brands, including Vantage brand cigarettes, with no failures. "It's vital to get a pilot product up quickly, test consumers' reactions to it, refine it, and get it going."

Speed, however, is not the hallmark of many companies. Up to seven years can elapse between the time a new product is proposed and its nationwide distribution. A product developed in 1976 may meet with

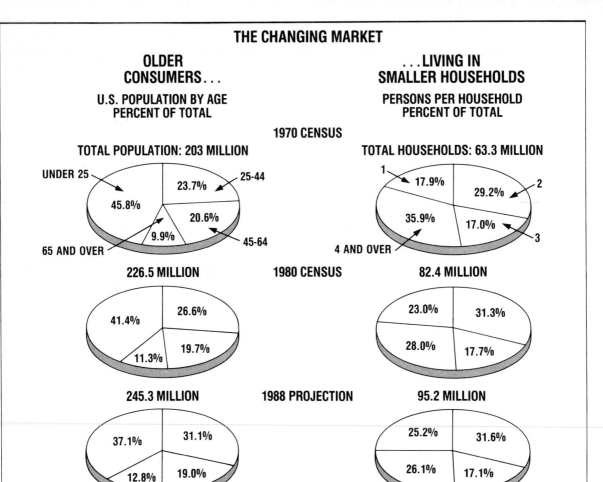

THE CHANGING MARKET

OLDER CONSUMERS...

**U.S. POPULATION BY AGE
PERCENT OF TOTAL**

...LIVING IN SMALLER HOUSEHOLDS

**PERSONS PER HOUSEHOLD
PERCENT OF TOTAL**

1970 CENSUS

TOTAL POPULATION: 203 MILLION

UNDER 25 — 45.8%
25-44 — 23.7%
45-64 — 20.6%
65 AND OVER — 9.9%

TOTAL HOUSEHOLDS: 63.3 MILLION

1 — 17.9%
2 — 29.2%
3 — 17.0%
4 AND OVER — 35.9%

1980 CENSUS

226.5 MILLION

41.4%   26.6%
11.3%   19.7%

82.4 MILLION

23.0%   31.3%
28.0%   17.7%

1988 PROJECTION

245.3 MILLION

37.1%   31.1%
12.8%   19.0%

95.2 MILLION

25.2%   31.6%
26.1%   17.1%

DATA: U.S. CENSUS. DONNELLEY MARKETING
INFORMATION SERVICES AMERICAN PROFILE

DATA U.S. CENSUS.
DATA RESOURCES INC.'S U.S. ECONOMIC SERVICE

wholly different market conditions when it finally makes its debut in 1983. "Developing a new product is like shooting a duck," observes Gary W. McQuaid, marketing vice-president at Hershey's. "You can't shoot it where it is; you've got to shoot it where it's going to be."

Aiming too far ahead of the market is just as risky, of course. But for some companies, such as auto makers, the lengthy time it takes to develop a new product leaves no choice. 'When we commit to a car, we're four years away from production," says F. James McDonald, GM's president. "How many people today know what they want four years from now? We really have to roll some dice."

The task of understanding and predicting consumer

behavior has led to a nearly insatiable hunger for market research. But experts in the field caution companies about switching from one new technique to another, and they suggest that keeping a steady information base will allow for more accurate projections and comparisons with previous years. Cutler believes that new products often misfire because they "are assigned to junior people at either the company or agency level, since the most experienced people do not want to take their eyes off the main brands. But it is imperative that the team have broad knowledge and have clout—in order to see the new product through review committees and then to get it on the shelf."

Given the slim odds for scoring a new-product hit, many executives are trying to breathe new life into dying brands. "There are dozens of older brands lying around that have been neglected over the years," says Chester Kane, president of Kane, Bortree & Associates, a new-product consulting group. "Companies must discover ways to make them viable for today's consumer."

RIGHT GUARD REBORN.   Gillette is trying for just such a comeback with its Right Guard deodorant, which dropped from a huge 25% share of the deodorant market in the mid-1960s to 8% today. The company was loath to let the bronze-canned brand die, since it had produced $500 million in profits during its 23-year life span. For the past two years, all departments—research, marketing, research and development, manufacturing, sales, and finance—as well as the product's ad agency, Young & Rubicam Inc., have been getting together monthly to coordinate plans for rejuvenating Right Guard. Last June, Gillette put the deodorant into new, bold-stripe containers and began a $28.2 million ad campaign—the most expensive in the company's 82 years. Gillette says the deodorant's sales are running 14% higher than planned.

Whether a product is new, old, or rejuvenated, the task facing all marketers is to differentiate it from competitors' offerings. The consumer must be made aware of its usefulness and given a reason to choose it over all other brands. "The financial-services companies are having trouble with this," remarks Russell Reynolds' Joys. "They all want a product portfolio that matches the competitors' offerings, but they also must come up with unique products—carrying higher gross margins—for the salesmen to really focus on."

Federated Department Stores Inc. is grappling with these issues. Fearful that its core department stores were losing their identity with consumers because of the rapid growth of designer labels and discounters, it has set up a buying office for the purpose of creating private-label goods that would be sold only in its better stores. As a first step, the company has brought out a line of sheets and towels under the "Home Concept" name. The idea is to develop unique, high-quality merchandise that carries a higher profit margin and is different from anything a consumer could buy at a rival department store or discounter—even a Federated-owned one, such as Gold Circle Stores.

Advertising plays a major role in carving out distinct identities for consumer products. The push is on for harder-hitting, product-selling ads and the increased use of sales-promotion devices, such as direct mail and rebates. Broadcast television is still the preferred medium, because cable is not yet in enough homes, and viewership data are still too sketchy to make it efficient as an audience-targeting device. However, specialty publications are getting more play from companies that wish to reach a particular market group—usually a working population that may not have the time to read more general media or watch TV.

NUKES AND BAGELS.   Furthermore, companies are consolidating their accounts at a few full-service agencies, rather than letting a number of agencies handle various brands. They are doing this on the theory that the more important an account is to an agency, the higher the quality of attention the client is likely to receive. Then, too, that policy promotes efficiency and more unified marketing, especially for companies that sell overseas. To capitalize on the consolidation trend, Bates has centralized in New York its operations for key multinational clients, including Colgate-Palmolive Co. and Mars Inc. The strategy is to develop "benchmark ads" that can be launched in the U.S. and then adapted for use all over the world.

The need to reorganize corporate priorities to meet the changing marketplace has caused several companies—quietly and almost surreptitiously—to start their own in-house venture-capital operations. Companies such as Seagrams, R.J. Reynolds, and Gillette have begun either funding or acquiring small, diverse businesses in market segments that hold promise. By experimenting in areas as disparate as nuclear medicine (Seagrams) and bagel chains (Reynolds), these companies can explore the intracacies of the medical or fast-food businesses—categories that are likely to become increasingly important—with little risk.

Gillette North America's just-begun ventures council—composed of its domestic divisional presidents and three corporate executives—has been charged with ferreting out opportunities, not necessarily in the consumer packaged-goods area. "The level of maturity of some of our businesses says to us that it is very important that we invest dollars today to grow higher-yield businesses for tomorrow," says Gillette's Phillips. "We are trying to motivate people inside and outside the company to help us develop new opportunities for the future."

THE COUNTERFEIT TRADE

ILLEGAL COPIES THREATEN MOST INDUSTRIES—AND CAN ENDANGER CONSUMERS

DECEMBER 16, 1985, PP. 64-68, 72

A worker rigging parachutes for military pilots in a Brunswick (Me.) plant picked up several pieces of cord. They felt too light, and he examined them closely. They turned out to be counterfeits that could tear apart during an ejected pilot's descent.

If the rigger had not been so vigilant, the substandard cord might have gone into service. Any pilots who tumbled to their deaths would likely be written off as victims of freak accidents.

That's the nature of the counterfeit trade these days: Perhaps the world's fastest-growing and most profitable business, it involves big dollars and, all too often, the possibility of quiet death. Products now routinely counterfeited include chemicals, computers, drugs, fertilizers, pesticides, medical devices, military hardware, and food—as well as parts for airplanes and automobiles.

This is a long way from the aspect of counterfeiting most familiar to consumers: the sale of imitation Gucci wallets, Louis Vuitton bags, Cartier watches, and Cabbage Patch dolls. Today's counterfeiters operate at all levels of the economy. Part of the problem stems from the growth of world trade. As U.S. companies do more manufacturing offshore, developing countries acquire the technology to crank out bogus goods. But not all offenders are foreign. Experts estimate that 20% of the world's fakes are made in the U.S.— often the work of marginal producers who can't turn a profit legally.

The business has a hierarchy all its own. At the highest level are true counterfeit products. These look as much like the original as possible and use the same brand name. Then come look-alikes, or knockoffs. These duplicate an original but carry a different name. Down the line are reproductions— close, but not exact, copies. Perfumes such as

Channel No. 5 and Chanel No. 6 are clearly intended to pass as the real thing. At the bottom of the heap are imitations. These cheap, unconvincing copies fool no one.

As the lines between such distinctions continue to blur, trade experts believe copying of some items will become epidemic. Says James L. Bikoff, president of the International Anticounterfeiting Coalition *(IACC)*: "There is now no business not affected by the problem."

TABOO TOPIC. According to the House Energy & Commerce Committee, which presided over hearings on the subject in 1983, direct losses tied to counterfeiting approach $20 billion a year. But that figure is, at best, a guess. No one knows the size of the market. Says Eugene C. Goodale, a patent attorney for Caterpillar Tractor Co.: "For every case you know about there are at least 10 others." The Counterfeit Intelligence Bureau in London estimates that up to $60 billion in annual world trade is in fakes. But it, too, cannot be sure.

This much is certain: The problem is far more costly than the mere market value of bogus goods. Counterfeiters are undermining legitimate business and obscuring long-held legal distinctions about who owns ideas and inventions. The disputes they cause create tensions between highly regulated industrialized nations and developing countries. Producers there typically defend their right to copy products with patents they see no need to buy— and can't afford.

Despite the growth of counterfeiting, businessmen everywhere still treat it as a dirty secret. Few want to admit they've been affected. They fear publicity will encourage others to copy their goods. They also fear that, if the quality of their parts is suspect, customers may go elsewhere. "The subject is still taboo," says the *IACC*'s Bikoff. Although membership in his anticounterfeiting group has jumped from 15 companies when it started in 1978 to more than 300 today, commitment varies. Manufacturers newly hurt by counterfeiting join to find out how to fight back, but some prefer to downplay the problem, unwilling to be perceived as victims.

Boeing Co., for example, describes an incident in 1977 this way: A small manufacturer made fake parts from stolen Boeing blueprints. "The parts turned out to be pretty good," says a Boeing official. But the Federal Aviation Administration didn't see it that way. It recalled the fake fire detection and control units from around 30 Boeing 737s and 727s. And in 1983 a Defense Dept. contractor was convicted and sent to prison for 10 years for supplying the agency with fake Boeing and Grumman Corp. parts. The faulty parts were manufactured in Florida machine shops, and Boeing and Grumman markings were later added without the companies' knowledge.

At the moment, the biggest worry for the aerospace industry is the proliferation of bogus "high-strength" fastening bolts. There are "tens of thousands" of such fasteners on every commercial and military plane, says Thomas Roach, an engineer for *SPS* Technologies Inc. The Newton (Pa.) company is a leading manufacturer of such bolts, used on airplane engines, wheels, brakes, and wings. *SPS* now publishes a sheet alerting customers to phony parts.

One of the aerospace companies most victimized by counterfeiters is Bell Helicopter Textron Inc. Fake parts were found in more than 600 helicopters sold to *NATO* military and civilian U. S. units. The parts included transmission and landing-gear assemblies made without heat or stress tests. Some of these parts may have caused crashes in the U. S. and abroad, says Bell. It reports that a Peruvian Air Force helicopter crash in late October was the result of a worn-out Bell tail rotor blade recycled by a Miami-based company. Several people died in the crash.

Airplane crashes create headlines, but the counterfeits that have quietly taken a higher human toll are pharmaceutical drugs and medical devices. The American Medical Assn. says an unknown number of deaths and cases of paralysis have been caused by fake amphetamines and tranquilizers. In 1984, G. D. Searle & Co. suddenly recalled more

THE LANGUAGE OF COUNTERFEITING

Counterfeiting—the unauthorized copying of a product—is an often murky subject with a jargon all its own. Some of the terms, such as copyright, patent, and trademark, are well known. Here are some of the less-known expressions:

ASSOCIATIVE COUNTERFEIT, IMITATION
Illegal use of a name or product shape that differs from the original product but that the consumer will associate with the original.

DIVERSION
The distribution and sale of legitimate products through unauthorized dealers.

GRAY MARKET
Goods available through diversion, usually cheaper and without service guarantees.

KNOCKOFF
A product that copies another design closely but carries its own name. Also used as slang for counterfeit.

LOOK-ALIKE, FAKE
Slang for counterfeit or knockoff.

PARODY
The intentional mockery of a product through imitation that results in an infringement of the original product's trademark.

PASSING OFF
The simulation of a trademark to closely resemble the original.

PIRACY
Similar to counterfeiting but broader. The unauthorized publication, reproduction, use, or imitation of an invention, creation, or product with the objective of having the result pass as genuine.

PRODUCT SUBSTITUTION
The Pentagon's official term for the use of counterfeit or substandard parts in defense equipment.

REENTRY
Purchasing goods from a domestic manufacturer, allegedly for overseas destinations, then returning them and selling them at lower cost in the domestic gray market.

REPLICA, REPRODUCTION
A close but not exact copy.

than 1 million fake birth control pills distributed without their authorization and made with insufficient levels of estrogen (box, page 43). A search for the fakes was touched off after women taking the pills complained to their gynecologists about unexpected, heavy bleeding.

Two years earlier, the Food & Drug Administration recalled more than 350 intra-aortic pumps, used to keep hearts beating during open-heart surgery. Investigators had found a bogus $8 part in the $20,000 pumps that threatened to stall.

CHALK GARDENS. In foreign countries where laws and regulations concerning counterfeiting are lax, product-quality problems are even more widespread. Farmers in Zaire and Kenya, for example, bought what they thought was Chevron Corp.'s top-quality pesticide six years ago. Unfortunately, it was a counterfeit made of chalk. The result? The two nations each lost two-thirds of their cash crops in the one year.

This situation raises a nagging enforcement problem. In many developing nations, the imitation of U.S. products is considered a route to growth, so enforcement is often half-hearted, if it exists at all. "In the long term," says Anthony R. Gurka, founder of Commercial Trademark Services Ltd., a Hong Kong agency that specializes in tracking fraudulent goods, counterfeiting "is a natural thing for any country in the world to go through that wants to modernize its industry."

Indeed, a developing America was a haven for counterfeiters a century ago. For postwar Japan, counterfeiting was the first step up the economic ladder. Spurred on by the Japanese example, other Asians followed suit. Today, Taiwan is probably the region's leading counterfeiting center, having replaced Japan. South Korea and Thailand are coming up fast. In Europe, Italy is first among imitators. Mexico and Brazil lead in Latin America, followed by Argentina. A growth area: the Middle East.

To make money, of course, every counterfeiter needs a buyer. And who doesn't love a good deal? Young professionals from New York to Tokyo proudly sport Cartier, Dunhill, or Rolex fakes. They enjoy the cachet that comes with being a smart shopper: A gold-plated clone costs $40, the real thing $1,000 and up. Says one satisfied customer: "Japanese-made fakes keep better time than genuine Cartiers because the fakes have Japanese-made movements." Cartier, of course, disagrees.

Just who are these counterfeiters, so quick to cash in on everyone's penchant to pay less? Some, of course, are seedy opportunists who grab a quick buck wherever they can. But the modern counterfeiter is often an otherwise respectable small-company owner who goes astray when he sees an easy dollar to be made. "They get greedy," says Daniel J. Elliott, director of security for *GM*'s Service Parts Organization. So they let their production lines go a few extra runs and either strike deals with retailers directly or make reasonable facsimiles they hope to wholesale as genuine.

FENDER FAKERS. So far, organized crime has played a surprisingly small role, at least in the U.S. But most government authorities and outside experts expect its activities to expand rapidly. The mob is already strong in certain markets, especially the garment trade and drugs. "The counterfeiting business is the drug business of the 1980s—only a lot safer," says Daniel J. Bianchini, executive vice-president of a Boston-based private investigation agency. Maybe so, but for now "there's no Mr. Big," explains one San Francisco attorney. "It's a bunch of little guys."

The little guys are causing big problems. The counterfeit trade is now sizable enough and sophisticated enough to endanger America's future economic growth. John A. Young, president of Hewlett-Packard Co. and chairman of the President's Commission on Industrial Competitiveness, says "technology is the only true American competitive advantage" left. Counterfeiting has become so sophisticated and high-tech, he adds, that it now threatens to erode that advantage.

Indeed, within days of reaching the market, or even as soon as a patent is published, any product can be duplicated. Take a new model of an American Telephone & Telegraph Co. telephone. The telecommunications giant showed a brand-new phone design at a Las Vegas trade show in 1983. Before it could hit the market, a Taiwanese company that had seen the display had copied, produced, and marketed the new phone. *AT&T* pro-

A BOGUS PILL, AN UNEXPECTED BABY, A WEB OF LAWSUITS

Beverly Butler was in Augusta, Ga., sitting in the trailer she and her husband Keith had just bought. It was the fall of 1984, and she was watching the noon news on television. That's how she heard that the birth-control pills she was taking were counterfeit. "I was shocked," she recalls. "I never doubted that I was getting the medication I was supposed to be getting."

The pills were labeled Ovulen 21, a drug made by Monsanto Co.'s G. D. Searle & Co. subsidiary. But the company discovered in October, 1984, that counterfeit versions of its product were being distributed—with reduced levels of hormones. Searle notified the Food & Drug Administration, and the bogus goods were quickly taken off the market. Meanwhile, Beverly Butler, 22, had become pregnant with her second child.

Zachary Scott, now five months old, is a cheerful, healthy boy whose parents love him. But the Butlers, who have an older son with a heart condition, weren't ready for him. "I didn't know who to be mad at," says Keith.

Eventually, he found out. Two months ago, the Butlers sued the Southside Pharmacy in Augusta, Richie Pharmaceuticals Co., and Interstate Drug Exchange Inc., a Long Island (N. Y.) drug distrib-

utor, for $1.6 million. Their attorney, Michael C. Walls, alleges that the bogus pills were manufactured in Panama and shipped to Interstate, which in turn sold them to Richie. The pills eventually wound up in Southside's drugstore.

HOW COMMON? If the pharmacy had purchased supplies from a Searle dealer, Walls contends, it would have received genuine goods. Southside, meanwhile, has cross-filed complaints against Richie and Searle, based in Skokie, Ill. Searle has also sued Interstate for damages related to patent infringement and trademark violation.

Richie Pharmaceuticals, a 13-year-old company in Glasgow, Ky., buys drugs mostly from manufacturers, but some come from other distributors, says a spokesman for owner Elmer Richie. Interstate Drug Exchange, a privately held company, refused to comment.

Beverly Butler is now working full time, and with two incomes, the Butlers are able to care for their two sons. Their birth-control pill ordeal is over, except for the lawsuit. But, says Beverly, "I want everyone to know what has happened to us, so it can help others. I'm afraid of how common this is. There is no telling how many women there are who were working and didn't get to see it on the news."

By Jan Jaben in Augusta

---

tested privately, and shortly thereafter the Taiwan company dropped the product.

It is also now incredibly cheap to make fakes that once required factories with heavy equipment and hundreds of workers. Today one man in an auto repair shop can copy the contours of a fender

---

'Technology is the only true American competitive advantage' left—an edge that counterfeiting could erode

---

on a home computer. He can then make a plastic die and run off hundreds of copies. A wholesaler can buy the fake for $25 and sell it to a local repair shop for $50. The shop, in turn, sells it to a customer for $110—the price of the brand-name product. Since the fenders are not made of corrosion-resistant coated steel, they rust out faster than the genuine article. When they do, the unsuspecting consumer blames the legitimate manufacturer, not the phony one.

SITTING DUCKS. Costs are passed along to workers, as well—who pay with their jobs. According to the Commerce Dept., at least 750,000 U. S. jobs have been lost because of forgers. Often companies and workers have no idea why sales suddenly slump. If fakes are top quality, they are rarely detected. If they are discovered, it is typically in the local distribution network, whether in the U. S. or overseas. Apart from producing a nondetectable facsimile, distribution is the single important factor facing a would-be counterfeiter.

As counterfeiting becomes big business, with substantial investment in plants and equipment, stability is making it vulnerable. It is now harder for the big operators to move around, changing locations or products. That's one reason why such measures as raids and lawsuits, which were once considered useless, are increasingly effective.

In 1984, Ford Motor Co. launched a counterattack. In the first nine months of the year, the car company, with government officials and police, confiscated more than 1 million phony parts in raids on 28 distributors and manufacturers. Ford has sued the 28 companies, and five cases have been settled so far—all in Ford's favor.

Such raids have also been made more effective by the Trademark Counterfeiting Act of 1984, which makes counterfeiting a federal crime punishable by fines of $250,000 and prison terms of five years. For corporations, the maximum fine is $1 million.

Like Ford, General Motors is also fighting back. In the New York City area, the company has discovered replacement brake shoes so soft they could be scratched with a fingernail. It also found corrosive antifreeze and transmission fluid that solidified below zero. And in the Middle East, the company even discovered entire copycat engines. Says *GM*'s Elliott: "Nearly 40% of all *GM* parts in the Middle East are counterfeit." Since mid-1984, it has conducted five raids in Saudi Arabia and four in Kuwait.

'COCO CHABEL.' Because counterfeiting is only now being recognized as a widespread problem in the U. S., government enforcement of trademark and patent infringements has been sporadic at best. "We found a lot of companies are doing their own investigations because they can't get help from government," says Representative John D. Dingell (D-Mich.), who chaired the House Energy & Commerce Committee hearings on the subject.

Dingell points a finger at the Administration for its cuts in U. S. Customs personnel. Rather than save taxpayers' money, he says, the cutbacks are inefficient: Because counterfeiting has become such big business and fakemakers tend to stay put longer than ever before, the cost-benefit ratio of tracking down pirates is improving. For every dollar paid out in salary to customs officials, they bring in $18 in additional customs receipts. There are 1,000 import specialists among a total of 13,000 agents who cover 300 ports around the country.

The best defense for businesses victimized by counterfeiters, say experts, is to strike back rather than rely on government agencies, the police, or the courts. Even Alexander H. Good, Deputy Assistant Commerce Secretary, concedes that private businesses "have been our front-line defense."

One of the companies doing the most to protect itself is Paris-based Chanel, which spends roughly $1.2 million a year on security. Chanel competitors include near-names such as Channel, Chabel, or Replica No. 5—reproductions that boldly claim on the bottle to be "a good imitation of Chanel No. 5."

TOKYO TOLERANCE. Chanel goes after these copiers by computer, keeping track of protected brand names in various countries as well as the names of suspected counterfeiters. The company also takes 40 to 60 cases to court each year. "If we did not," says General Manager Bernard Lehmann, "there would be 20 times more of them. The damage would be catastrophic."

Cartier is also fighting back in some creative ways. Officials in Mexico were being uncooperative about pursuing a Mexico City retail-store owner who was selling fake Cartier products—despite 49 legal decisions against him. So Cartier opened up its own store directly across the street and forced the retailer to strike a deal: In return for not selling forgeries, he would become Cartier's sole local distributor.

The Union des Fabricants, the Paris-based association that protects patents and trademarks, had an even tougher problem in Toyko recently. It found fake Cartier belts for sale in the Ministry of Trade & Industry building. *MITI* is one of the government agencies charged with combating counterfeiters, about 30% of whom are believed to be involved with the *yakuza,* the Japanese Mafia. Only after they were publicly embarrassed did Japanese officials act—arresting 484 counterfeiters in October, 10 times more than in earlier months of the year.

Such crackdowns, however, are often short-lived, and dealers usually find ways around them. The current practice in Japan is to display the genuine article and sell the cheaper fake under the counter. In Seoul, shoppers in a busy district are offered Members Only-style jackets without the identifying label. That comes separately, to be stitched on at home.

To put pressure on developing nations, Congress last year passed the Tariff & Trade Act. The act is intended to do internationally what the Trademark Counterfeiting Act does domestically: put teeth into existing laws. It requires the U. S. to deny tariff preferences and duty-free imports to developing countries that are havens for counterfeiters.

Already, the act is getting results. Because of it—and quiet but firm protectionist talk—Taiwan and other nations have begun to crack down on counterfeiters. Last year, Taiwan passed a law that makes trademark infringement a crime punishable by a five-year prison term. It also revised its copyright law. The government is also working on a fair-trade bill that would outlaw products with packaging that is intended to confuse consumers.

JEAN RESEARCH. Taiwan also has the distinction of making some of the shoddiest and most dangerous products. So far, not one bogus auto part discovered there has been able to meet federal safety standards—and auto accidents caused by phony parts are one of the most serious threats counterfeits have posed to date. In the late 1970s, a bus in Canada careened over a cliff because it was equipped with Taiwanese brake linings. Fifteen people were killed.

If Taiwan gets tough, however, the counterfeiters headquartered there will undoubtedly pack their bags and move elsewhere. Even without a crackdown, the action is likely to shift. "Within three years, there's going to be a serious problem in China," predicts an expert in Hong Kong. "Copying has been a way of life there for thousands of years. It's a form of flattery."

Wherever counterfeiting moves, some companies think they'll be ready to cope by means of state-of-the-art technology. Levi Strauss & Co., for example, weaves a microscopic-fiber pattern into its fabric that is visible only under a special light. When the company spots dubious merchandise, it buys a sample from a retailer and tests for authenticity.

The device was developed by a Los Angeles company called Light Signatures Inc., which also does the checking. Light Signatures, a subsidiary of Telecredit Inc., is part of an industry that didn't even exist five years ago. Today there are more than a dozen such anticounterfeiting companies. They are all going after slices of the more than $50 million that victimized American businesses will spend this year on high-tech solutions to the problem.

No matter how hard companies work for solutions and how exotic their protection becomes, counterfeiting will never disappear. It may, in fact, be the world's second oldest profession: In the Paris office of the Union des Fabricants sits a lid from a wine jar. It's very pretty, it's fake, and it was made during the first century B. C.

By Thomas C. O'Donnell and Elizabeth Weiner in New York, Hazel Bradford in Washington, Amy Borrus in London, and Dorinda Elliott in Taiwan, with bureau reports

THE HOLLOW CORPORATION

THE DECLINE OF MANUFACTURING THREATENS THE ENTIRE U.S. ECONOMY
MARCH 3, 1986, PP. 57-59

"American companies have either shifted output to low-wage countries or come to buy parts and assembled products from countries like Japan that can make quality products at low prices. The result is a hollowing of American industry. The U. S. is abandoning its status as an industrial power."

Akio Morita
Sony Corp. chairman and co-founder

While economists engage in an eerily detached debate about whether the U. S. is losing its industrial base—and even whether it matters—Sony's 64-year-old chief affirms what American business leaders have been seeing for more than a decade: In industry after industry, manufacturers are closing up shop or curtailing their operations and becoming marketing organizations for other producers, mostly foreign.

Autos, steel, machine tools, videorecorders, industrial robots, fiber optics, semiconductor chips—these are some of the markets in which the U. S. is losing dominance or has been driven out. More markets are destined to feel the bite of foreign competition.

The result is the evolution of a new kind of company: manufacturers that do little or no manufacturing and are increasingly becoming service-oriented. They may perform a host of profit-making functions—from design to distribution—but lack their own production base. In contrast to traditional manufacturers, they are hollow corporations.

Unchecked, this trend will ultimately hurt the U. S. economy. The traditional industrial sector has long been the leader in U. S. growth in productivity, the wellspring of innovation, and the generator of a rising standard of living. The spectacular rise in employment in the fast-growing service sector will continue to offset the loss of jobs in manufacturing. But services, on average, do not measure up well against manufacturing in productivity growth (chart, page 47) or in personal income. In short, the idea that a post-industrial America can become increasingly prosperous as a service-based economy appears to be a dangerous myth.

No one who finds this threat a bit remote right now will be accused of economic myopia. The U. S. economy appears to be enjoying a period of unusually well-balanced growth. The collapse of oil prices has revived a three-year-old expansion that seemed to be winding down only a few months ago. Economists are scurrying to raise their forecasts for growth, employment, and personal income. The oil plunge, along with a general weakness in commodity prices, has blown away the specter of inflation for the foreseeable future. The dollar continues to soften against most foreign currencies. Interest rates, reflecting the improved inflation outlook, are declining. And the stock market is just wild about all of the above.

Unfortunately, however, this is only part of the story—the short-term chapter. Beneath this shiny surface, U. S. industry is undergoing fundamental changes whose full impact on the economy may not be seen for a decade. If the hollowing process continues in industrial America, the economy of the mid-1990s will look vastly different from the one that is generating the current prosperity. And there are serious reasons to doubt that the long-term picture will be as bright as today's.

It may be some consolation that Sony, Honda Motor Co., and other foreign producers make many of their products in the U. S. That keeps some jobs in this country and may help to defuse protectionist pressures in Congress. Indeed, foreign companies are now pouring money into their U. S. operations faster than American companies are investing abroad. Ironically, however, as foreign producers move into the U. S., American manufacturers continue to take their operations overseas. Low wage bills in South Korea, Taiwan, and other Asian countries clearly are part of the attraction, but all too often it appears that American companies are simply giving up on the U. S.

as a suitable place to make their goods. Says Sony's Morita: "We are not taking away your manufacturers' business. They are giving it up. If they move out factories and depend on the Far East, that means the hollowing of American industry."

Indeed, U. S. manufacturers are pursuing a strategy of outsourcing—buying parts or whole products from other producers, both at home and abroad—with a vengeance. Outsourcing breaks down manufacturers' traditional vertical structure, in which they make virtually all critical parts, and replaces it with networks of small suppliers. Even such proud giants as International Business Machines Corp. and General Electric Co. are doing it to varying degrees. In the short run, the new system may be amazingly flexible and efficient. In the long run, however, some experts fear that such fragmented manufacturing operations will merely hasten the hollowing process.

NEW FOUNDATION? What is happening to the U. S. economy, some futurists and economists say, is simply progress. It reflects the adaptation of a mature industrial economy to the realities of international competition. According to this view, the U. S. is undergoing a transition to a new foundation of services and information-based high technology—a changeover potentially as sweeping and beneficial as the industrial revolution or the mech-

---

The U. S. advantage in services is no more invulnerable than the ones it had in steel or autos

---

anization of agriculture. What survives of manufacturing will be done in the totally computerized and robotized factory of the future, where employment will be so low that wage costs become irrelevant.

But to others, all of this is wishful thinking. They consider it a given that the U. S. cannot prosper without a strong manufacturing base.

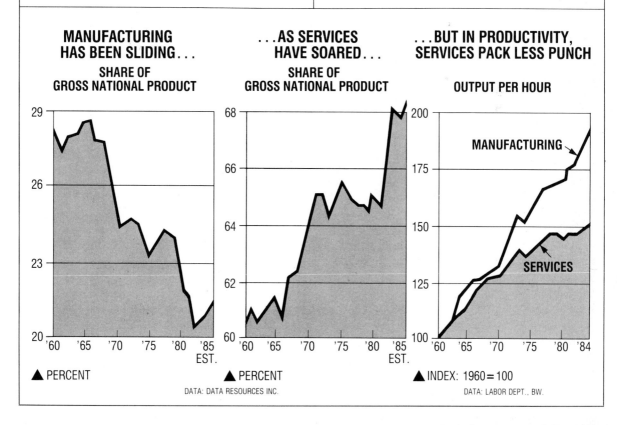

MANUFACTURING HAS BEEN SLIDING...
SHARE OF GROSS NATIONAL PRODUCT
▲ PERCENT

...AS SERVICES HAVE SOARED...
SHARE OF GROSS NATIONAL PRODUCT
▲ PERCENT
DATA: DATA RESOURCES INC.

...BUT IN PRODUCTIVITY, SERVICES PACK LESS PUNCH
OUTPUT PER HOUR
MANUFACTURING
SERVICES
▲ INDEX: 1960=100
DATA: LABOR DEPT., BW.

"The growth of manufacturing has historically paralleled that of the overall economy," says Roger E. Brinner, chief U. S. economist for Data Resources Inc. "It's useless to ask which is the chicken and which is the egg. They go together, and if manufacturing keeps slipping, it may drag down the rest of the economy." Adds *DRI*'s Sara Johnson: "Past gains in manufacturing are what enabled our economic system to afford to increase its demand for services."

Another Japanese industrialist, Tsutomu Ohshima, senior managing director of Toyota Motor Corp., puts it even more strongly: "You can't survive with just a service industry." Ohshima finds it hard to understand that U. S. policymakers are not talking about what he and many other foreigners see as a clear need for America to reindustrialize.

Is concern over deindustrialization, or a hollowing of industry, justified? By most measures, manufacturing is a disaster area. In current dollars, the sector has plunged from a peak of 30% of U. S. gross national product in 1953 to about 21% in 1985, with much of the decline coming in the last decade (chart). Durable goods production alone has tobogganed from 17.8% of *GNP* in 1953 to about 12% last year. That's a drop of 30% or more in both cases. In 1953, one of every three nonfarm workers was in manufacturing; today the ratio is roughly one out of five.

Some economists complain that it is torturing the data to look at manufacturing's slide only in current dollars. Says Robert Z. Lawrence of the Brookings Institution: "If you look at manufacturing's share in real dollars, using 1972 as a price base, the numbers are virtually trendless until the last couple of years, and that decline is just a function of the strong dollar." As for the drop in current dollars, Lawrence says that it largely represents productivity gains and technological improvements, particularly in computers and other office equipment, and therefore is nothing to worry about.

But this view is not shared by the nonpartisan Congressional Budget Office. The *CBO* examined the measurement problem as it prepared a study on industrial policy two years ago and decided that the current-dollar numbers are the ones that count. Explains one *CBO* economist: "Those are the dollars we care about. They tell you what business has to invest today, what income and value-added you are creating, and whether business can increase employment now. They give you the social value of your output."

U. S. manufacturers doubt the dollar's realignment and the plunge in world oil prices will bail out American industry. They note that their major foreign competitors are even more dependent on imported oil than are American manufacturers—and therefore benefit even more from the price slide. The drop in the dollar gives the foreigners a further bonus since everyone pays for oil in dollars. The perception remains that the tide of foreign competition is inexorable, and U. S. manufacturers must continue to position themselves to live with the new realities. For many producers, the answer will continue to be to manufacture less.

One way or another, U. S. industry has been engaged for the past decade in a massive drive to lower the costs of doing business, whether through outsourcing, squeezing concessions out of unions, closing inefficient plants, or opening plants abroad. Companies long identified with making goods of all sorts now often only produce the package and the label.

Says economist Nestor Terleckyj of the National Planning Assn.: "For corporate managers the central question is not necessarily what product their companies make but whether their companies make profits. If Ford Motor, for example, can make money by making loans, it will become a bank and let the Japanese make more and more of its cars."

Robert E. Lipsey of the City University of New York cites U. S. multinationals as an example of successful adaptation to international competition, with business moving abroad to take advantage of lower wages and capital costs. "These firms prove that American business can compete on a firm-by-firm basis," says Lipsey, though he concedes the resultant job losses in the U. S. and other macroeconomic effects "may not be beneficial for the economy in the aggregate."

Lipsey's concern about the aggregate is a masterpiece of understatement. Yes, individual companies can adjust to Asian competition by making their products in Taiwan or South Korea. They may revitalize domestic operations through infusions of Japanese management and production technology. They can also hammer down wage costs by farming out production jobs and buying services from outside vendors. And others find it pays better to ride the merger wave and shuffle existing assets than to raise capital to invest in new plants and equipment.

But does all this add up to a healthier U. S. economy? Probably not. It is true that the growth of the service sector has been phenomenal in recent years. The retail and wholesale trades, transportation, communications, finance, and personal services have added almost 10 million jobs to the U. S. economy since 1979, in contrast to 1.5 million lost in manufacturing. Just since 1960, services have grown from 60.4% of *GNP* to more than 68% in 1985.

COUNTER JOBS. What's more, the service tide shows no sign of ebbing. In the next 10 years, services will provide roughly 90% of all new jobs, according to Labor Dept. projections. But economists, political scientists, and other experts raise serious questions about how much punch that growth will carry when it comes to keeping the U. S. competitive in world markets and raising Americans' standard of living.

For one thing, the new service jobs will, on average, pay less than the median wage for U. S. workers. Highly valued jobs in leading-edge technologies, finance, and the professions will be a large part of that market, but so will jobs for janitors and clerks. As one economist puts it: "The McDonald's counter jobs will offset the McKinsey consultant jobs."

Nor can the U. S. count on services for the growth in productivity that is essential for a rising standard of living. Services have historically trailed manufacturing in gains in output per hour by a wide margin. They are likely to continue lagging behind for at least a decade until automation becomes more widespread in offices and shops. And judging by experience to date, such productivity gains are not immediately reflected in the income of service workers.

But the greatest shortfall in services is a basic inability to fill the void in trade that is being left by manufacturing. Right now the U. S. holds a powerful edge in high technology. But Lester C. Thurow of Massachusetts Institute of Technology asks: "If U. S. industries lose their production base, how can their engineers and scientists keep coming up with the software to sell overseas?" Most advances in technology are generated along the learning curve of an ongoing production process, not in the vacuum of a university laboratory.

Private U. S. research and development expenditures in nondefense industries already have slipped behind those of the country's keenest competitors as a share of *GNP*. Business and, more important, government, may be reluctant to keep funding *R&D* even at present rates if the resultant products wind up being produced in Taiwan or Brazil.

Finally, there is no reason to think the U. S. has an invulnerable advantage in services any more than it had one in making steel or autos. Foreigners are playing all sorts of trade-barrier games to limit inroads by U. S. service companies while they nurture their own. Indeed, the rapid growth of telecommunications is making it as easy to farm out such service jobs as keypunching as it is to outsource hardgoods production.

'A NICHE ECONOMY.' In short, the U. S. still needs a strong and growing industrial base. And the need may be greater than ever because that base is so vitally linked to the most promising service and high-tech businesses. Says economist Stephen Cohen of the Berkeley Roundtable on the International Economy at the University of California: "If you lose your industrial base, you can't be a prosperous service economy. The U. S. is too big to be a niche economy."

Cohen cites a vast variety of services—from trucking to banking to computer programming— that have a "direct linkage" to the goods-producing industries. And he notes that "to sustain U. S. incomes and productivity, it really matters who does the manufacturing. In a global input-output model, it may not matter where the goods come from, but a huge core of this economy depends on what's made on these shores."

The manufacturing-vs.-services debate comes down to competitiveness. And if lowering wages is the only way for the U. S. to regain its edge, then the solution may be worse than the problem. This clearly is the answer for many less developed countries, which can easily sell their wares on the world market by keeping wages at subsistence levels. But American business has long known—at least since Henry Ford made it an economic axiom—that its welfare ultimately depends on having workers who make enough to buy its products.

Says political scientist Bruce R. Scott of the Harvard business school: "U. S. competitiveness means the ability to employ U. S. resources, both human and capital, so that Americans earn increasing returns while in open competition with other countries." The U. S. can temporarily meet the competition by lowering the wage base, by outsourcing, by literally turning its industries inside out—in short, by hollowing. But enduring prosperity will require investment in human and physical resources, in innovation, and in raising productivity in both manufacturing and services. The first step is to take a careful look at the phenomenon of the hollow corporation.

By Norman Jonas in New York

BUSINESS CELEBRITIES

MOVE OVER, HOLLYWOOD—THE CORNER OFFICE IS A TICKET TO STARDOM, TOO

JUNE 23, 1986, PP. 100-104, 107

Browsing in a New York bookstore one day in April, T. Boone Pickens Jr. began tapping to the beat of the background music. When he asked to buy the record, the clerk said he'd just sold the last copy. Turning away, Pickens encountered a stranger who pulled out the record he'd just bought—the one Pickens liked—and handed it to the Texan. "I know who you are," said the man, adding that he'd made a bundle on the Gulf takeover. "I owe you one."

Pickens made a lot of people a lot of money when he attempted in 1984 to take over Gulf Oil Corp. He also made himself famous. He has appeared on the cover of 20 magazines, on all the network news shows, and on programs ranging from *Lifestyles of the Rich and Famous* to *Face the Nation*. Houghton Mifflin Co. is paying a $1.5 million advance for his memoirs. Promoters want to use his name on everything from miniature oil barrels to a board game called Takeover. Lately, a raft of foreign journalists have called on the maverick from Amarillo, Tex. No wonder he's recognized on the street—or in stores.

Pickens isn't alone. The public also knows Lee A. Iacocca. And Ted Turner. Steven P. Jobs. Peter Ueberroth. Malcolm S. Forbes. Donald J. Trump. Leona M. Helmsley. Felix G. Rohatyn. Victor K. Kiam II. Frank Borman. Those who didn't know H. Ross Perot a month ago probably do now: *NBC* portrayed the founder of Electronic Data Systems Corp., who in 1979 engineered the swashbuckling rescue of two *EDS* employees from an Iranian jail, in a miniseries broadcast in May.

Their numbers and their renown are growing. "I expect to see the day when, just as most Americans can name 10 or 15 major entertainers and 10 or 15 major athletes, they can name an equal number of corporate executives," says Lester B. Korn, chairman of Korn/Ferry International, executive recruiters.

At least twice before in American history—during the Gilded Age of the 1890s and the Roaring '20s—many business executives were well-known and often celebrated. Now, as then, the economy is rolling along without recession, Wall Street is booming, and entrepreneurs are creating empires and making fortunes. Business, viewed with contempt by some in recent years, is now popular. Making money is an acceptable ambition once again on college campuses. The rise of the executive celebrity reflects these trends—and encourages more people to seek the limelight.

Within limits, the trend seems healthy. If society needs heroes, executives seem as worthy as athletes or movie stars. And the adulation may even draw more creative people into the business world. But there is a dark side, too: The pursuit of fame can expose an executive and his company to unrealistic scrutiny. It can eat into the time he needs to spend on the job and make him overconfident. And it can make grooming a successor unusually difficult.

None of today's executives is more celebrated than Chrysler Corp.'s Iacocca. He achieved perhaps the ultimate celebrity feat on May 9 with a guest appearance on the hit *TV* show *Miami Vice*. His autobiography led the best-seller list in 1985 for the second year. He writes a syndicated newspaper column; he regularly makes the news and gossip columns. His fan mail runs to 300 to 500 letters a day. In 1984 and 1985 Gallup polls, Iacocca ranked among the 10 most admired men—the first businessman to make the list since Bernard M. Baruch in 1958. There has been a groundswell of grass-roots support for an Iacocca

Presidency. And as chairman of the Statue of Liberty-Ellis Island Foundation, he'll be front-and-center when America celebrates the Lady's centennial this July 4.

Wherever Iacocca goes, he attracts a crowd of gawkers. At one recent Chrysler reception in New York, guests pressed to get near him. "I want to go shake his hand," one man said to his companion. "He may be the next President of the United States." As others surged close to take his picture, Iacocca made the rounds surrounded by four aides. "We keep him from getting knocked over," explained one.

FAME BY ASSOCIATION. Like Iacocca, some executives earn fame. Some manufacture it with advertising campaigns for their companies. Some, like Borman, were famous before they went into business. Some achieve fame by associating with celebrities. Others, usually those with adventurous lifestyles and means, are just celebrated for their celebrity.

There have always been high-profile business executives. In the past, though, most of them targeted their quest for fame, concentrating on making themselves known in the highest circles of Wall Street and Washington. They didn't care if the general public knew them. Now many execs aren't content with the behind-the-scenes influence wielded by the likes of Irving S. Shapiro and Reginald Jones 10 years ago.

"I envy Iacocca. If they asked me, I'd do a Miami Vice *episode; I'd even do* Hill Street Blues.*"*
—W. Jeremiah Sanders III, founder, Advanced Micro Devices Inc.

Jerry Sanders may be one of the few executives who admit outright that they'd like to bask in celebrity. But he's not the only one to desire it. Many business people today believe that being famous can further their goals. "Having a high profile is a positive thing if it stimulates people to look into the company," says the flamboyant Sanders.

Ten years ago, Boone Pickens barely talked with the local newspaper. Then he realized he could turn publicity to his advantage. So he honed his story-telling abilities and learned to make better speeches. He billed himself as a champion of the common man, wrestling with the buttoned-up *CEO*s of big business to reap rewards for long-suffering shareholders. He was well-versed for his role as a folk hero when he began making raids—in 1982, on Cities Service Co.—and the limelight began to shine.

Pickens now makes himself readily available to the press—after all, it is the media that create celebrities. He accepts 100 speaking engagements a year, saying it's all just part of his job as chief of Mesa Petroleum Co.—and he makes it sound credible. "It's very important that corporations are personalized," Pickens explains. Insiders concede that he also enjoys the attention. Now that a buoyant stock market has curbed Pickens' takeover yen, he's keeping his celebrity alive by starting a nonprofit association to advance shareholder rights.

ELECTRIC SHAVER. Victor Kiam didn't set out to be a star. He just needed a marketing ploy for Remington Products Inc. And when he made commercials saying that he liked his new electric shaver so much he bought the company, fame followed. It was so exhilarating that Kiam is now trying to turn his book, a primer for entrepreneurs, into a best-seller. He's spending $1 million of his own, in addition to $150,000 laid out by his publisher, William Morrow & Co., to promote *Going for It!*

Armand Hammer, a veteran headline-chaser, made a typical dash in mid-May, when he flew to Moscow with medical supplies for the victims of the Chernobyl nuclear disaster. Hammer has also underwritten a glossy picture book, *The World of Armand Hammer.* One chapter, "The Beautiful People," showcases Hammer with such luminaries as Jacqueline Onassis and Frank Sinatra.

Oilman Marvin Davis hankers after another brand of celebrity. He dislikes talking with the press, but he has been striving to get back into the entertainment business since he sold 20th Century-Fox Film Corp. last year. These days his Hollywood parties, once peopled with stars, lack glamour. That's one reason, industry observers say, that Davis made a recent bid to take over *CBS*.

On a smaller scale, scores of normally conservative executives are stepping into public roles. Each Sunday night on *ABC*, Walt Disney Co. Chairman

Michael D. Eisner introduces the Disney movie—just as Walt used to do. Before Eisner took the part, Disney considered using Cary Grant or Ron Howard for the role. J. Willard Marriott Jr. has taken to doing ads not only for his own hotels but also for USA *Today*, Hathaway Shirts, and Monopoly. J. Peter Grace has turned his campaign against government waste into a highly visible crusade, and for the past year he has been a commentator on public *TV*'s *Nightly Business Report*. Even An Wang, once nearly a recluse, is capitalizing on his reputation as a legend in computers by appearing in Wang ads.

"It is axiomatic of a society that we are who we celebrate."
—Historian Barbara Goldsmith, in *The Meaning of Celebrity*, *The New York Times Magazine*, Dec. 4, 1983

Sometime in the late 1970s, America's mood changed. No more radical chic. Instead, there was a resurgence of raw capitalism and an emphasis on self-reliance. Making money was in. Business was where the action was. Ronald Reagan was elected President. Corporate America, meanwhile, was changing fast. Foreign competition, deregulation, and a start-stop economy made it tough to turn a profit. Institutional investors, fixated on quarterly earnings, pressured executives to perform. Corporate raiders triggered mergers and restructurings.

In such challenging, uncertain times, those executives who perform well or take a lot of risks—like Iacocca or Turner—look larger than life, compared with the ordinary folk around them. "If we're insecure, heroes tend to emerge," explains James W. Kuhn, a professor at Columbia University's Graduate School of Business. And, when business is newly popular, who better to adulate than born-again capitalists?

RIGHT-WING AIRLIFT. Perot's celebrity is a startling sign of the changed times. When he first turned up on the front pages in 1969, he had bankrolled the flight of a planeload of medicine and food to U. S. prisoners of war in North Vietnam. For the effort, he was scorned by the antiwar movement as a right-wing crackpot. Nor was his Iranian rescue, at the time, greeted with cheers. All along, critics ridiculed *EDS* for its militaristic corporate culture. Perot hasn't changed. But now he's widely praised.

Admiration for Iacocca is more understandable. In saving Chrysler, he looked like a miracle worker. Besides, Americans like underdogs, especially those who go on to win. And though Iacocca didn't think so at the time, it was a blessing that Henry Ford II fired him as Ford's president. Ford provided an excellent antagonist, a real enemy for the son of immigrants to vanquish.

Iacocca, however, is an aberration—an interventionist in an era of laissez-faire. Ted Turner is more emblematic of the age. "Turner is an aggressive, no-holds-barred capitalist," says sociologist Amitai W. Etzioni. Steve Jobs, too, embodies the successful entrepreneur many people want to be. Pickens thrives by taking on the Establishment.

MAGIC FORMULA. Like them, other executive celebrities often exhibit an individualistic, risk-taking streak—qualities Americans applaud. As a result, such executives are heroes. The public wants to learn their magic formula.

Such adulation can thrust business celebrities into roles beyond their expertise. Just as Henry Ford's views were sought on many topics, and just as he ran for Senate in 1918 and talked of running for President in 1924, so it goes for many in business today. Republicans have asked Ueberroth, Frank Perdue, and William F. Farley of Farley Industries Inc. to run for the Senate in California, Maryland, and Illinois, respectively (all declined). "The average cost of a Senate campaign is $3 million," says Thomas C. Griscom, executive director of the National Republican Senatorial Committee. "With a price tag like that, you'll look closely at anyone who doesn't have to spend time and money building name identification."

These days, news shows that once paid little attention to business are giving some executives "personality" treatment, stressing their lifestyles more than their business acumen. So are newspapers and magazines. In New York, *Manhattan inc.*, a 22-month-old glossy monthly, celebrates money-makers. One recent cover story chronicled the climb into respectability of Saul Steinberg, "the nation's most notorious greenmailer." "*Manhattan inc.* couldn't have existed in 1970," notes

David Corvo, acting executive producer of CBS *Morning News.* Even more interesting, many of *Manhattan inc.*'s subjects are eager to cooperate.

"There is so much show biz in business today that working with people who are not show biz is a real experience."

—Felix Rohatyn

It seems only fitting that the invisible hand worked when it came to business celebrities. With the increase in demand came a new supply.

Some businesses have always been so glamorous that the glitter spills over onto their executives. Sports, fashion, and entertainment have made the public familiar with the likes of George M. Steinbrenner III, Calvin Klein, and Grant Tinker. But for most others, the celebrity life was not proper.

Now a little flamboyance is acceptable, even for the ordinary executive. In many respects, a *CEO*'s life has grown imperial, with personal assistants, corporate apartments, and other perquisites attached to the job. It has also grown more public. As a result, ordinary business executives—let alone the celebrities—are better at using the media. Even investment bankers, who once preferred to work behind the scenes, are leaping to take credit for their deals. Rohatyn became a star when he "saved" New York from bankruptcy. Today he might have made it by just doing deals.

Executives have also learned that it pays to have a positive image to draw on in times of trouble—a takeover threat, a bizarre incident such as the Tylenol murders, or an industrial accident. So they're actively seeking higher profiles. "*CEOs* that were telling me a few years ago that they never gave interviews are giving interviews now," Korn says.

First, though, they've got to have a message, or at least an excuse for attracting attention. "*CEOs* can't turn the spotlight [just] on themselves," Korn notes. "Boards won't stand for it, and others in the corporation don't like it. There has to be a corporate interest being served." Unless, like Steinberg, they run private companies.

Short of causing a scandal, rescuing an institution, or amassing a fortune with the panache of a Vanderbilt, the marketing trail is the most common route to stardom. Most people learned of Iacocca when he went on the air to plump for Chrysler.

Advertising also turned Perdue, Kiam, and Helmsley into household names. More locally, it has made familiar faces of discount broker Charles R. Schwab, Sanford C. Sigoloff of Wickes Cos., Robert Brennan of First Jersey Securities, and Stephen A. Wynn of Golden Nugget casinos. Others want to duplicate those successes. Some are endorsing other companies' products: Malcolm Forbes is hawking the *New York Post* in *TV* ads, and Robert K. Jarvik, the heart surgeon and president of Symbion Inc., is among several execs posing in Hathaway shirt ads.

EXPRESS LANE. Steve Jobs never made a commercial for Apple Computer Inc., but he was nearly synonymous with the company. "People like symbols, and in looking for a symbol for Apple, many times they latched on to me," he says. Jobs believes that Apple needed a personality when it started out. "Other competitors were fairly impersonal, organizational entities, whereas Apple was in many ways like a person in formation, like somebody growing up."

"Since we're available, the media becomes our critic."

—Boone Pickens

Fame exacts a price. John DeLorean began his odyssey from middle manager at General Motors Corp. to superstar in the early 1960s when he was working with the rock group Ronny & the Daytonas. Their song, GTO, was supposed to get the new Pontiac *GTO* into the express lane. DeLorean, viewing the glamorous life close-up, decided to pull out into the fast lane himself—to his detriment. "It interfered with his work at *GM*," says Eugene E. Jennings, an auto industry expert at Michigan State University.

SIREN SONG. When he struck out on his own, DeLorean used his celebrity to get financing from dealers and from Hollywood contacts like Johnny Carson, on whose show he had appeared. Again, celebrity had its costs. "He was too tempted to spend his time seeking celebrity at a time when he had to give his total person to the job," Jennings says. (DeLorean was later acquitted on charges of selling cocaine.)

There are other risks. Highly visible executives have no place to hide if things don't work out. They have turned up the intensity of the scrutiny they and their companies get. Jobs, who left Apple last summer after a public brouhaha, feels that both he and Apple were held to higher standards.

Having a celebrity at the top makes grooming a successor difficult—and the successor's job nearly impossible

---

Pickens resents the attention the press gives his high salary.

Even Iacocca is drawing criticism. In April, Peter F. Drucker, the usually low-key management guru, lambasted Iacocca for collecting $11.4 million during 1985, while his auto workers got a 2.25% increase and a $2,120 lump sum. Iacocca's megabuck salary threatens Chrysler's comeback, Drucker said, according to three people who heard him speak. He claimed that Chrysler workers will no longer make sacrifices for Iacocca. (Drucker neither confirms nor denies the account.) And at Chrysler's annual meeting on May 14, corporate gadfly Evelyn Y. Davis wondered if Iacocca was spending enough time on company business.

Kenneth E. Clark, former director of the Center for Creative Leadership, points to another danger. "Any *CEO* begins to have more feelings of confidence in his plans than he deserves. After a while you think you're something special. You think you can handle every problem, and you can't. That's worse among celebrity executives."

Then there's the succession problem. While having a celebrity executive often fosters good morale within a company, it makes grooming a successor difficult. Worse, it makes his job, once he gets it, nearly impossible. "The shoes are too big," says management consultant Harold Levinson. People always compare.

For their part, the executive stars report that there are personal costs, too. "It's a two-edged sword," Kiam says. "It lengthens my day. I don't have a minute to myself." Adds Advanced Micro's Sanders: "It's a little disconcerting to have to be 'on' all the time." Worse, celebrity creates personal security risks.

"I worked for 27 or 28 years in anonymity. All of a sudden, when you get recognition, there's a glow."

—Victor Kiam

No doubt about it, celebrity is alluring. Steve Jobs says that when people come up to him, "usually it's someone saying, 'God, I really love my Macintosh,' or 'I really love my Apple II—thanks a lot.' It's nice to hear." Being a celebrity is also fun. It opens doors. Iacocca can do almost anything he wants. He says he'll shun politics, and he claims he didn't like acting on *Miami Vice*, which is probably just as well. But Iacocca is using his stardom in other ways: He is now bottling and selling his own label of wine, made from grapes grown at his Tuscan villa. Will oenophiles be impressed? Who knows? Paul Newman's salad dressing became an instant success.

Ted Turner, meanwhile, exploits his fame to the utmost. Besides the predictable outlets like *60 Minutes*, he's appeared on *The Tonight Show*, on *Donahue*, and he may soon host—yes, host—*Late Night with David Letterman*. He makes some 10 "personal appearances" a year at $15,000 to $25,000 a crack. Not that he needs the money—Turner is worth at least $300 million, and his agent turns down engagements that could bring in an additional $150,000 to $200,000 annually. But his Goodwill Games with the Soviet Union (BW—June 16) might never have gotten off the ground if a lesser light had tried to organize them.

"The attention is a motivating factor," says Frank H. Farley, a professor of psychology at the University of Wisconsin. Farley, an expert on heroes and on personality, has devised a "T" scale that rates people for thrill-seeking, stimulation-seeking, and creativity. Virtually all executive celebrities are "Type Ts," who seek out and relish new challenges.

Farley believes that, with such visible role models, more and more Type Ts will go into business. "I think this bodes well for the business world,

THESE HOTSHOTS JUST 'WANT TO BE ALONE'

Call financier Carl H. Lindner to ask for an interview, and the likely answer is a firm "no." Ask his staff to confirm a fact about one of Lindner's many interests, and the response is often stony silence. Few photos of Lindner exist, and his office tower in Cincinnati is unmarked.

For every Ted Turner or T. Boone Pickens Jr., there's a Carl Lindner, D. K. Ludwig, Stephen D. Bechtel, or Sid Bass. These high-powered executives could easily merit celebrity treatment by the press. But finding the glitzy life unappealing, they avoid the public eye. Many reclusive executives even hire public relations firms to keep their names out of the paper.

Partly, it's a matter of personality. Partly, it's because they have powerful reasons to avoid celebrity. First among them: security for themselves and their families. While kidnappings of the rich happen much more frequently overseas, they're not unknown in the U. S.

In business, secrecy offers more room to maneuver. As head of privately held American Financial Corp., Lindner—like the others at private companies—does not have to disclose most of what he does. He can explore ventures in private, let them develop or not outside the media's gaze, and have most mistakes go unnoticed.

SPARE CHANGE? Then, too, keeping a low profile prevents a flood of requests for donations. Just take a look at Boone Pickens' mail. An Italian woman wrote, enclosing a picture of her children and a deposit slip for her bank account. A prisoner wrote, asking Pickens to pay for an indoor firing range at the prison. A woman recently sent him a check for $500 with orders to invest it for her children's college fund.

Some companies such as Procter & Gamble Co. and Teledyne Inc. are also devoted to lying low. And they frown on the trend toward personality journalism. The chairman of one consumer-products company says he deflects questions of a personal nature because it's not "his" company and he doesn't want a personality cult to develop.

For most executives, however, avoiding publicity is getting more difficult. Companies don't necessarily want a Lee Iacocca at the top, but they do want someone able to speak out when situations demand it. "When we do 90% of our searches now, one thing the directors ask us to search for is executives who can represent the corporation well and communicate its goals and objectives," says Lester B. Korn, chairman of Korn/Ferry International. "That's not in place of being able to make a profit or manage assets. It's in addition to [it]." Privacy is now a luxury only a few executives can afford.

and it's long overdue. Business needed to be personalized. Better, more creative people will be drawn to the business world," he says.

But will it last? Corporate improprieties—from insider trading to Pentagon contract fraud—could lead people to downgrade business. After the 1929 crash, some executives needed protection from people who'd lost their savings in the market. That could happen again.

Etzioni believes that the outlook for executive celebrities depends on the economy. If the U. S. is headed for another recession, they are likely to lose favor. If a long period of prosperity is in store, their popularity might wane as people turn to other priorities, taking the good times for granted. But if the nation continues to muddle through with adequate but not spectacular economic growth, then executive celebrities may have long runs.

Etzioni, too, believes that having executive celebrities—particularly executive heroes—is a good thing. "Who is a celebrity reflects values," he reminds. Then he asks: "Who would you prefer to be celebrities—movie stars?"

By Judith H. Dobrzynski in New York, with Jo Ellen Davis in Houston and bureau reports

WHY AT&T ISN'T CLICKING

ITS FLASHY NEW INFORMATION BUSINESSES ARE DRAGGING DOWN PROFITS

MAY 19, 1986, PP. 88-91, 94

Talk about a hard sell. Instead of old magazines strewn on a coffee table, visitors to *AT&T*'s divisional headquarters in Berkeley Heights, N. J., are entertained by futuristic color *TV* monitors placed next to nearly every seat in the lobby. Each of the touch-sensitive screens promotes American Telephone & Telegraph Co.'s technological prowess. Press a spot on one and discover the wonders of the 3B20D, a minicomputer that "never stops working." Press another and learn about the world of Unix, *AT&T*'s much-heralded computer software system. The message is clear: *AT&T* is now a high-tech powerhouse, not just a big utility.

Yet *AT&T*'s results tell a far different story. Its regulated long-distance operation is stronger than ever. In the two years since its breakup, *AT&T* has also continued to do well selling equipment to the Bell phone companies. But the part of *AT&T* that was supposed to lead the $35 billion company to new heights is instead dragging down these traditional businesses. Sales of computers and phone systems to businesses and consumers racked up estimated operating losses of $1.6 billion in 1985, and profitability seems years away. Overall net earnings, projected by *AT&T* at $2.1 billion for 1984, fell far short that year and in 1985. In brief, it's turning out to be a lot harder than anyone expected for *AT&T* to transform itself into an Information Age superstar.

Part of the reason is bad timing: *AT&T* moved into computers just as the industrywide slump started. More troubling, it has been slow in learning to think like a free-market competitor. Its costs are too high. And many staffers say the company seems directionless.

GLACIAL PACE. Even *AT&T*'s rosy first quarter betrayed its problems. The 50% profit increase was from long distance and a change in pension-fund accounting. Margins on product sales fell substantially. "*AT&T* is in real trouble, much graver than people realize," says a former high-level executive, an *AT&T* veteran who seems genuinely concerned about the company. "The question is, will they evolve into anything other than a long-distance supplier and anything the old Western Electric can produce? The cards are stacked against them. They don't have the management talent and resolve to get it done."

Some observers are more optimistic. They cite the marketing savvy *AT&T* has picked up while taking its lumps—plus its financial strength and the unmatched technology of *AT&T* Bell Laboratories. But computer customers aren't waiting for *AT&T* to get its act together. And the company faces a long-term threat from the Baby Bells. By 1990 they may be freed from most restrictions of the breakup. Then they could eat away at *AT&T*'s long-distance business and make their own equipment instead of spending billions on *AT&T*'s.

The task of solving these problems will fall to James E. Olson, who is expected to move into the *CEO*'s office at *AT&T*'s Manhattan headquarters when Chairman Charles L. Brown retires in August. Olson's promotion from president and chief operating officer, though not public yet, is considered virtually guaranteed and may be announced after the next board meeting on May 21.

Many *AT&T*-watchers welcome the change. Rather than face an uncertain fate in a Justice Dept. antitrust suit, Brown made the courageous decision to break up the Bell System, then managed the divestiture well. But a Bell executive says that taking apart the close-knit company "took so much out of Charlie that I don't think he had the heart to continue the destruction at the new *AT&T*—even when it was warranted." Cost-cutting has proceeded at a glacial pace. "There's no hard-nosed management at *AT&T*," says one former executive. "Nothing happens when people don't produce results."

Brown argues that "any business, and this one in particular at this juncture in history, makes progress in increments." He adds: "Whatever you do, if the earnings are not as good as expected, people say you should have done something else."

One "something else" that critics mention is infusing *AT&T*'s 333,000 employees with a vision to replace the old corporate theme of public service. In an annual series of executive meetings a few months back, Brown gave a speech that one insider says "boiled down to little more than, 'Be the best that you can be.' People thought that was a little ludicrous. It's not the kind of corporate philosophy that people can latch on to."

Outgoing and energetic, the 60-year-old Olson is likely to be more forceful. "At least some decisions will be made," says Edward Goldstein, formerly corporate vice-president for strategic planning at *AT&T* and now an industry consultant. But Olson's critics note that he headed *AT&T*'s troubled equipment operations before stepping into the president's slot last June. In his 42 years with *AT&T*, Olson's forte has been operations; most observers expect him to focus more on cost-cutting than strategic planning.

Few experts foresaw *AT&T*'s problems. It seemed that the company's executives had pulled a coup by spinning off the slow-growth, capital-intensive local phone companies while retaining Bell Labs, the profitable long-distance arm, and the $13 billion Western Electric Co., the world's largest maker of communications equipment. Management wanted to keep as much of these traditional businesses as possible while moving *AT&T* into faster-growth areas: the international market and integrated computer and phone systems. The betting was that, after taking a year to

---

'The question is, will they ever evolve into anything other than a long-distance supplier?'

---

overcome the chaos of the breakup, *AT&T* would be off and running.

In long distance, saturation advertising featuring actor Cliff Robertson, plus a raft of new services and lower prices, has kept rivals such as *MCI* Communications Corp. and *GTE* Sprint Commu-

nications Corp. on the run. The company's long-distance market share, expected by some to drop as low as 60% by 1990, has stabilized at around 80%. Its long-distance operations are well managed, too. Analyst Jack B. Grubman of PaineWebber Inc., a former *AT&T* accounting manager, expects operating profits from *AT&T* Communications Inc. to hit $3.6 billion this year, up 50%.

The story is similar at *AT&T* Network Systems, Western Electric's successor as supplier of equipment to phone companies. In the late 1970s the company fell behind Canada's Northern Telecom Ltd. in digital switching technology. By 1983, Northern sold almost all the digital switches in the U. S. By last year, however, *AT&T*'s impressive research and manufacturing let it draw even with Northern in the $4 billion U. S. market.

TOO MANY SALESMEN. The company was counting on similar success in advanced phone equipment and computers. At divestiture, it still had a 25% share of the $3 billion market for business phone systems. It owned a huge amount of phone equipment rented to businesses and homes. And it had been building computers into its switching systems for years. "We felt we were the equal of anybody in our knowledge of processors," recalls William M. Ellinghaus, who retired as *AT&T*'s president in 1984.

But troubles mounted from day one. The marketing of these high-tech systems fell to *AT&T* Information Systems, a division created after the Federal Communications Commission ruled that *AT&T* had to separate competitive equipment sales from regulated long-distance operations. So *AT&T* had two sales forces calling on major customers— one from *AT&T* Communications, the other from Information Systems. "It was a terribly inefficient organization that was forced on us," says Brown.

The revenues to support Information Systems' 110,000-employee payroll never materialized. The market for business phone systems, known as *PBX*s, turned down in 1985 just as computers slumped. That was exacerbated by post-breakup confusion and poor marketing. *AT&T* salespeople, recalls Nicholas D. Kaltneckar, manager of voice communications at Johnson & Johnson, "didn't know their products that well, and their prices

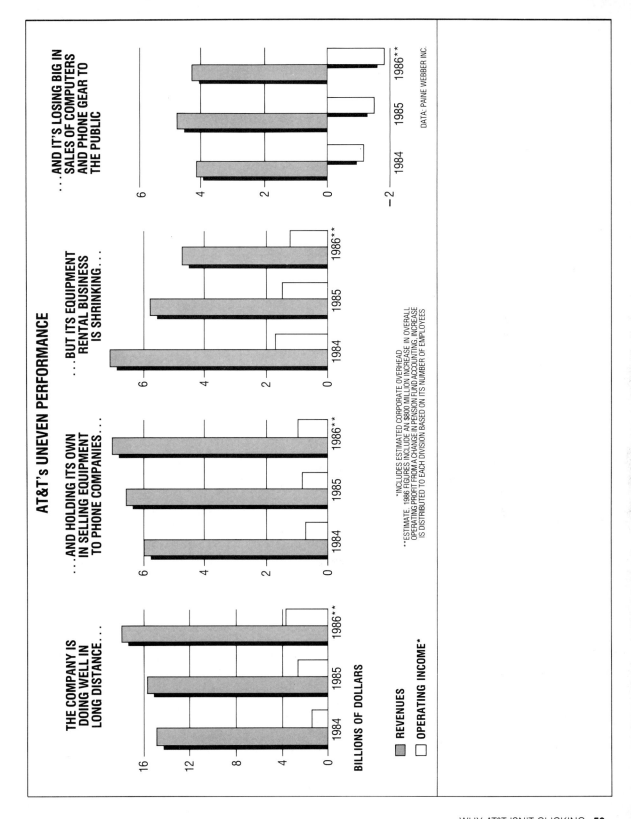

AT&T's UNEVEN PERFORMANCE

THE COMPANY IS DOING WELL IN LONG DISTANCE...

...AND HOLDING ITS OWN IN SELLING EQUIPMENT TO PHONE COMPANIES...

...BUT ITS EQUIPMENT RENTAL BUSINESS IS SHRINKING...

...AND IT'S LOSING BIG IN SALES OF COMPUTERS AND PHONE GEAR TO THE PUBLIC

BILLIONS OF DOLLARS

■ REVENUES
□ OPERATING INCOME*

*INCLUDES ESTIMATED CORPORATE OVERHEAD
**ESTIMATE. 1986 FIGURES INCLUDE AN $800 MILLION INCREASE IN OVERALL OPERATING PROFIT FROM A CHANGE IN PENSION FUND ACCOUNTING. INCREASE IS DISTRIBUTED TO EACH DIVISION BASED ON ITS NUMBER OF EMPLOYEES

DATA: PAINE WEBBER INC.

were 40% over the competition." *J&J* just started buying *AT&T PBX*s again after a two-year hiatus. **'DAMN HIGH.'** Alarmed, *AT&T* "bought market share," recalls the *CEO* of a large rival. To win a contract at the University of Colorado last July, *AT&T* underbid many rivals and donated $1.5 million worth of computers to the school's engineering labs. Such tactics, plus a host of top-quality new products, helped increase *AT&T*'s *PBX* market share from 19.6% in 1984 to 25% in 1985, says Northern Business Information Inc.

However, *AT&T* set off a price war, and its margins suffered the most. "Their costs were too damn high, every single cost you could name: components, manufacturing, and marketing," says Goldstein, the former *AT&T* strategic planner. In mid-1984, in a dramatic videoconference beamed to employees nationwide, Olson pledged to cut costs by 20% at *AT&T*'s equipment arm by year-end. Insiders say actual cuts fell far short of that. Meanwhile, the computer side of Information Systems was burdened by slow growth and larger-than-expected losses (pages 62-63).

The only thing forestalling disaster was the division's "embedded base" of phone equipment rented to homes and businesses. But salespeople were encouraged to sell rental systems or replace them with new *AT&T* gear, even though gross profit margins on rentals topped 50%. Rentals shrank by 19% annually. "If you're losing money on each product you ship and making a lot of money on the embedded base, then why replace the embedded base with new products?" asks a former sales

---

The company's bid to grab more of the PBX market set off a price war— and its margins suffered the most

---

executive. "It seemed to take a long time for somebody to figure that out." This year, *AT&T* finally began offering lower rates to customers who extend their leases and changed its sales compensation to discourage raiding the rental base.

By mid-1985, Information Systems' financial situation was deteriorating so rapidly that Robert E. Allen, who had become chairman of the division in February, 1985, eliminated 24,000 jobs. Critics say the move was overdue. But given *AT&T*'s history of almost unparalleled job security, "it was a difficult and wrenching thing to do," says Brown.

'PARALYSIS BY ANALYSIS.' Information Systems is still bogged down by bureaucracy. "Trying to negotiate a contract with these people is impossible," complains Jeffrey S. Lipton, director of telecommunications service for the University of Colorado. "It took seven months to get a signed contract, even though we had agreement on major issues within three months. It all has to be reviewed and approved [at headquarters] in New Jersey." One disgusted sales manager, who recently joined a rival, calls *AT&T*'s problem "paralysis by analysis." He complains about too many task forces and committees. "That's how they put off making decisions—they study them to death."

Customers report that *AT&T*'s marketing has improved, though it's not up to that of other big suppliers. Allen, who is expected to succeed Olson as president, concedes that big problems remain: "This is still very much a business in transition. It'll probably be another three years before we feel better about our direction and successes." Still, he denies rumors of new layoffs. He says 1986 results will "absolutely" be better than last year's estimated $250 million operating loss on revenues of $11.5 billion. Analyst Grubman, though, predicts operating losses will double this year.

To speed the turnaround, top officers are pinning high hopes on cooperation between *AT&T* Information Systems and *AT&T* Communications, the long-distance unit. The *FCC* ruled last fall that the divisions could combine some functions. As a first step, *AT&T* plans to integrate the duplicate sales teams that call on major customers. The idea is to spur sales of both *PBX*s and computers, given the good rapport the long-distance sales force has with big clients. More important, *AT&T* is determined to use its communications skills to tie together all of a client's information equipment— from phones to *PBX*s to computers. "There are a lot of box vendors out there," says Olson. "We are a strategic vendor, who can walk in and do total systems engineering."

Customers welcome the changes. "I'm tired of dealing with two sides" of *AT&T*, says William T. Houghton, Chevron Corp.'s general manager of communications technology. In fact, he's "disappointed" that he won't get a unified sales team for at least a year. The reason: Insiders say the company is moving gingerly to mesh the sales forces. They have a historic animosity, and infighting over who will lead the merged account teams is fierce.

NOT MUCH ROOM. *AT&T* may have a better future in its other big push, overseas equipment sales. "It's a great growth area, with big money at stake," says Desmond F. Hudson, president of rival Northern Telecom Inc. Olson wants to get 25% of *AT&T*'s equipment revenues from overseas by 1995, up from less than 5% now. To do so, he has set up a host of ventures and strategic alliances in Europe and the Far East.

It's too soon to tell whether the international moves will pay off. Italy's Olivetti, in which *AT&T* took a 25% stake in 1984, sold only 1,000 *AT&T* minicomputers in Europe last year. But Olivetti has been a good supplier of personal computers that *AT&T* resells in the U. S., and *AT&T*'s $254 million investment is now worth $1.2 billion. A joint venture with the Netherlands' Philips to sell switching gear has gotten few orders but could make a breakthrough in France soon. Other projects are just getting started, including a venture to produce microchips in Spain. Rivals say *AT&T*'s overseas thrust is poorly focused. But Olson says he's "very optimistic" about long-term success.

With a payoff in international markets years away and the thrust into computers disappointing, *AT&T* must rely for the next few years on its workhorse: long distance. But it doesn't have much running room. *AT&T*'s long-distance revenues are expanding at about 8% annually, says Lap Lee, an analyst at Wertheim & Co. He adds: "I just don't see earnings growing rapidly there." Moreover, long-distance profits have begun to exceed the *FCC*'s 12¾% target return on investment—making an *FCC*-ordered refund possible.

POT OF GOLD. Perhaps to forestall that, the company in late April filed for a huge 9.5% average rate cut, effective in June. *AT&T* says the cut offsets lower fees it will pay to connect to local phone networks, part of an *FCC*-mandated change in phone-industry pricing. In any case, *AT&T*'s long-distance earnings probably will level off for the next few years.

After that, there could be a resurgence in long distance as new services and lower prices stimulate use of its network. *AT&T* also is trying to convince the *FCC* that it deserves a higher rate of return, given the greater risks in a competitive world. Even without that, a request for faster depreciation of equipment—already made to the *FCC*—would boost profits. The real pot of gold may come when *AT&T* frees itself from most regulation, perhaps in the early 1990s. Able to price its services at will, and with more freedom to introduce advanced technology, the company should be able to capitalize on an exploding demand for ways to move information.

Ironically, the spun-off Bell companies are the biggest threats to these plans. In trying to redefine their marketing focus after divestiture, the Baby Bells and *AT&T* hit on the same strategy: selling large customers a package of communications equipment and services. The Bell companies already had the local-network part of the puzzle, and the breakup settlement allowed them to market equipment, as well. Now, with *AT&T* and others being allowed to bypass local Bell networks with direct hookups to customers, the Baby Bells think they deserve the final piece—long distance. "We'd produce some real competition to *AT&T*'s dominance," says Thomas E. Bolger, chairman of Bell Atlantic Corp. That's something *MCI* and its smaller brethren may never do.

U. S. District Court Judge Harold H. Greene, who presided over the breakup settlement, could loosen some restrictions on the Bell companies as early as next year. Although few observers expect him to act so quickly, they believe the Baby Bells will be permitted to sell long-distance service, at least within their regions, by 1990. One Bell official boasts that even such a partial change would let the seven spinoffs cut *AT&T*'s market share from 80% to 60% in three years. "That'll suck one hell of a lot of profit away from *AT&T*," says a former high-level *AT&T* executive.

COMPUTER MARKETING: AT&T KEEPS BANGING ITS HEAD

When American Telephone & Telegraph Co. burst into the computer business in March, 1984, shortly after divesting its regional phone companies, industry analysts predicted an epic battle with International Business Machines Corp. Computers, after all, were the cornerstone of the "new," unregulated *AT&T*. The analysts' "expectations were almost superhuman," recalls James D. Edwards, president of *AT&T*'s Computer Systems division. They thought "we would somehow overwhelm *IBM*."

Far from that, *AT&T* has achieved spotty results in computers. It has done well with some products, such as *IBM*-compatible personal computers and small minicomputers. But a personal computer that uses *AT&T*'s Unix software is a flop. And the company has been unable to develop a wide market for its large minicomputers (chart). Sums up *AT&T* Chairman Charles L. Brown: "We've done reasonably well, picking up our share in the computer business, though not as much as we would have liked."

Revenues of $2 billion last year made *AT&T* the world's ninth-largest computer maker, but analysts estimate that it lost as much as $250 million in the process. Now the experts are rolling back their expectations. "Instead of looking to 1990 for a leading role for *AT&T*, try 1995 to 2000," says William C. Rosser of Gartner Group Inc.

SLOW START. One reason for the setback is the 15-month computer slump. "We probably couldn't have picked a worse time to enter the computer business," says Robert E. Allen, chairman of *AT&T* Information Systems.

But *AT&T*'s problems go deeper. Despite decades of in-house computer development, it has failed to produce successful commercial systems of its own. It has turned to Convergent Technologies Inc. to build its Unix *PC* and to startup Counterpoint Computers Inc. for an engineering workstation. Its only truly successful commercial product, the *AT&T* PC6300, is a clone of the *IBM PC* built by Italy's Olivetti.

AT&T's slow start on the commercial side has a lot to do with Unix, its operating system software that controls such basic computer functions as storing information on disks and printing it out. There's no standard operating system for the hundreds of thousands of midrange computers now in use. Unix, which runs on 140 different models, was supposed to fill the gap—and help *AT&T* sell machines. But it has a reputation for being hard to use—and lacks any major advantages to offset that. McKesson Corp., a San Francisco-based pharmaceuticals distributor, is typical of many buyers: It has 400 PC6300s but isn't interested in other *AT&T* models. "We don't have any applications for Unix at this point," says John W. Fitzgerald, McKesson's vice-president for technical services.

As a result, even though all but the largest of *AT&T*'s minis are regarded as reasonably competitive in price and power, they have limited appeal. Only the regional phone companies, the U. S. government, corporate engineering departments, and universities have bought many. "Unix remains unknown and uninteresting to 80% of commercial data processing customers," says Jean L. Yates, a vice-president at market researcher International Data Corp.

Trouble with the regionals also threatens to erode *AT&T*'s dominance of another profitable business. *AT&T*'s Network Systems division is the largest seller of equipment to the Bell companies, including Centrex systems, which the Baby Bells use to provide phone service to big companies. At the same time, *AT&T* Information Systems is trying to sell the same big companies its own *PBX*s, which do essentially the same thing as Centrex. "We're competing with *AT&T*, using their equip-

AT&T learned that the hard way. Last March it brought out the Unix *PC*, a machine that it hoped would serve as an inexpensive introduction to Unix for commercial buyers. Industry watchers figure *AT&T* sold as few as 5,900 in 1985, instead of the expected 40,000. The lesson, says Edwards, is that customers don't want a whole new set of software for desktop computers—or for any system.

Instead of trying to replace existing computers and software, *AT&T* now wants to make Unix work alongside the software in existing machines. Unix's major role would be to smooth communications between computers. A new version, due this summer, translates files from different computers for transmission across networks. "We will reach out to the computers that are in place," says Edwards. "That's very different from how *AT&T* began."

Even if the company can develop the software to make this strategy work, it must vastly improve its approach to customers to compete with the likes of Digital Equipment Corp. and *IBM*. "It comes down to marketing," says Richard J. Matlack, president of InfoCorp. "There's a lack of marketing tradition and culture in the company."

'HIT-AND-MISS.' Even customers who like Unix and praise *AT&T*'s product quality complain about its lack of marketing savvy. "It's kind of hit-and-miss," says James W. Mathis, director of telecommunications for Trailways Corp., a new customer. "On the follow-through, they've got some problems." At Lincoln National Corp., which has ordered 35 *AT&T* minis, "when it came to Unix, we had to figure it out for ourselves—there was nobody to call," says George F. Modzelewski, an assistant vice-president.

AT&T's marketing is weakest where *IBM*'s is strongest—in large companies. Computer Systems is only one of several product groups in *AT&T*

AT&T COMPUTERS: PHONE COMPANIES ARE THE BIGGEST CUSTOMERS

Product category	1985 sales (millions of dollars)	
	To Bell operating companies and AT&T	To others
Personal computers & small microcomputers	$30	$603
Minicomputers	420	255
Superminis	650	12
TOTAL	**$1,100**	**$870**

DATA: GARTNER GROUP INC. ESTIMATES

Information Systems. *ATTIS*'s sales teams on major accounts generally concentrate on telephone switches and have more contacts with telecommunications managers than with data processing departments. The company is trying to solve that problem by combining the *ATTIS* sales force with that of *AT&T* Communications Inc., which sells data lines to large *IBM* customers.

Nobody expects a sudden surge in *AT&T*'s computer business. And the company can't afford to absorb losses forever. "No business—no matter how well funded—can continue without making money," says Edwards.

But many customers would like to see *AT&T* succeed. "I would love for *IBM* to have a viable competitor," says McKesson's Fitzgerald. And Edwards says *AT&T* can fill the bill with "careful planning and a little bit of patience." InfoCorp analyst Grant S. Bushee likens *AT&T*'s computer efforts to the experience of Japanese companies entering U. S. markets: "Their initial attempts were sometimes ludicrous, but they were plodding and determined. They keep banging their heads on it, and they eventually succeed. *AT&T* is approaching the computer market the same way."

By Geoff Lewis in New York, with Alice Z. Cuneo in San Francisco

ment and technology, against equipment sold by another division," complains a top official at a Bell regional.

The Bell companies worry that *AT&T* will withhold advanced technology from them, crippling their ability to compete. Olson counters that he intends to give the Bell companies the best available technology, "and to the extent that *AT&T* [Information Systems] gets hurt, that's a fact of the marketplace." The regionals aren't convinced, and they're lining up other suppliers. They're also pressing Judge Greene and Congress to let them make their own equipment, primarily through joint ventures with established manufacturers.

'SERIOUS HARM.' Any move away from *AT&T*'s equipment will take a while: Only Northern Tele-

---

AT&T's cost-cutting plans will be tested soon—when it tries to win a raft of union concessions

---

com now sells big-ticket switching gear comparable to *AT&T*'s. But the Baby Bells are already going to Japanese companies for optical-fiber equipment. And the strains promise to get worse. One option, says a Bell executive, is for *AT&T* to spin off either Network Systems or Information Systems. "They're going to have to do something," he adds, "or in the long run cause serious harm to our relationship."

What are the prospects that *AT&T* can turn itself around soon? After last year's disappointing earnings of $1.6 billion, or $1.37 a share, up from $1.25 a share in 1984, most Wall Street analysts aren't too hopeful. Once an investor darling, *AT&T* stock dropped from 25 to 22⅛ in the first quarter, during the biggest bull market in history. The stock got a boost from the surprising first-quarter earnings of 47¢ a share. But analysts say that was mostly because the 9¢ increase from the change in pension-fund accounting—which should continue each quarter for several years—made *AT&T* attractive to institutions looking for stocks with low price-earnings ratios.

Analysts who are still bullish hope for dramatic cost-cutting this year, and the first test will be upcoming labor negotiations. Contracts with the Communications Workers of America and the International Brotherhood of Electrical Workers, who together represent 196,000 *AT&T* employees, expire on May 31. *AT&T*'s prime goal is to win lower starting wages for 107,000 clerical employees and operators, who it believes earn 20% to 30% more than counterparts at rival companies.

HUNGRY TO BUY. The unions will resist that. They want an employment-security provision that would force *AT&T* to retrain and relocate excess workers with seniority. Though a strike is unlikely, Wall Street is watching. "Given the problems in the equipment area, *AT&T* can't afford a bad contract," says Kenneth M. Leon, an analyst at L. F. Rothschild, Unterberg, Towbin.

Once he takes over, Olson could cut other costs. One possibility: writing off a huge chunk of outdated equipment, which would clear the way for improved profits next year. More layoffs could be in store. Also, Olson has "an appetite for an acquisition," says a close associate. Rumors abound that *AT&T* may gobble up a computer maker, perhaps Digital Equipment Corp. But Olson says he has "no current plans to make a major acquisition of a computer company."

No matter what Olson does, *AT&T*'s transformation into a high-flying technology company will be a long time in the making. Five years from now, it'll probably look much as it does today—with most revenues and profits coming from long distance.

Former President Ellinghaus speculates that ignorance of the challenges that lay ahead may have been *AT&T*'s tragic flaw. "Maybe there was a lot of thinking that because we were so good, with such fine manufacturing and such great *R&D*, others couldn't compete with us as fast as they did," he says. "It wasn't because we were stupid or arrogant but because we had a lot to learn." Analyst Leon titled a recent report critical of *AT&T*'s performance in high tech *The Wrong Stuff*. So far, he seems to be right.

By Mark Maremont in New York, with Randy Welch in Denver and John Wilke and Michael Pollock in Washington

GENERAL MILLS STILL NEEDS ITS WHEATIES

HAVING SPUN OFF ITS UNRELATED UNITS, THE SLUGGISH GIANT IS TRYING TO PEP UP ITS MATURE FOOD BUSINESSES

DECEMBER 23, 1985, PP. 77, 80

Whether bounding across television screens or beaming from the covers of cereal boxes, well-known athletes have been hawking Wheaties for years. The current champions of breakfast are Mary Lou Retton, 17 years old, and Pete Rose, who, even at 44, personifies vitality. That's a quality missing lately from the maker of Wheaties, General Mills Inc. The company's slow-poke sales and profits have left it near the back of the pack among packaged-food companies.

Until now, General Mills has had a handy explanation for its lagging performance. The Minneapolis company was running a three-legged race, its managers said, with the food business strapped to the limping fashion and toy divisions. Those units were acquired starting in the late 1960s, and General Mills never grasped the ins and outs of such trendy businesses (BW—Feb. 11). These days, however, General Mills no longer has that excuse. The company spun off those subsidiaries on Nov. 7. Now, to regain its prominence in foods, Chairman H. Brewster Atwater Jr. is shaping up the company and promoting younger, feistier managers. The question is whether he can instill some of Pete Rose's pep into the 57-year-old company.

FRESH IDEAS. Ironically, to reach a goal of 6% real annual growth, Atwater is stressing two mature, slow-growth industries. Packaged foods are growing a mere 1% a year, and restaurants are creeping along at 3%. "The secret to getting good returns and good growth is to get yourself in the right segments," he says. He will concentrate on General Mills's Big G cereals and its Red Lobster Inns restaurants.

A new generation of managers—described by a former executive as "more entrepreneurial"—will be working to realize those goals. Atwater, 54, is a 27-year veteran who rose through the marketing ranks to become president in 1977 and chief executive in 1981. Last month, he made 43-year-old

Mark H. Willes president and put him in charge of operations. Willes, formerly chief financial officer, joined General Mills in 1980, after serving as president of the Federal Reserve Bank of Minneapolis. He is an articulate executive who isn't tied to the policies of the past. Former executives believe it was his analysis of each unit, in which he contrasted results with those of competitors, that led to the spinoff of the toy and fashion divisions.

In addition, Atwater shifted control of consumer foods away from 58-year-old F. Caleb Blodgett, the vice-chairman, and assigned it to two executive vice-presidents. Steven M. Rothschild, 40, will command the high-growth convenience lines, including Yoplait yogurt, granola snacks, and fruit rolls and bars. Rothschild, regarded as a market-

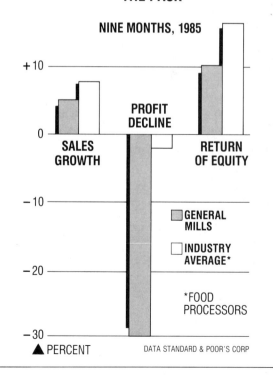

GENERAL MILLS IS TRAILING THE PACK

NINE MONTHS, 1985

PROFIT DECLINE

SALES GROWTH

RETURN OF EQUITY

GENERAL MILLS

INDUSTRY AVERAGE*

*FOOD PROCESSORS

▲ PERCENT

DATA STANDARD & POOR'S CORP

ing whiz, led Yoplait, a tiny venture the company bought in 1977, to a 15% market share. Arthur R. Schulze, 54, will oversee mature products such as Big G cereals and Betty Crocker mixes.

General Mills needs the kind of boost a shakeup can provide. The company's performance during Atwater's four-year reign as *CEO* has been disappointing. Earnings dropped 4.8% in 1984. And a $73 million loss in the 1985 fiscal year, ended last May, was the company's first, brought on by a $188 million write-off for the planned divestitures. Meanwhile, sales increased only 4%, to $4.3 billion, not including the divested units.

FIERCELY COMPETITIVE. Atwater is targeting cereals for growth because he believes that they will benefit from a growing demand for convenience foods. Sales of the cereal division, under the Big G trademark, have grown 13% annually for the past five years, to more than $800 million last year. But the market is fiercely competitive. With a 21% share, General Mills holds second place behind Kellogg Co. Big G will increase advertising by 20% this year. Also, Schulze says, the company is counting on product reformulations and packaging changes to sustain its older brands, such as Cheerios, Wheaties, Total, and Trix. General Mills "doesn't wildly innovate," says a former cereal executive from General Foods. "They just add wrinkles here and there that turn out to be profitable."

Indeed, the stars of the Big G line are well into middle age. Seven of the company's top 15 brands are more than 20 years old. But Schulze points out that last year, Big G brought out three new products instead of the usual one. Two—Fiber One and Bran Muffin Crisp—were late entrants in the growing fiber cereal market. They have grabbed 1% of the market. S'Mores Crunch, a new children's brand, has 0.5%. Schulze says he hopes to have two more new brands by June.

Red Lobster, the company's other expected growth vehicle, is a chain of family-oriented seafood restaurants. Made up of three restaurants when General Mills bought it in 1970, it ended fiscal 1985 with 375 units and sales of $828 million. Since 1980, sales have jumped at a 16% annual rate, and they should make up 19% of the company total in fiscal 1986. General Mills plans 25 new U. S. outlets each year through 1990, as well as others in Canada and Japan.

As the only national seafood dinner chain—and therefore the only one that advertises nationally—Red Lobster scares off potential competitors. *S&A* Restaurant Corp., a Pillsbury Co. unit, is starting a more upscale seafood chain that avoids Red Lobster's niche. "We have purposely chosen not to take on the Goliath of the industry," says Lane Cardwell, an *S&A* senior vice-president.

NEW GLAMOUR. Atwater is also looking for growth from the company's other lines. Yogurt, snacks, Gorton's frozen fish, and Talbots women's clothing, he says, will expand 13% a year. He is seeking new segments, too. Recent acquisitions include Vroman Foods, a maker of ice cream snacks, and Leeann Chin's, a group of Twin Cities Chinese restaurants that is being tested as a dinner chain, a takeout chain, or both. And the company is expanding its eight-restaurant Italian chain, the Olive Garden. Predicting that it will hit $400 million in sales by 1990, Atwater says: "It's the first restaurant concept that we've seen that has the same kind of promise that Red Lobster has."

Atwater's plans could be stymied, however, if the takeover mania in consumer products makes General Mills a takeover target. Analyst Alan S. Greditor of Drexel Burnham Lambert Inc. estimates the company's breakup value at $97 per share—67% above the current price.

"We're substantially less vulnerable than we would have been had we not done all the streamlining," Atwater insists. The spinoffs did add some glamour to the once-frumpy stock. When the

> The company's plan could be stymied if the takeover mania in consumer products hits General Mills

plans were announced last January, the price soared 32%, to 65¼. Since the spinoffs last month, General Mills's revalued stock has risen slightly to about 58. While part of the recent gain comes from takeover speculation, some may stem from better results. In the quarter ended Aug. 31, net earnings from continuing businesses rose 13%, and sales were up 5%. Atwater says second-quarter results will be better, too.

Now that General Mills has shed one-fourth of its sales and assets, Atwater sounds like a man who's recaptured some of his old vigor. "I feel more comfortable about where we're going than I have for a long time," he says. Whether he can translate that into a championship performance at General Mills remains to be seen.

By Patrick Houston in Minneapolis and Rebecca Aikman in New York

THE NEW BREED OF STRATEGIC PLANNER
NUMBER-CRUNCHING PROFESSIONALS ARE GIVING WAY TO LINE MANAGERS
SEPTEMBER 17, 1984, PP. 62-66, 68

After more than a decade of near-dictatorial sway over the future of U. S. corporations, the reign of the strategic planner may be at an end. In a fundamental shift of corporate power, line managers in one company after another are successfully challenging the hordes of professional planners and are forcing them from positions of influence.

Two examples out of many make the point: At Sonat Inc., planners from headquarters were accustomed to write a blueprint for each subsidiary and "present" it to the management of the operating unit. Now members of a greatly reduced planning staff report directly to the operating units—not to corporate headquarters. And what they do is considered a "support" function. "We've gone 180 degress," says Ronald L. Kuehn Jr., chief executive officer of the Birmingham-based energy company.

At General Motors Corp., the change is even more striking. Chairman Roger B. Smith is known throughout *GM* as the man who introduced strategic planning to the company in 1971. But he is also known as the man who, after three "unsuccessful tries" at establishing a strategic planning system at headquarters, decentralized the process and decreed that operating-division managers, not planners, should carry the ball. Now, says Michael E. Naylor, *GM*'s general director of corporate strategic planning, "planning is the responsibility of every line manager. The role of the planner is to be a catalyst for change—not to do the planning for each business unit."

KEY FORMULA. Perhaps the most telling sign of change is at the famed Boston Consulting Group, which is widely considered the parent of strategic planning. Even *BCG* is abandoning some of the planners' buzzwords in favor of a new emphasis on "implementation."

The revolution against the planners is especially impressive considering the enormous impact that

> 'The notion that an effective strategy can be constructed by someone in an ivory tower is totally bankrupt'

the strategic-planning discipline made on business operations in the late 1960s. Planning offered—for the first time—a systematic means of analyzing the economic and competitive prospects for corporate operations and charting a long-term course of action. Among the leading theorists was *BCG*, which developed a couple of key formulas that helped plot strategies for gaining market share and for determining how to deploy assets.

Another important force was General Electric Co., which, along with consultant McKinsey & Co., added other seminal concepts. These enabled diversified companies to focus more intensely on the market outlooks and competitive factors for each of their operations.

From these ideas emerged a profession of strategic planners that, by the mid-1970s, emerged as a separate function. Its practitioners became dominant figures in their companies. But as their power grew, the influence of operating managers waned, and hostility between the two escalated. The result: Few of the supposedly brilliant strategies concocted by planners were successfully implemented. Says *GM* Chairman Smith: "We got these great plans together, put them on the shelf, and marched off to do what we would be doing anyway. It took us a little while to realize that wasn't getting us anywhere."

The disenchantment runs deep. In a refrain that is echoed in dozens of companies, Roger W. Schipke, the senior vice-president in charge of General Electric's Major Appliance Business Group, talks of "gaining ownership of the business, grabbing hold of it" from "an isolated bureaucracy" of planners.

Depicting the upheaval as a bloody battle between planners and managers may sound extreme. But judging from the way line managers tell their stories, it has been nothing less. There have been plenty of casualties, too. In a bid to return strategic planning to its original intent—forcing managers to take "a massive, massive look outside ourselves"—*GE* Chairman John F. Welch Jr. has slashed the corporate planning group from 58 to 33, and scores of planners have been purged in *GE*'s operating sectors, groups, and divisions.

'PLANOCRATS.' Cleveland-based Eaton Corp. finally reacted to a rebellion of operations people against planners by cutting its staff of corporate "planocrats" from 35 to 16. And in the wake of cutbacks at U. S. Steel Corp., Rockwell International Corp., and many other companies, the two trade associations for planners—the Planning Executives Institute and the North American Society for Corporate Planning—are negotiating a merger.

If operating managers display new confidence in challenging the mystique of strategic planning, one reason may be that they themselves are thoroughly at home with the concepts by this time—educated by the business schools and tutored by the consultants. And—despite all the drawbacks—they have had to participate in "the process" or "the ritual" of putting together what was supposedly their business' strategic plan, but in too many instances was only the planner's plan.

The *CEO*s of the generation now coming to power feel they are the "strategic thinkers"—and believe that their key operating lieutenants should be as well. "Those who succeed in thinking strategically and executing strategically are the people who are going to move ahead at this company," says Hicks B. Waldron, chairman of Avon Products Inc. The same is true at Norton Co., the Worcester (Mass.) abrasives maker. Says *CEO* Donald R. Melville: "You can't get ahead just thinking in terms of operations. You won't become a top manager unless you think strategically."

Strategic planning's fall has another explanation as well. Managers not only know how the magic trick works; they question whether the magic is there at all. To put it bluntly, it has become obvious that very few strategies seem to succeed. Indeed, a reassessment of 33 strategies described in *BUSINESS WEEK* in 1979 and 1980 found that 19 failed, ran into trouble, or were abandoned, while only 14 could be deemed successful (table, pages 69-70).

The companies in the survey were drawn from a random sample of hundreds of stories on corporate strategies that appeared in the magazine in those years. These reviews are snapshots of how the strategies are currently faring, not reports on their ultimate outcome. But even taken as a rough measure, the survey's findings are not good news.

Clearly, the quantitative, formula-matrix approaches to strategic planning developed by *BCG* in the 1960s are out of favor. One reason is that these concepts grew out of the boom decade of the 1960s, when growth seemed eternal and market structures were relatively stable.

These overly quantitative techniques caused companies to place a great deal of emphasis on market-share growth. As a result, companies were devoting too much time to corporate portfolio planning and too little to hammering out strategies to turn sick operations into healthy ones or ensure that a strong business remained strong. In too many instances, strategic planning degenerated into acquiring growth businesses that the buyers did not know how to manage and selling or milking to death mature ones. Notes Stephen R. Hardis, the executive vice-president who oversees

A SAMPLING OF STRATEGIC PLANNING'S TRACK RECORD

Companies were selected from those whose strategies were described by BUSINESS WEEK in 1979 and 1980 and reassessed since by BUSINESS WEEK

PLANS THAT DIDN'T WORK

Company	Strategy	BW assessment	Company	Strategy	BW assessment
Adolph Coors	Regain lost market share and become a national force in the beer industry	Largely unsuccessful because of weak marketing clout	Napco Industries	Become the dominant distributor of nonfood items to grocery stores	Ran into trouble through bad acquisitions, logistical and management problems, and the recession
American Natural Resources	Offset sagging natural gas sales by diversifying into trucking, coal mining, oil/gas exploration, and coal gasification	Ran into trouble because anticipated gas shortages and higher prices failed to materialize	Oak Industries	Diversify into subscription TV and cable TV equipment	Failed because cable TV competition was underestimated; it also did not keep abreast of TV equipment technology
Ashland Oil	Sell off energy exploration/production business and diversify into insurance and other nonoil areas	Largely unsuccessful, partly because of industry problems in refining and insurance	Shaklee	Streamline product lines and become the leading nutritional products company	Ran into trouble because of the recession and sales-force turnover
Campbell Soup	Diversify away from food	Abandoned by new CEO who successfully expanded into new food products	Standard Oil (Ohio)	Use the cash flow from giant Prudhoe Bay oilfield to expand energy base and diversify into nonoil businesses	Largely unsuccessful so far. Kennecott acquisition is still a big loser, and efforts to find new oil have met with mixed success
Church's Fried Chicken	Build modular, efficient fast-food outlets aimed at the lower end of the market	Failed because upscale chicken restaurants are capturing most of the market growth	Toro	Capitalize on brand recognition and reputation for quality in mowers and snow-blowers by expanding into other home-care products	Failed because of snowless winters and distribution mistakes; new management changed strategies
Exxon	Diversify into electrical equipment and office automation, offset shrinking U.S. oil reserves by investing in shale oil and synfuels	Failed because of poor acquisitions, management problems in office automation, and falling oil prices	Trailways	Survive in the bus business by striking alliances with independent carriers and persuading regulators to hold Greyhound to 67% of intercity bus traffic	Failed because of deregulation and Greyhound's market-share war
Foothill Group	Diversify from commercial financing into leasing—especially oilfield drilling equipment	Failed because the equipment market slumped and the company failed to obtain adequate collateral from borrowers	Union Carbide	Reduce dependence on commodity chemicals and plastics and build up six faster-growing, higher-margin lines	Deep economic slump hit all chemical markets and delayed sale of undesired businesses
General Motors	Gain market share by outspending U.S. competitors in the race to offer more fuel-efficient, downsized cars	Failed as import market share grew. Modified strategy to pursue diversification	U.S. Home	Use economies of scale in land development and financial clout to take a commanding position in homebuilding	Ran into trouble when interest rates rose and its home sales sank
International Multifoods	Diversify away from flour milling by developing niche products in consumer foods and expanding restaurant business	Largely unsuccessful because of management timidity, problems overseas, and the recession	Wang Laboratories	Become the leader in the office-of-the-future market by introducing new products to combine data and word processing	Largely unsuccessful because of rise of personal computers
Lone Star Industries	Focus entirely on cement-related businesses and sell off other operations	Ran into trouble because cement shortages and higher prices did not materialize			

Company	Strategy	BW assessment	Company	Strategy	BW assessment
Abbott Laboratories	Become less vulnerable to cost-containment pressures in traditional hospital products	Won a leading share of the diagnostic products market through acquisitions and internal development and built a highly profitable dietary supplements business	**Hershey Foods**	Diversify into noncandy foods, nonchocolate candy, and food services	Reduced dependence on chocolate via new candies and snack foods. Expanded pasta and restaurant divisions
American Motors	Capitalize on a consumer shift to small cars by building autos designed by Renault to broaden its product line	New Renault cars perked up AMC, breaking 14 quarters of consecutive losses. Product timing still a threat	**National Intergroup**	Improve efficiency of and reduce dependence on steel operations	Became an efficient steelmaker by modernizing. Diversified into financial services, sold a steel plant to workers, and sold a 50% share of steel operations to Nippon Kokan
Bausch & Lomb	Regain dominance in soft contact lenses through intensive marketing and aggressive pricing. Become a major force in lens solutions	Boosted share of daily-wear lens market to 60%	**New England Electric System**	Reduce dependence on oil by switching to coal, developing other fuel sources, and promoting conservation	Switch to coal saved over $200 million, cut oil consumption 58%
Bekins	Return to profitability by selling real estate, building market share in basic moving business, and remedying poor diversification moves	Increased moving's market share through improved marketing. Divested bad businesses	**Ralston Purina**	Refocus on basic grocery-products and feed business	Shed mushroom and European pet food divisions, revitalized core business through product development and improved marketing
Borg-Warner	Offset the cyclicality of manufacturing-related businesses	Expanded into financial and protective services through acquisitions and internal development; services now account for a third of earnings	**Southern California Edison**	Reduce dependence on oil and gas	Developed alternate energy sources and is well on the way to generating 2,200 megawatts from new sources by 1992
Dayton Hudson	Maintain impressive sales and earnings growth by diversifying retail operations	Jumped to No. 5 in retailing by dramatically expanding Target, Mervyn's promotional apparel, and B. Dalton Booksellers chains	**Triangle Pacific**	Become less vulnerable to swings in housing market	Sold off wholesale lumber business and expanded kitchen cabinet fabrication operations
Gould	Move from an industrial and electrical manufacturer into an electronics company via divestitures and acquisitions	Built electronics to 100% of earnings by buying nine high-tech companies and divesting old-line operations	**Uniroyal**	Revive ailing tire business and abandon lackluster businesses	Shut two U.S. tire plants, shed many foreign and U.S. operations, and is expanding in specialty chemicals

strategic planning at Eaton: "It's great to say, 'Why don't we all go into growth businesses?' But those are not all highly profitable. If there's a hell for planners, over the portal will be carved the term 'cash cow.'"

Many companies painfully learned about the shortcomings of the formulas and matrixes. Mon-

santo Co.'s President Richard J. Mahoney notes that his company recently had "to terminate" a unit in the "enchanted land" of high share and high growth "because we were losing our shirts."

Thanks to the *BCG*-type formulas, Monsanto also made an acquisition in a bid to become No. 2 in polyester—on the assumption that leisure suits

HOW GM TAKES PLANNING INTO THE TRENCHES

Only eight years ago, General Motors Corp. had no strategic planners in its divisions, let alone in a lowly car plant. But as Raymond K. Fears, the strategic planner for *GM*'s Buick City complex in Flint, Mich., amply demonstrates, times have changed. Fears, who turns 30 in mid-September, moved from *GM*'s corporate strategic-planning group in 1983 to Buick City—the trio of 60-year-old plants that *GM* aspires to turn into the world's most efficient auto factory. His assignment: "To get [operating managers], who are used to thinking in terms of nuts and bolts, to think in strategic terms." That, he concedes, "is a major educational job."

Fears's transfer is part of *GM* Chairman Roger B. Smith's master plan to integrate strategic planning "into our daily lives." In Smith's book, that means "true integration with the operating organization."

MARCHING IN STEP. Fears served as a product planner for three years in *GM*'s Chevrolet Motor Div. before moving in 1982 to corporate, where he worked as a business-plan consultant to nine *GM* divisions. At Buick City, which will begin cranking out full-size 1986 cars a year from now, Fears's job is to aid in devising and implementing its piece of Buick Motor Div.'s strategy.

Chairman Smith insists that "the guy in charge of strategic planning is the general manager." Indeed, Fears's job will probably be phased out next year when the plant manager assumes all strategic-planning duties. One of Fears's tasks is to coordinate the strategic committee charged with insuring that all corporate groups involved in pilot production are marching in step. He also has helped to scout the competition to make sure Buick City will not be made obsolete—even by newer *GM* plants that adopt the facility's manufacturing practices.

Does he have regrets about moving from headquarters to the down-in-the-trenches atmosphere of a car plant? Absolutely none, says Fears, who aspires to an operating job. "I see the move as getting closer to the action."

---

would stay in style forever. "Using conventional analysis, we thought it might be possible that we could be a strong No. 2 and [enjoy] a lot of good things that would accrue to a strong No. 2," says Mahoney. A few years later, leisure suits went out of style, and Monsanto sold the entire business. Sighs Mahoney: "Our assumption that there was growth enough disappeared in a hurry."

Formula planning, warns *GM*'s Naylor, also tends to make a company's strategy "dangerously transparent" to its competitors. "It was a search for shortcuts," says Frederick W. Gluck, a director of McKinsey & Co. "It took the thinking out of what you had to do to be competitively successful in the future." This is why Mead Corp. has dumped analytical formula planning—along with a slew of businesses ranging from ink-jet printing to a foundry. Now the company is focusing on forest products and data services. In establishing strategy, each of its business units now compares itself with its intra-industry competition.

SECOND-CLASS CITIZENS. "The belief that you didn't have to look at the specific industry just didn't work," says Michael Raoul-Duval, Mead's former chief strategic officer. "The old process was just too mechanized. The real world is just too complicated for that." Adds Donald J. Povejsil, vice-president for corporate planning at Westinghouse Electric Corp.: "The notion that an effective strategy can be constructed by someone in an ivory tower is totally bankrupt."

The big problem is that strategic planning grew further and further away from the external world of customers and competitors. Companies hired consultants and *MBA*s schooled in the latest techniques, making operating people feel like second-class citizens. As more elaborate formulas and theories sprang up, bigger staffs were needed to collect more data from operations. Pretty soon the size of the planning bureaucracies and their demands on operating managers grew out of control.

At Mead, Raoul-Duval recalls, "plans became much too voluminous. We had the feeling that people prepared their business plans as a matter of routine, trying to add more papers and numbers than [were in] the previous year's plan."

Robert M. Lockerd, vice-president for corporate staff at Texas Instruments Inc., says his company let its management system, which can "track the fall of every sparrow, creep into the planning process so we were making more and more detailed plans. It [became] a morale problem because managers knew they couldn't project numbers out five years to two decimal points."

'US VS. THEM.' The end result is that strategic planners disrupt a company's ability to assess the outside world and to create strategies for a sustainable competitive advantage. The experiences of *GE*'s Major Appliance Business Group serve as an excellent case study of how disruptive strategic planning can be.

The relationship between the Appliance Group's operating managers and strategic planners was "us vs. them" from the start. Many of the planners, whose numbers grew to more than 50 by the late 1970s, were recruited from consulting firms. "A lot of operating people—and I was one of them—[interpreted the buildup to mean that] we were not smart enough to think our way through these things," says Roger Schipke, who ran the dishwasher business before assuming the Appliance Group's top job in 1982.

A "natural resistance" that escalated into out-and-out hostility meant that even when the planners were right, operating managers often would not listen to them. In the 1970s, planners correctly recognized the internationalization of markets, including appliances. But operating managers, who then saw Sears, Roebuck & Co. as the competition, paid them little heed. Only recently—now that the planners are gone—has the Appliance Group awakened to the threat that is being posed by the Japanese.

If the planners were sometimes right, they were frequently wrong—usually because they relied on data, not market instincts, to make their judgments. Says Schipke: "An awful lot of conclusions were drawn by that group somewhat in isolation. We had a lot of bad assumptions leading to some bad strategies."

WASTE FROM HASTE. When data indicated that houses and families were shrinking, for instance,

planners concluded that smaller appliances were the wave of the future. Because the planners had little contact with homebuilders and retailers, they did not realize that kitchens and bathrooms were the two rooms that were not shrinking and that working women wanted big refrigerators to cut down on trips to the supermarket. Moreover, top management, which also lacked contact with the market, did not see that the planners' data failed to tell the true story. The result: *GE* wasted a lot of time designing smaller appliances.

Even more harmful to the Appliance Group was the planners' obsession with predicting the unpredictable—such as oil prices—and then hastily reacting when events did not turn out as expected. When the energy crunch hit, planners predicted that the government would set energy-efficiency standards for appliances. "They thought the refrigeration business was going to come to an end because of the energy crunch," says Schipke. The reaction: a crash program to improve refrigerator insulation. As it turned out, efficiency standards never came to pass. And Schipke notes that improving the refrigerator's compressor—not the insulation—is the best way to increase energy efficiency.

But by the time these facts were realized, the damage had long been done. The comprehensive program for building state-of-the-art refrigerators in state-of-the-art facilities now under way—and which Schipke calls "our No. 1 priority"—was sidetracked for four years. Instead, says Schipke, Appliance Park's automated dishwasher plant was built "because the program looked like a nifty program." Though the dishwasher plant is successful, Schipke insists the returns would "definitely have been better if we put the same effort into refrigeration."

Schipke also blames planners for hurting the relationship between *GE*'s top management and the Appliance Group's management. When planners rushed into headquarters "raising red flags" such as energy, says Schipke, "top management would say, 'Gee, didn't this dumb [operating] guy know about this energy issue?'" Schipke says the energy *cause célèbre* in refrigeration cost at least four general managers their jobs.

As strategic planning became less of a creative

HOW GE TURNS MANAGERS INTO STRATEGISTS

No senior executive in General Electric Co. can boast of a strategic planning staff leaner than Roger W. Schipke's. The senior vice-president, who heads *GE*'s Major Appliance Business Group, has none.

Soon after assuming the top job at Appliance Park in Louisville in early 1982, Schipke finished the job that Vice-Chairman John F. Welch Jr. began before becoming *GE*'s chairman. Welch had slashed the planning staff from more than 50 to 25. As far as Schipke was concerned, that was still 25 too many. He now takes his "visions" for the group to his top operating managers, who "hash out a consensus" and then "drive it" through the organization. Insists Schipke: "For any strategy to succeed, you need [operating] people to understand it, embrace it, and make it happen."

Schipke is just as adamant in his belief that being a strategist means being externally focused. That explains his obsession with Whirlpool Corp.,

GE's major competitor in appliances. One of Schipke's pastimes is trying to understand how Jack D. Sparks, his counterpart at Whirlpool, thinks—and he expects his lieutenants to do the same.

'WE WOKE UP.' Upon assuming his current job (he previously headed *GE*'s dishwasher operation), Schipke ordered an analysis of Whirlpool. One lesson: the danger of an internal focus. For instance, by introducing new features, Whirlpool had almost eliminated *GE*'s share lead in side-by-side refrigerator-freezers. *GE*'s model had remained virtually unchanged since 1970. Says Schipke: "We were sitting here and saying, 'Gee, our figures look good. We're holding our share. Nothing must be happening.' We woke up."

He is now paying just as much attention to the Japanese. That explains why *GE* improved the evaporators on some single-door-refrigerator models—to make sure the Japanese could not use the niche to expand in the U. S.

Schipke, who replaced three of his top four appliance executives, says being good operationally is no longer enough at *GE*. "Now it's a question of, 'Can they develop a strategy for their business?' ", he says. "Some will make that cut. Some won't."

thinking exercise and more of a bureaucratic process, its original purpose was lost to *GE* and other enthusiastic corporate disciples. Managers began to confuse strategy with planning and implementation. To *GE* Chairman Welch, that is the difference between being externally or internally focused. Making sure that his managers understand the difference is an obvious obsession.

'HERE TO THERE.' Strategy, says Welch, "is trying to understand where you sit today in today's world. Not where you wish you were and where you hoped you would be, but where you are. And [it's trying to understand] where you want to be in 1990. [It's] assessing with everything in your head the competitive changes, the market changes that you can capitalize on or ward off to go from here to there. It's assessing the realistic chances of getting from here to there."

A strategy, says Welch, can be summarized in a page or two. "It is different from plan appropriation requests, building a plant, developing a product," he explains. "That's implementation of a strategy of where you want to be."

This distinction has been lost and has hurt plenty of companies. Of the 19 companies in *BUSINESS WEEK*'s survey whose strategies failed, ran into trouble, or were abandoned, 14 appear to have made the wrong assumptions about the business environment—ranging from interest rates to competitors' strategies.

By focusing on its plant's capacity and not on the market, Hydril Co., a Los Angeles manufacturer of oil-field equipment, chose not to build the new capacity that might have prevented new competitors from entering its market. An inward focus caused some of *TRW* Inc.'s industrial and automotive businesses to suffer from changes in distribution patterns because they had seen distributors—rather than end users—as their customer. "We did not try to anticipate what our competitors might do to the extent that we should have," says Richard L. Erickson, vice-president for planning and development at *TRW* Automotive Worldwide.

To correct the mistakes of the past, *GE*, Westinghouse, and scores of other companies are tearing down their rigid strategic-planning structures. Westinghouse's Povejsil has cut the strategic planning instructions for operating units "that looked like an auto repair manual" to five or six pages. To make sure that strategies are not presented at the annual meeting and then forgotten, both *GE* and Westinghouse have abandoned the practice of holding "a strategic planning month" each year. For each unit at *GE*, says Schipke, "the meeting would last 15 to 20 minutes. It was 'Pass Appliance through, bring in Television.'" The Appliance Group's most recent strategic review with Jack Welch lasted from 8:15 a.m. to 3:30 p.m.

ONE JOB INTO TWO. *GE* and other companies are also taking pains to separate operational and budget issues from strategy. Avery International, a Pasadena (Calif.) maker of labels, tape, and office products, has split its planning vice-president's job into two. One focuses on such long-term strategic issues as competition, technology, and acquisitions. The other concentrates on operational issues. *GE* and, reportedly, Shell Chemical and Fluor discuss budget and strategy issues with operating managers at separate sessions to make sure ideas—and not numbers—dominate strategies.

The very way strategic planning—or "strategic thinking"—is done is dramatically changing. At Millipore Corp., a maker of high-tech filtration systems, the planners are noticeably absent: Chairman Dimitri V. d'Arbeloff fired the company's six. Instead, "environmental" task forces of operating managers meet every 18 months to two years to brainstorm on what is happening in their markets and where those markets are likely to go in the next 5 to 10 years. This approach has enabled Millipore to keep apace of the increasingly demanding filtration needs of the semiconductor industry by introducing new technology. "One

reason we're a leader today in contamination control in microelectronics is because we took this approach," says Anthony J. Lucas, director of microelectronics marketing. "We just had to be there at an operational level rather than at a top-down corporate level."

Some companies are also incorporating their contingency or "what-if" planning into overall strategy. This contrasts with the old approach of creating a separate, rigid contingency plan that was often proved to be worthless. The new approach enables such companies as Monsanto to take the initiative to shape events—such as the public acceptance of biotechnology—rather than simply to react to them.

The role of strategic planners is also changing in a big way. Borg-Warner Corp.'s three corporate planners—down from 10 three years ago—now serve as consultants to business units. The heads of its seven groups act as their "chief strategists," says Donald C. Trauscht, vice-president for corporate planning.

At *GE*, David W. Keller, manager of strategic planning for the Aerospace Business Group, says that the time he spends pestering divisions and departments for information ordered by the corporate and sector offices has dropped about 90%. "People mired in their markets are asking us how we can bring a broader perspective to them in assessing their new opportunities," he says.

For example, Keller is helping managers of *GE*'s simulation and training business assess a possible move into the graphics market. "In the past," he says, "they wouldn't dare to call us and ask for our help or another point of view, fearing it would more likely generate more requests of them rather than be more help to them."

At *GM*, planners are "facilitators" to help operating managers do the planning themselves. Raymond K. Fears, the planner in *GM*'s Buick City complex, says he is "working my way out of a job." Fears figures Buick City's plant manager will be ready to handle strategic planning without his help in a year.

Some companies, though, may find it a lot harder to turn operating managers into strategic thinkers. Many operating managers at a Midwestern manufacturer continue to fill out strategic-planning forms that headquarters no longer requires. "You almost had to rip them out of their hands," says an executive.

PRESSING THE FLESH. Still, management gurus believe the biggest challenge in strategic planning will be turning *CEO*s into true strategic thinkers. A McKinsey study found that corporate executives now spend only 10% to 15% of their time thinking. That the rest of their time is devoted to meetings, crunching numbers, and pressing the flesh is not an encouraging sign.

Perhaps this explains why so few companies appear to have a bona fide corporate strategy. Harvard business school's Michael E. Porter says this should be more than a compilation of individual business units' plans—it should be a device to integrate business units and enable the parent company to capitalize on synergies so that the whole of the corporation is more than just the sum of its units. Some examples of companies trying to do just this: American Express, Citicorp, and *GE*. Declares Porter: "Companies that are on top of forging integrated strategies are the companies that are going to succeed in the future."

THE FUTURE CATCHES UP WITH A STRATEGIC PLANNER

CRITICS SAY THE ONCE-HOT BOSTON CONSULTING GROUP DID NOT KEEP PACE AS ANALYSIS MATURED

JUNE 27, 1983, P. 62

Four years ago, Bruce D. Henderson, founder and chairman of Boston Consulting Group Inc. and, many argue, the architect of modern corporate strategic planning, wrote: "Success in the past always becomes enshrined in the present by the overvaluation of the policies and attitudes which accompanied that success."

Ironically, critics contend, it is now BCG and other "strategy boutiques" that are wedded to "overvalued" policies that brought wild success in the past two decades. A growing number of companies now recognize that a brilliant strategy does not always guarantee bottom-line success. Confronted with brutal competitive conditions, they are more concerned with product development, productivity improvement, and cost-cutting. And technology that is rejuvenating mature markets and making young products obsolete has tarnished the allure of the portfolio-management approach that BCG helped spawn.

Says Alexander R. Oliver, a partner at Booz, Allen & Hamilton Inc. and a BCG alumnus: "Strategic analysis has not been a particularly successful and sustainable sales vehicle. Unless you can implement plans, they have no value whatsoever." Adds a planning official at a major company: "What BCG does, it does well. But it's limited in scope."

'EXPERIENCE CURVE.' BCG took corporate America by storm by coining two concepts that became the heart of strategic planning. Its "experience curve" helped companies develop pricing strategies by projecting how costs fall as units produced rise. And its "growth-share" matrix aided in the evaluation of businesses and their potentials by analyzing market share and growth rates.

Armed with these tools, BCG under Henderson averaged 25% annual increases in billings in the past decade. Such competitors as McKinsey & Co. and Booz Allen scrambled to beef up their strategic-planning departments as customers defected to BCG. "BCG was at the center and in many ways created the field," says Michael A. Carpenter, who left BCG to join General Electric Co. in February as a planning vice-president.

Competitors say the new emphasis is taking a toll at their prestigious rival. BCG posted a 7% increase in billings last year, which, though respectable in a recession, "is a number they would have sneered at in the past," notes one alumnus. Concedes Alan J.

Zakon, who succeeded Henderson as chief executive in 1979: "This is not a boom time."

In fact, industry sources say, BCG—which in the past rarely dismissed people—recently axed 6 of the 20 middle managers at its Boston headquarters. BCG denies that they were fired, saying all are leaving voluntarily. Zakon has, however, revamped the company's compensation system to rein in a pay scale that had 28-year-olds earning $70,000.

The underlying reasons for these actions, BCG critics contend, owe less to a soggy economy than to the marked change in what corporate managers want from consultants. Increasingly, they want assistance in implementing strategies and in finding out "what customers want and how I can get it to them," says Christopher J. Samuels, a BCG alumnus and now director of the Center for Strategy Research Inc., a Cambridge (Mass.) consultant.

Moreover, growing numbers of chief executives—and consultants—realize that the successful implementation of a strategy depends on having the right resources, organization, compensation program, and culture. "We are trying to approach [customers] with an awareness of the need to look at management processes as an interrelated system rather than as fragmented pieces," says Walter I. Jacobs, a partner at Hay Management Consultants.

Noting BCG's traditional devotion to strategic analysis, competitors question whether BCG can change easily. One rival says that BCG's transition from the Henderson era has been fraught with "intellectual debate as to how they should recast their mission."

BACK TO BASICS. Zakon agrees the market has shifted but insists BCG is adapting smoothly to its new priority of "making it happen for the client." In what Zakon labels "a mutual learning process," BCG is entering into longer-term relationships with clients to understand better "what will really happen when [a strategic plan] gets rolling." And for the first time, BCG is recruiting from industry, breaking away from its tradition of hiring from elite business schools.

Nonetheless, many observers believe that BCG has not fully come to grips with the maturing of strategic analysis. They contend that other consultants—such as Bain & Co. (one of several BCG spinoffs), as well as Booz Allen and McKinsey, which offer a wide range of services—have taken the lead with their back-to-basics approaches. One BCG alumnus recalls making a presentation when he was in his mid-20s to the directors of a major U.S. corporation who interrupted him with applause. "I was stunned," he says, "but it demonstrated the impact BCG's product had on people. Now the applause has definitely stopped."

UP FROM $4.95 FUDGE: FANNY FARMER TRIES TO BE A *CHOCOLATIER*

DECEMBER 10, 1984, P. 102

Chocolate lovers visiting some Fanny Farmer candy stores these days are likely to find a surprise. There among the $4.95-per-lb. fudge, the 50¢ French mint bars, and the $6-per-lb. boxed chocolates are handmade cream-filled chocolate truffles selling for $1.25 each. Fanny Farmer Candy Shops Inc., the 65-year-old candymaker named after a Victorian cooking school matron from Boston, is putting on the ritz.

In an attempt to erase Fanny Farmer's chronic multimillion-dollar losses, President William L. Jorgenson is changing the Bedford (Mass.) company's recipe to appeal to upscale chocolate fans.

Jorgenson, brought in last June by Fanny Farmer's new French owner, Poulain, may seem an odd choice for the job. Glancing at boxes of factory-fresh bonbons waiting for an executive taste test, the trim 41-year-old confides he never has been much of a chocolate eater. But he earned laurels as a marketing executive at Quaker Oats Co. and then in 1980 became president of Ward-Johnston Inc., which makes Bit-O-Honey and Raisinettes. Now, clad in jeans, he often spends weekends behind shop counters to see which candies are moving.

UPHEAVALS. His skills are sorely needed at Fanny Farmer, which dominated the retail candy business in the 1950s. In recent years, although the candy business got more competitive, the company paid scant attention to the market as it endured two proxy fights and nine presidents in

22 years. Fanny Farmer slipped into the red in 1981 and has remained there. It expects to lose at least $2.5 million in 1984, on sales of $45 million.

But Jorgenson's timing may be good. Americans are still watching their waistlines, but they are also indulging in chocolate again. In 1983, the average American ate nearly 18 lb. of confections—about 65% chocolates—up from a low of 16 lb. in 1975. And the market for upscale chocolates is growing fast. Chocolates are again popular gifts for dinner parties—providing a boost to candymakers, who have traditionally relied on Easter, Christmas, and Valentine's Day for some 55% of sales and largely on "chocoholics" for the rest. Nestlé Co. pegs the 1984 boxed-chocolate market at about $1.8 billion and expects it to reach $4 billion by 1990.

Jorgenson plans to introduce rich new specialty chocolates at $8 to $15 per lb.—just below the $20-per-lb. designer chocolate world dominated by Godiva, a subsidiary of Campbell Soup Co., and imports such as Perugina of Italy, and a cut above Russell Stover and Fannie May Candy Shops, whose chocolates average $6 per lb. "There's a giant void in the market," agrees Gino A. Marinelli, president of Miss Saylor's Candies Inc., a candy wholesaler. Jorgenson also intends to dress up his aging shops—either in wood and brass or in a modern red, white, and blue decor.

Poulain, a $389 million food company that bought the ailing company in June from Amoskeag Co., a Boston holding company, says it will pump $15 million into Fanny Farmer during the next two years. "It's the first real chance to turn the company around," says former Fanny Farmer President Peter S. Kurzina. "We were cash-starved."

Besides the truffles, which Fanny Farmer began to test-market in Boston stores in mid-November, Jorgenson next year will roll out new lines of by-the-pound chocolates at three prices: $8, $12, and $15. "We're going to make basic bonbons bigger," he says. The average 1-lb. box will now hold 26 pieces, instead of 32, for $12. The chocolates will also get new decorations. And Jorgenson is shav-ing shop inventories from 12 weeks to 3 weeks to ensure freshness.

'MORE THAN CANDY.' Even some competitors endorse Fanny Farmer's strategy. Says Curtis C. Rogers, president of Palm Beach Confections Inc., a four-store regional rival selling $15-per-lb. chocolate: "The market hasn't come anywhere near its potential." Adds Albert J. Pechenik, president of Gourmet Resources Inc., which imports $20-per-lb. Michel Guérard boxed chocolates from Belgium: "Jorgenson is in a position to take over the chocolate business in this country. He's a bright guy, he's marketing-oriented, he has the base, the Poulain money, and there's a tremendous opening in the market."

But there are obstacles. Jorgenson, who predicts that Fanny Farmer will break even on 1985 sales up 9%, to $53 million, will have a tough time changing Fanny Farmer's image. "A lot of people will buy a $5-per-lb. box of chocolate for Granny in the hospital, but if they are going to dinner at Joe and Mary's they'll buy a box of Godiva," says Kurzina. Entrenched premium chocolatiers use snooty names and fancy wrappings to draw consumers. "You're selling more than candy," says Sven E. Tilly, a vice-president of Gourmet Resources.

Competitors in Fanny Farmer's traditional low-price class are beginning to scout the middle market, too. In late November, See's Candy Shops Inc., which has 214 stores in the West, started test-marketing its boxed chocolates—sold on the West Coast at $6 per lb.—for $9.60 in Bloomingdale's stores in the East.

But Jorgenson believes Fanny Farmer's street-corner locations—325 shops in 23 states in the East and Midwest—new packaging, and lower prices, compared with costly rivals, will entice young buyers. The pricy truffles already account for 15% of sales in the test stores. Nonetheless, he is looking for an acquisition, perhaps a deluxe *chocolatier* like Guérard. He wants another line of candy, sold under another name, to help change Fanny Farmer's grandmotherly image.

By Barbara Buell in Boston

INFORMATION POWER

HOW COMPANIES ARE USING NEW TECHNOLOGIES TO GAIN A COMPETITIVE EDGE

OCTOBER 14, 1985, PP. 108-112, 114

For all the talk about the Information Age, most computers are still just workhorses—churning out payrolls, reports, numerical analyses. But slowly, stealthily, companies are turning their machines into a lot more.

No longer handmaidens to the back office, office automation and data processing are fast becoming indispensable allies in marketing, customer service, product development, human resource management, strategic planning, and many other jobs. "The diffusion of technology is changing the way we do business and the way companies relate to customers and suppliers," says James I. Cash Jr., a Harvard business school professor. "This is no longer a technological phenomenon but a social one."

FRESH MIND-SET. In part, the change simply reflects the proliferation of computers. But there's more to it than that. Information technologies are reaching a critical mass. Business is beginning to reconfigure things from the ground up—this time with the computer in mind. The result: entirely different approaches to existing markets and whole new product lines that didn't seem a logical extension of the business before. Retailer J. C. Penney now processes credit card transactions for Shell Oil and Gulf Refining & Marketing as a way to leverage its investment in its information network. Who would have foreseen such relationships 10 years ago?

At the same time, computers, telecommunications, and video technology are merging into something bigger and better than the individual components. What is a telecommunications system these days without a computer? As the technologies become more entwined, the potentials of each suddenly multiply. And as they become part of everyday life, more people are perceiving new ways to use them. What becomes essential is a fresh mind-set, a new way of perceiving the role of information technology in business.

The ability to use computers and telecommunications creatively to collect, make sense of, and distribute information is already spelling the difference between success and mediocrity in industries ranging from banking to bicycle making, at companies as large as General Motors Corp. and as small as automobile body shops. "The difference between now and five years ago is that then technology had limited function. You weren't betting your company on it," says William H. Gruber, president of Research & Planning Inc., a Cambridge (Mass.) consulting firm. "Now you are."

How so? Consider three classic cases, mythologized in Harvard business school case studies and preached with evangelical fervor by a growing cadre of information management experts:

■ **Merrill Lynch & Co.** used computers to create one of its most successful new products ever: the Cash Management Account. By combining information on a customer's checking, savings, credit card, and securities accounts into one computerized monthly statement and automatically "sweeping" idle funds into interest-bearing money market funds, Merrill Lynch has lured billions of dollars of assets from other places since it introduced *CMA* in 1978. It now manages $85 billion. And though rivals eventually concocted similar offerings, it still has almost 70% of the market.

■ **American Hospital Supply Corp.**, which distributes products from 8,500 manufacturers to more than 100,000 health-care providers, saw its market share soar in the 1970s after it set up computer links to its customers and suppliers. Hospitals

TEN WAYS TO GET AHEAD WITH INFORMATION TECHNOLOGY

TELEMARKETING
Testing cold leads by telephone first—using computer runs to ferret out the best prospects—helps slash sales-force expenses and boost productivity.

CUSTOMER SERVICE
By letting customers tap into your data base to track their orders and shipments, you build loyalty and smooth relations.

TRAINING
Training or retraining workers using videodisks lets them learn at their own speed—and lets you cut training costs.

SALES
Giving salespeople portable computers so they can get messages faster and enter orders directly adds up to quicker deliveries, better cash flow, and less paperwork.

BETTER FINANCIAL MANAGEMENT
By setting up computer links between the treasurer's office and your banks, you can obtain financial information faster—and that means better cash management.

PRODUCT DEVELOPMENT
By providing a toll-free number for consumer questions and complaints, you get ideas for product improvements and new products. In-house electronic publishing can help turn out product manuals faster for speedier introductions.

MARKET INTELLIGENCE
By assembling and manipulating data on demographics and competitors, you can spot untapped niches, develop new products, and avoid inventory crunches.

NEW BUSINESSES
Information technologies make whole new operations possible. Federal Express, for one, could not work without computer-equipped trucks and facilities.

LOCKING IN CUSTOMERS
By creating exclusive computer communications with customers for order entry and exchange of product and service data, you can help thwart competitors.

SELLING EXTRA PROCESSING POWER
You can use off-peak processing power to develop completely new services for outsiders. That way, you can transfer some of the high costs of building your information network.

---

could enter orders themselves via *AHS* terminals. The technology let the company cut inventories, improve customer service, and get better terms from suppliers for higher volumes. Even more important, it often locked out rival distributors that didn't have direct pipelines to hospitals. Now, *AHS*, which agreed to be acquired by Baxter Travenol Laboratories Inc. in July, stays ahead of competitors by analyzing the industry data it collects to spot order trends and customer needs more quickly.

■ **American Airlines Inc.** has used computer and communications technology to build an entirely new business with sky-high profit margins. American provides its Sabre reservation system, which lists the flight schedules of every major airline in the world, to 48% of the approximately 24,000 automated travel agents in the U.S. They pay

American $1.75 for every reservation made via Sabre for other carriers. American's parent, *AMR* Corp., which earned $400 million pretax last year on $5.3 billion in revenues, expects Sabre alone to earn it $170 million before taxes this year on $338 million in revenues. "We are now in the data processing as well as the airline business," says President Robert L. Crandall, a data processing expert who conceived Sabre a decade ago, when he was American's marketing chief.

Such success stories have sent companies in every industry scrambling to find ways to harness the power of information technology—from computers and telephones to communications satellites and videodisks.

As the use of information technology escalates, every industry will be affected, and businesses that stay out of the fray will suffer. But upstaging a rival today is no guarantee of superiority tomorrow. Often competitors respond in kind, bringing the situation back to parity. The aggressor must keep innovating to maintain its edge. Five months after American started installing Sabre, United Airlines began delivering its Apollo system, and now Eastern, Delta, and *TWA* have systems, too.

Often the biggest beneficiary of such competitive thrusts is the customer, who gets a cheaper air fare, faster service, or a new product. When banks began offering computer linkups between themselves and corporate treasurers in the early 1980s, companies were able to determine earlier how much cash was in their accounts—and thus to manage it better. "Bankers used to live by the '3-5-3 rule': Borrow at 3%, lend at 5%, play golf at 3 p.m.," says consultant Michael Hammer, president of Hammer & Co. in Cambridge, Mass. "But not any more. Now treasurers are managing much more actively, and I think one of the reasons behind many banks' problems is they don't have a lot of the float from corporate accounts."

HUNGRY FOR MORE. Although most companies may not have thought of information as a competitive weapon, for years they have been putting in place the infrastructure needed to make it one. In the past decade, according to Harry F. Bunn, senior vice-president at *PA* Consulting Services Inc., a management consultant in Princeton, N. J., corporate spending on information processing gear has gone up an average of 16% a year, and raw computer power for crunching data faster has increased 18-fold.

> 'Get the right information
> to the right guy at the right time to
> make the right decision'

But using technology to gain a competitive edge has gotten its biggest boost from the personal computer. Until the early 1980s, computers were the preserve of distant data processing managers who spoke a different language than managers. Data processing shops had months or years of backlogged requests for programming, so management rarely took advantage of data locked in corporate computers.

Now, though, managers can manipulate data themselves on personal computers, and they are hungry for more and better information. The most forward-thinking companies have come up with ways to give it to them. The information can come from sources as diverse as portable computers for salespeople in the field, external data bases that provide intelligence on competitors and markets, and inventory management systems. General Electric Co. found that by creating a toll-free hotline for customer complaints and questions, it could generate a wealth of information that helped it improve old products and develop new ones.

Most companies still have a long way to go, though. "There are a lot of personal computers and word processors out there, but most of them are not hooked up," notes Joan C. Trude of Booz, Allen & Hamilton Inc. "Most companies have exploited little of the potential." A look at American's development of its Sabre system shows how difficult this can be.

American started designing Sabre when United Airlines Inc. announced plans for its own reservation system for travel agents, who then made about half of all airline bookings. "Bob Crandall said we had to have a competitive tool—we couldn't allow United to dominate," says Max Hopper, who designed Sabre. The reason: Travel agencies are the distribution system for the industry's commodity—seats.

United's system was just for its own routes. "They thought that would be enough, that it would give agents 70% of what they needed," Hopper says. "We made the decision to provide all airlines' schedules. We wanted agents to use the system all the time." By creating total dependence on its system, American gained market share. It listed its own flights first, and many travel agents never went further. "We saw it as a marketing tool from day one," says Hopper, who is now in charge of information systems at Bank of America. "It took United a year or more to catch up."

Eventually, Sabre and Apollo proved to be such powerful competitive tools that other airlines cried foul. Now, under government pressure, the two big carriers have eliminated the bias of listing their own flights first. But they are making up the difference by charging for bookings on other carriers. And Sabre is now also a marketing pipeline. Travel agents can use it to get visas and book hotels. American gets a cut on all the services the agents sell.

It's no surprise that management experts would try to capture the secrets of information strategy in a formula. In his new book, *Competitive Advantage*, Harvard business school professor Michael E. Porter discusses his "value chain" analysis. "The firm is a collection of activities: You have to tear it apart into discrete activities, determine what it costs to do each activity, and what makes it unique," he says. "Information technology can affect how every activity is and can be performed."

'NEGLECTED FORCE.' Others feel Porter's approach is simplistic. "I would only spend 20% of my time on [the value chain]," says Richard L. Nolan, chairman of Nolan, Norton & Co., a Lexington (Mass.) consultant. "I'd spend the other 80% creating the culture to make it happen." He says employees must be computer-literate and management must have learned how to apply information technology. "The reason technology can be such a potent force and is frequently a neglected one is that it often takes a number of years to build the technical infrastructure and skills base with which to compete," asserts Research & Planning's Gruber.

With or without a formula, companies are finding they have to be more creative to make information technology part of their business strategies. Irwin J. Sitkin, vice-president for corporate administration at Aetna Life & Casualty Co., now views his company as "one great big information processing business." The game, he says, "has really become 'Get the right information to the right guy at the right time to make the right decision to beat the other guys out in the marketplace.'" Aetna now gives customers access to its Aecclaims system, which processes group insurance claims. Now the client can do some analysis of his own—on the effectiveness of his own cost containment efforts, for instance—using Aetna's computer files.

MAKING DATA PROCESSING PAY FOR ITSELF

Most data processing managers don't think like business strategists. And most executives don't really understand what technology can do. That's a big problem for companies trying to use technology to gain a competitive edge. People are often on different wavelengths.

Security Pacific National Bank thinks it has a solution: Spin off data processing into a separate division, and make it support itself. That way, data processing people will have to think in business terms. If they don't come up with competitive ideas that sell, they'll be out of business.

That's the idea behind Security Pacific Automation Co., a new unit of the bank. The subsidiary will bid on internal bank projects, though bank departments are free to hire competing outfits instead. The unit will also sell its services outside the company, mostly to small and medium-size banks. That way Security Pacific can spread the cost of its data processing facilities. DuWayne J. Peterson, chairman of the new division, is optimistic about demand for its services. "In banking," he says, "you can't survive without technology—it's becoming a competitive weapon."

So far, the move is dramatically reducing rapid increases in the bank's data processing expenditures. This year's budget of some $250 million represents only a 4% rise from last year vs. annual increases of 28% for the two previous years.

And the division is already coming up with new services. It is putting terminals into car dealerships to link them with Security Pacific Credit Corp. That way, dealers can run credit checks and close deals faster and consumers can calculate loan payments.

Security Pacific's strategy is not without risks. Other banks have had little success selling data processing, and the division will break even this year at best. But Security Pacific expects some profits by next year, and it is looking for the subsidiary to contribute up to 5% of overall corporate earnings in 10 years.

Sometimes, whole new enterprises grow out of systems put in place just to provide information. Citibank, which offers financial services and data, has teamed up with McGraw-Hill Inc., which collects data on commodities, to create a 24-hour commodity trading venture called Global Electronic Markets Co. Now, traders can not only get information instantly but also make deals and transfer money in minutes. (McGraw-Hill also publishes *BUSINESS WEEK*.)

Being creative doesn't necessarily mean being first. In the New York City retail banking market, Chemical Bank was the first to put in automatic teller machines in 1969. Its goal was simply to automate the teller's job. But it didn't seem to work, and Chemical pulled back. Citibank, on the other hand, saw an entirely different opportunity. It thought that the primary value of *ATM*s lay in customer service and marketing. It did a lot of research on customer responses to technology and created much "friendlier" machines. By blanketing the city with them in the late 1970s, it more than doubled its checking and deposit balances and almost tripled its market share, from 5% to about 13% today.

To spot such opportunities, executives don't necessarily have to know how the technology works. But they do need to understand how to deploy it. Just as no general would leave tactical planning to his quartermaster, executives cannot expect their data processing lieutenants to wage this battle. "The technically sound people are often not creative [in business strategy]," notes Peter Keen, a former Massachusetts Institute of Technology professor who now consults on how to use information technology.

The data processing manager who can talk management's language and explain how to launch a preemptive attack in the marketplace is an invaluable asset. "Companies are competing on a national basis to find this rare commodity," says Herbert Halbrecht, president of Halbrecht Associates Inc., a Stamford (Conn.) executive search firm specializing in finding technical executives. "Salaries have been escalating very rapidly."

At $1 billion-plus companies where information technology is "the engine driving the company"— at major insurance companies and banks, for ex-

ample—annual salary packages for information managers often hit $150,000 to $250,000, almost twice what they were five years ago, Halbrecht says. One company with revenues in the $60 million range offered a salary package of $100,000 to $120,000 for a job whose last occupant, "a real techie," made $70,000 with a minor bonus, he reports.

As information technology becomes a strategic tool rather than simply a support function, data processing managers' roles—and jobs—will have to change, too. "They will have to delight in solving the business problem, not the crossword puzzle that was programming," notes John F. Rockart, a professor at *MIT*'s Sloan School of Management. William R. Synnott, senior vice-president in charge of information systems at Bank of Boston Corp., wonders how many data processing people will make the transition. "A lot won't," he says. "They have come through the technical ranks and have had little management exposure."

'BELIEVERS.' Synnott says his own role has already changed "quite dramatically." He has become progressively more involved in strategic planning and marketing and now spends an allotted time each month showing senior management how to use information technology. "The people in management have become believers," he says.

The companies that use information technology best are forging just this kind of partnership between their executives and their technical people. "Just as executives have always had to cope with operations, strategy, financial planning, and people, now they are going to have to deal with information technology as well," says *MIT*'s Rockart.

One executive who spearheaded a technological revolution at his company is Robert F. McDermott, president of the San Antonio-based insurer *USAA*, formerly the United Services Automobile Assn. When McDermott arrived in 1969 and found boxes of paper spilling into the hallways, he vowed to create a "paperless environment" at the company, which then handled most of its promotions and collections by mail, processed by hand.

Early on, *USAA* entered names, addresses, and other policy information into computer terminals and cross-referenced them to give service representatives easy access to the data. Other innovations followed. Now the National Insurance Consumer Organization in Alexandria, Va., recommends *USAA*'s Universal Life Policy to consumers largely because automation lets the company do sales and service over the telephone, eliminating agents that boost premiums. Consumers Union, the nonprofit publisher of *Consumer Reports*, ranks *USAA* at or near the top in customer satisfaction with automobile and homeowner claims handling.

Clearly, more businesses are starting to think hard about how to use information technology strategically. Many analysts have blamed the computer industry slump on buyers' hesitancy to make large-scale purchases until they understand better how the equipment can make them more effective, not just more efficient. Now, companies may be getting ready to buy. "Two years ago clients were hiring us for needs assessments and diagnostics. Now they want strategic planning," says Randy J. Goldfield, president of Omni Group Ltd., a New York market research and office automation consulting firm. "Now it's, 'Let's move ahead, let's implement.'"

These companies may be willing to spend more now than ever, suggests Harvey L. Poppel, a partner at Broadview Associates, a Fort Lee (N. J.) financial consulting firm. "Technology is starting to influence the revenue stream, not just the cost side, and people are becoming less cost sensitive," he says.

RISKY SAVING. But to get into the game, many businesses are going to have to change the way they justify technology expenditures. "The costs are certain, the benefits are not," notes consultant Hammer. Adds Theodore J. Freiser, president of John Diebold & Associates, a New York management consultant: "You have to be willing to make the investment without having a correspondingly measurable return. There's no measure we can construct that can isolate the contribution of information and not be also attributable to some other factors. It's subjective."

The key is to stay flexible. "If you're going to use information as a competitive weapon, you don't know what the environment is going to be like in three to five years," Freiser says. But it may be riskier not to spend the money. "If you wait until others make the technology an industry standard and then you do it," he warns, "you are left without the benefits but with all the costs."

The long-term implications of this information technology arms race scare some observers. Michael E. Treacy, an assistant professor at *MIT*'s Sloan School, worries that "the whole thing is being oversold." He fears many industries may cripple themselves. He cites the effects of computerized reservation systems on airlines: "One or two companies have gotten an advantage, but they have decreased the wealth of the whole industry. With all the information they now have access to, customers have a relatively better bargaining position" and prices have been eroding. Airline stocks, even American's, have performed poorly relative to other investments, Treacy says. The stock price of American's parent, *AMR* Corp., has risen only 10% since yearend 1983, to $40.

Treacy concedes, though, that other airlines have done worse. And that's the rub. Just as Star Wars-style programs are likely to proceed even though they may escalate the chances of nuclear war, business is so competitive that companies are likely to do anything to gain an edge, even though in some cases their industries may be the ultimate victims. And competitors have got to be willing to follow. So businesses must gird themselves for the information technology revolution. The ones who understand how to use the new tools will be the survivors.

By Catherine L. Harris in New York, with bureau reports

AT TODAY'S SUPERMARKET, THE COMPUTER IS DOING IT ALL

IT HAS MOVED BEYOND THE CHECKOUT TO TRACK EVERYTHING FROM PILFERAGE TO PROFIT

Ronald K. Springer isn't one to get nostalgic. When he started in the grocery business 25 years ago, one of his chores was to take home piles of invoices and figure his store's gross profit on truckloads of food. Today, as manager of the Super Shop 'n Save in South Portland, Me., Springer oversees a market that beeps and whirs as computers do everything from figuring those dreaded invoices to setting up work schedules for checkout clerks. "I don't think the old days were simpler," he says. "They were more difficult."

More than half of the nation's supermarkets are equipped with scanners, those computerized checkout machines that read the bar code on a box of Wheaties. At least one in four uses a central computer to help run the business. But now, food stores such as Springer's are going beyond that, becoming what might be called "electronic supermarkets" permeated by computers. Says Timothy M. Hammond, senior vice-president of the Food Marketing Institute, a grocers' trade group: "Within the last couple of years, the industry has moved to phase two—using the mound of scanning data to influence management."

"Phase two" is rewriting the rules of the trade, both for small outfits such as Gromer Super Markets Inc. in Elgin, Ill., and for giants such as Safeway Stores Inc. Data of unprecedented precision, on everything from pilferage to profit per item, are giving the best supermarket managers a competitive advantage that some analysts say could double profit margins, which today average only 1.2%. It's even having a major impact on foodmakers such as Campbell Soup Co. The numbers, for instance, can help tell a manufacturer that better packaging will sell more of his products.

The new system is working well at Hannaford Brothers, the Scarborough (Me.) owner of Shop 'n Save stores. In 1980, Hannaford posted a respectable 1% profit margin, then the industry average. Since that time, by using computers in all phases of its business, Hannaford has boosted margins steadily, to 1.8% in the first quarter of this year. "I would characterize what's happening as a revolution," says Hugh C. Smith, a product management specialist at Hannaford.

With data flowing from stores and warehouses to an *IBM* 4381 mainframe at headquarters, Hannaford calculates virtually every cost involved in getting its goods from manufacturer to consumer—including shipping expenses, warehouse handling requirements, bulkiness of display, energy needs at the store, and the time canned corn spends on the shelf before it's bought. Hannaford crunches these data for each of its more than 17,000 products and each of its 65 stores.

'EYE-OPENER.' The resulting richness of detail is staggering. "We can call up a report on the direct profit contribution of pickle Brand X at store Z during some seven-week period," says James J. Jermann, Hannaford's vice-president for merchandising. Armed with such information, retail buyers and marketers can for the first time make truly informed decisions on, say, which brands of gherkins to carry and how to price them. That's a far cry from the not-so-distant days when a grocer's only guide to profit contribution was the markup percentage on a given item, which often ignored variable costs such as transportation.

"Computerized profit calculations have been a real eye-opener for the retailer," says John R. Phipps of Touche Ross & Co. As the accounting firm's director for food industry consulting, Phipps is the guru of what the industry calls direct product profitability *(DPP)* analysis (table). The concept was born in the early 1960s, but it wasn't until the cost of mainframe computing power fell in the 1980s that *DPP* caught on.

Retailers have always known that certain items

USING INFORMATION TO MAKE SUPERMARKETS MORE EFFICIENT

STEP 1: Raw data flow from stores and warehouses to a mainframe computer, usually at chain headquarters. Included are sales records from checkout stands, data on product delivery schedules, employee work schedules, energy use, and the amount of time products spend in chain warehouses before they're shipped to stores.

STEP 2: The numbers are crunched to help make better decisions about what products to sell, how to display them, and how to make their storage and delivery more efficient. Headquarters can determine which brands of soap make the most money, for example, and cut back on the least profitable ones. Or it can use computer-projected cost estimates to gauge how profitable a new brand of soap might be. The numbers might also suggest whether products should be delivered directly to stores or go to a central warehouse first.

STEP 3: Headquarters sends its recommendations back to the store and to warehouse managers and their assistants. Sometimes called "Plan-a-Grams," these instructions include detailed schematics of every shelf, showing the store manager where to display each of the up to 17,000 products sold in large supermarkets. The plan may even recommend prices for these goods.

STEP 4: Headquarters also gives or sells the numbers generated in Step 1 to manufacturers, which may subsequently modify their products. For instance, the numbers may tell a soap maker that its products would sell better if they were packaged differently.

DATA: BW

---

must be priced as "loss leaders," carried primarily to bring shoppers into the store. But Phipps says that "*DPP* is showing that about 20% of the items in a typical grocery store actually lose money, which means that the more of those you sell, the more you lose." In these cases, *DPP* analysis serves two novel functions: It identifies exactly which products hemorrhage profit, and it offers clues about how to stop the bleeding.

UNEXPECTED WINNER. The results are often surprising. House brands, once considered big money-makers because of their low initial cost, turn out to be skimpy performers compared with better-advertised name brands that move faster. Paper products are also a drag on profit, given their bulk and small price. Stores must sell toilet paper, but *DPP* numbers suggest limiting variety and avoiding costly promotions.

One of the supermarket's unexpected winners, according to *DPP*, is the freezer section. It has traditionally been perceived as too energy-intensive to reap big returns. But frozen meals actually outperform the average grocery item almost two to one because of their large markups. Once enough frozen items have been sold to cover energy costs, profits soar. Soft drinks, dairy goods, snack foods, magazines, and other products delivered directly to stores by manufacturers also make more money than previously thought, because store employees aren't used to stock them.

The wealth of detail compiled by *DPP* often helps retailers and manufacturers streamline their operations. At Hannaford and other chains, *DPP* is translated into "Plan-a-Grams"—printouts that show store managers, shelf by shelf, exactly where to place their stock to maximize profit. A decision on whether to display three rows of Skippy peanut butter rather than two has never been trivial from a profit standpoint. But with Plan-a-Grams, that decision can be based on more than instinct.

NEW SOPHISTICATION. *DPP* information also helps Procter & Gamble Co., Campbell Soup, and other manufacturers design more efficient containers and shipping methods. *DPP* studies have shown that stores prefer to stock lighter-weight packages of detergent, so manufacturers have set out to limit the air and water content in their packages. "We get calls every week from manufacturers interested in our *DPP* findings," says Hannaford's Smith. Hannaford and an increasing number of other chains sell access to their scanning data and cooperate with manufacturers running *DPP* experiments. Some, such as Safeway, staff a separate office to design and run such tests for manufacturers they deal with.

Hoping to build on the industry's new sophistication, automation consultants, market research-ers, and hardware and software producers are promoting an expanding array of scanning spin-offs. Set to debut later this year in some markets is the "electronic shelf," which will offer shoppers cost and nutrition information at the touch of an electronic display—and let retailers constantly re-vise prices at the touch of their own buttons. Assuming that consumers don't mind having their privacy invaded, new identification cards tied to scanners will let stores track individual families' purchases and target them with coupons and ads. In the long run, scanning and *DPP* analysis will not be limited to supermarkets. Drug chains, con-venience stores, and even department stores al-ready are planning their own versions of the sys-tem.

The move toward *DPP* analysis could also trans-form the staff back at the headquarters of the new electronic supermarket. Managers who know com-puters are already in increasing demand. "Retail-ing has always had an image problem with *MBA*s," says Walter J. Salmon, an expert in the field at Harvard business school. "If in fact *DPP* leads to reorganizations in favor of sophisticated product managers, *MBA*s will be more attracted to the food industry."

Even so, store managers don't seem to see auto-mation as a threat to their authority or their intuition. Ron Springer says he needs help to manage his 250 employees and 17,000 products: "Bring it on. Bring it on."

By Gary Geipel in Scarborough, Me.

BANK OF AMERICA RUSHES INTO THE INFORMATION AGE

AFTER NEGLECTING COMPUTER TECHNOLOGY FOR YEARS,
THE BANK IS SPENDING $5 BILLION TO MODERNIZE SERVICES

APRIL 15, 1985, PP. 110, 112

Every year, Bank of America finances 250,000 California home buyers. But the San Francisco bank has no way of knowing whether those high-profile customers have bought any of its other products and services—from checking accounts to auto loans. Its customer in-formation has always been organized by product line, in separate data banks that can't be linked together. So it has been impossible for BofA to pull together complete customer profiles, even though such information would be instrumental in marketing new services.

But starting this spring, every time the bank approves a mortgage, a new loan-processing com-puter system will automatically generate a report about the buyer to the BofA branch office closest to the mortgaged property. When the client shows up for the closing on his property, he will be greeted by a sales rep already privy to his financial status and prepared to match the bank's repertoire of services to his needs.

This new approach to wooing customers is just one step in an all-out drive by BofA to become more competitive by using information more stra-tegically. "The name of the game is capturing the customer to sell him other products," says Execu-tive Vice-President Peter V. Hall. "If we can't do that, we won't survive as a bank."

Developing better information is becoming in-creasingly critical to all banks. Few thought about developing such strategic information as customer profiles before 1980, when deregulation began to remove price protection. But now that such flashy marketers as Sears, Roebuck & Co., and Merrill Lynch & Co. are luring away customers, BofA and other banks are scrambling to compete.

The 140 largest U. S. banks will spend at least $45 billion on automation and new data systems over the next five years, says Input, an informa-tion market researcher. And BofA, the second-biggest bank in the country after Citicorp, says it will spend $5 billion on new technologies as well as on the maintenance of its old systems. That is as much as Manufacturers Hanover Trust, Chase Manhattan, and Chemical combined will spend, according to management consultants Nolan, Norton & Co.

Samuel H. Armacost, BofA's president for the last four years, is serious about moving BofA squarely into the information age. Three years ago he recruited Max Hopper, an information systems hotshot from American Airlines Inc., to serve as executive vice-president in charge of BofA's new systems development. In January he appointed Hopper to head a new division that will centralize the bank's technology policies and systems development. "This is the first time BofA has treated information as a corporate resource," says Russell J. Harrison, senior vice-president for strategic technology management.

Hopper developed American's Sabre reservation system, a highly competitive weapon that allows the airline to keep track of its most frequent fliers, business travelers who are generally not sensitive to price and whom marketers consider the *crème de la crème*. Among other things, Sabre can tell if these customers stop flying regularly and send them personal letters asking why.

The personable Texan is already leading the charge. Known as Hopper the Chopper for his demanding style, he spent $45 million last year on computer technology borrowed from Sabre. As he retools BofA's systems, it's no surprise that he is building in the ability to generate a wealth of information.

'We've been sitting here
with a gigantic
battleship that was built
...before subs'

Hopper faces no easy challenge: BofA management, anxious to hold on to profits, invested little in new technologies during the 1970s, and the bank fell behind archrival Citicorp and some new nonbank competitors. "We've been sitting here

with a gigantic battleship that was built to compete before nuclear subs and long-range fighter aircraft ever came along," Armacost says.

SHEER SIZE. Not only did BofA fail to automate many back-office procedures, it also put off developing an efficient international telecommunications network. And it ignored tying data bases together to permit better marketing of its products to customers. In addition, BofA has had to march double-time in the last three years to overtake its California competitors in installing automated teller machines *(ATMs)*, which lower the cost of delivering services.

To make matters worse, BofA has traditionally treated its huge network of 950 California branches and international operating units as independent businesses. As a result, many have different reporting methods and incompatible computer systems. That has hampered the consistent gathering of information and made BofA less competitive.

Armacost, 46, is counting on the bank's sheer size to create unmatched economies of scale as it automates. The bank boasts 4 million customers on the West Coast and a large network of international offices. It also processes more financial transactions than any other private bank in the world—some 14 million every day. "We have a volume capability that very few competitors can match," notes Hopper.

Using the new systems that Hopper brought in, BofA can already process such electronic transactions as *ATM* cash withdrawals and fund transfers five times faster than standard banking systems and at about one-third less cost. Over the next two years, Hopper will spend at least $50 million more to consolidate BofA's 20 different telecommunications systems into a single, flexible network. As processing and communications costs plummet, "BofA is going to reverse the economics of the banking industry," predicts consultant Bruce J. Rogow of Nolan Norton. "All the other guys will have to catch up."

While many of the informational benefits of such systems are still years away, some advantages are beginning to show up. They are coming from a $200 million prototype system for the bank's international operations starting up this year in

Europe after four years of development. Corporate lending officers can now pull up an electronic file on a customer's current account balances, loans outstanding, foreign exchange positions, and other data anywhere in Europe—and eventually around the world. That enables officers to know which of the bank's products to push, and gives them more complete information to assess a customer's creditworthiness. Tracking a total relationship with a client was virtually impossible before.

And on the newly automated money market trading floors of BofA's European offices, supervisors can now electronically track each trader's buy and sell positions by currency. As a result, they can instantly detect any unauthorized trades and spot when an individual exceeds a specified limit. Such management capability, insiders say, could have prevented the embarrassing loss of $95 million last year when BofA found that some escrow department employees had unwittingly entangled the bank in an alleged mortgage-backed securities scam. Instead, almost three years passed before upper management was alerted to the scandal.

"Our controls will be modified to identify things like that," says Derrald K. Johnson, the vice-president who headed the bank's investigation.

By 1990, similar benefits should become more widespread as systems like the one in Europe are installed in the bank's other international regions and in its California retail operations. But Wall Street analysts are not looking out that far. They are already distressed over Armacost's spending for equipment and facilities—up 25% last year to $783 million. Those expenditures have combined with mounting problem loans to chop earnings of BankAmerica Corp., BofA's parent, by 46% since 1980 to $346 million in 1984. Return on equity weighed in at 6.4%—the worst performance of the 10 largest U. S. banks except for disaster-plagued Continental Illinois National Bank & Trust Co.

Armacost is cool to criticism and determined to "manage for the long term." But after four years of deregulated competition and declining profits, the sooner he retools the battleship the better.

By Jonathan B. Levine in San Francisco

PART 2

TARGET MARKETS

Ask those in business today to describe their customers and you will quickly realize they are engaged in target marketing. They segment their customers into homogeneous groups and develop marketing programs for each group or market.

The yuppies have been a big market and still are. However, marketers now realize that older consumers have created a huge market with special needs. Coke is after the teen market. Dips of ice cream have created a $1.9 million market. The industrial market is extremely large with firms such as McDonnell Douglas purchasing and selling millions of dollars' worth of products.

PART 2 ARTICLE SYNOPSES

DEMOGRAPHICS AND BUYING POWER

LAST YEAR IT WAS THE YUPPIES—THIS YEAR IT'S THEIR PARENTS

Though people over 50 have almost 50 percent of the U.S. disposable income, and though marketers are waking up to the fact that by the year 2000 76 million Americans will be 50 or older, it is no easy task to reach them; what is required is innovative marketing. People over 50 indulge in spending patterns that reveal greater discretionary income than the baby boomers, but such spending is focused on both brand preferences and specific areas. At the same time, marketers must be cautious about overplaying the age factor; research indicates that older Americans increasingly push back the age parameters that define an "old" person.

PRICEY ICE CREAM IS SCOOPING THE MARKET

When it comes to ice cream, give me quality, rich taste, and a popular name, and I'll pay the price. That's what consumers of highly priced, high-butterfat brands of ice cream like Häagen-Dazs and Frusen Glädjé seem to be saying. Customer loyalty has resulted in a 20 percent annual growth in superpremium ice creams. The leader, Häagen Dazs, is owned by Pillsbury; sales have more than doubled since Pillsbury's acquisition. Dart & Kraft purchased Frusen Glädjé and within a year tripled the brand's market share. Since 1980, sales of superpremiums have doubled to a $1.9 billion market. Smaller companies that hope to survive in this market must differentiate their product, as Dove Bar did by making superpremium ice cream bars.

THE INDUSTRIAL MARKET

MCDONNELL DOUGLAS TRIES MORE BUTTER AND FEWER GUNS

With defense orders tapering off, defense contractors are having to move into the nonmilitary market. McDonnell Douglas has been facing losses. Its attempt to enter the information system market has been a failure. However, the company has been successful in selling new commercial planes based on old designs.

LAST YEAR IT WAS YUPPIES —THIS YEAR IT'S THEIR PARENTS

MARKETERS DISCOVER OLDER CONSUMERS— TRICKY TO WOO BUT EAGER TO SPEND

MARCH 10, 1986, PP. 68, 72, 74

For years, Joe Smith felt left out. As president of Oxtoby-Smith Inc., a New York research firm, he has plenty of discretionary income. Yet few advertisers seemed to court him. Whenever Smith turned on the *TV* or opened a magazine, he found lots of ads—but few of them were pitched to him. How come? Smith is over 50.

Now marketers are paying plenty of attention to Smith and his contemporaries. His Long Island mailbox is brimming with catalogs from Neiman-Marcus and brochures describing time-share condominiums. "There are fewer pitches assuming I am feeble and lame," says the 59-year-old Smith. "The world has discovered I did not fall off a cliff when I turned 50. I am a desirable consumer."

Indeed he is. Today older is definitely in. Consider these recent developments:

■ Sears, Roebuck & Co., the nation's largest retailer, is wooing customers over 50 with discounts up to 25% on everything from eyeglasses to lawnmowers. Started just two years ago, the Mature Outlook Club has already attracted 400,000 dues-paying members.
■ Airlines such as American and United are rushing to offer discounts to older passengers. These recently introduced promotions could become as widespread as frequent-flyer bonus programs.
■ Southwestern Bell Corp. is publishing a series of telephone directories aimed at senior citizens. Revenue from the Silver Pages is exceeding projections.

These efforts go well beyond the 10% discounts local drugstores traditionally offer older customers. They represent a fundamental shift by marketing executives, who now recognize that a consumer's preferences can still be influenced at 49 or even 65—and the potential gains can be enormous. "Just as baby boomers and yuppies were hot last year, this year it is the 49-plus market and seniors," says Peter S. Kim, a vice-president at J. Walter Thompson *USA*.

The decline of traditional marketing strategies explains much of this new direction. "With the growing diversity in consumer lifestyles, mass-marketing is less efficient," says Jeffrey Prupis, a vice-president at Yankelovich, Skelly & White Inc., a New York research firm. "Advertisers are becoming more selective. Everyone is looking for areas of disproportionate affluence."

And that's where older Americans top the charts. People over 50 make up about 25% of the population but have nearly 50% of the nation's disposable income. They buy $800 billion worth of goods and services each year, according to a study by the Conference Board, an independent research group. More important, they are the fastest-growing age segment. In the next 15 years, the number of adults will grow by 14%, but the number of people over 50 will increase by 23%. By the year 2000, 76 million Americans will be 50 or older.

Now consider spending patterns. For the over-50 crowd, child-rearing costs are often over and done with. Homes either are paid for or have old, low-cost mortgages. Baby boomers are burdened with major expenses their parents have already met. Says Prupis: "Older people have put off benefiting themselves for the sake of the children. Now they are saying things like, 'Let's buy the *VCR*, because we don't have to pay Johnny's dentist bill.' "

PAYING DUES. Still, reaching this group is tricky. Typically, older people have established brand preferences. What's more, their spending tends to be concentrated in specific areas. "Seniors already own all the household goods they need and make replacements only as necessary," says Terrence L. Foran, Touche Ross & Co.'s national director of retail consulting. "They have their wardrobes and are not overly fashion-conscious."

That's why clever marketing is needed. One innovative effort is Sears' Mature Outlook Club, created to attract customers over 50. For a $7.50 annual fee, members receive benefits tailored to their needs. Older people, for example, purchase more than one-third of all garden tools. So club members have a standing 20% discount on any garden tool they buy at Sears. Similarly, they get lower rates on auto insurance through Sears' Allstate unit. This approach supplements Sears' conventional advertising. "The focus there is on younger customers," says William B. Strauss, Mature Outlook's executive director. "We are targeting an older audience. These people have money and the time to consider what you offer them."

Although Sears is the first major retailer to target older customers, both Strauss and Kurt Barnard, publisher of *Barnard's Retail Marketing Report*, an industry newsletter, predict the idea will catch on. "You are starting to see ads and catalogs that show older people," says Barnard. "The infatuation with the very young is fading, for the simple reason there are fewer of them."

'LOVE TO TRAVEL.' The trend extends beyond retailers. People over 50 account for a disproportionately large amount of vacation travel and by some estimates spend 30% more than their younger counterparts when they go. To attract them, many lodging chains now offer discounts. Travel agencies, too, have stepped up their efforts. Boston-based Grand Circle Travel, which targets customers over 50 by direct mail, will send out 7 million catalogs this year, nearly triple last year's mailing. Says Chairman Alan E. Lewis: "These people love to travel, and they have the money."

Airlines have gotten the message and have begun offering discount programs for seniors. Michael W. Gunn, senior vice-president for passenger marketing at American Airlines Inc., says the

OLDER AMERICANS LEAD IN SPENDING POWER

Age	Discretionary income
Under 35	$2,628
35-50	2,904
50-55	3,685
55-60	4,494
60-65	4,571
65 and over	5,219
U. S. AVERAGE	**3,444**

DATA: THE CONFERENCE BOARD

recent decision to offer a 10% discount to people over 65 represents "a significant opportunity" to get a bigger share of the growing seniors' market and to encourage more older people to fly. Gunn says those 65 and over now account for nearly 7% of American's customers.

The same types of studies that prompted American to enter the market also lured Southwestern Bell. While independent directory companies had previously targeted groups such as Christians or gays, there had never been a widespread effort to reach seniors, says Al C. Parsons, president of Southwestern Bell Publications. By June, 1984, Southwestern Bell had a prototype in St. Louis, where the company is based. Success there led to the creation of a 1,000-person sales force that will sell advertising in directories for 91 cities by year-end. "We think we've got a win-win-win situation," Parsons says. "Seniors win because our ads offer them discounts. Companies placing the ads win because they attract more business. And we win by getting more advertising."

BENCHES AND RESTROOMS. Parsons says Southwestern is spending "many millions" to produce its directories, and he is pleased with the initial results. "We are in our second year in Kansas City, and we were expecting a 20% increase in revenues," he says. "We actually achieved 41%, even with a 5%-to-6% increase in rates."

This sudden focus on people over 49 has some marketers bemused. "We have been selling to the older customer for years," says Mark C. Hollis, president of Publix Super Markets Inc., the large Florida chain. To make shopping easier, Publix places benches in front of its stores, has restrooms, and teaches employees how to make things easier for the elderly. Checkout clerks, for example, give customers two light bags instead of a single heavy one. Says Hollis: "When they are most of your population, you take care of them."

While Publix' attitude may become widespread, there is no guarantee the attempts to lure older people will pay off. With a market this large, generalizations can be tricky. And if companies go overboard in attracting people over 49, they may see a backlash. Young women won't be eager to shop in a store perceived as being for old ladies. **OVERDRAWN IMAGE.** Older Americans, too, can react negatively to an overdrawn age image. The median age is now 31, and studies show that as the population ages, Americans keep pushing back the point at which they are willing to be called old. Most people from 60 to 75, for example, now identify themselves as "middle-aged." Moreover, vanity doesn't decrease with age. People 60-plus commonly say they feel 10 to 15 years younger. For marketers, that means a 65-year-old man may more readily identify with *Miami Vice* star Don Johnson than with George Burns.

It will be years before marketers know if their increased emphasis on older people will pay off. For the time being, though, it seems that many of them believe Linda Evans is right. In the opening line of a current Clairol commercial, the middle-aged *Dynasty* star says: "Let's face it, 40 isn't fatal." *By Paul B. Brown in New York*

PRICEY ICE CREAM IS SCOOPING THE MARKET

JUNE 30, 1986, PP. 60, 61

Myron Jennings, manager of Bi-Lo supermarket No. 119 in Spartanburg, S. C., knows why Frusen Glädjé ice cream— priced at $2 a pint—is the hottest item in his freezer chest: "It's the quality and the name. People don't care what it costs."

Such dedication by customers is propelling growth in superpremium ice creams by about 20% annually. It's enough to make mouths water in the sluggish food business. That's why giant packaged-goods marketers such as Dart & Kraft Inc. and Pillsbury Co., which have scooped up the largest positions in the superpremium ice cream market, are pulling out all stops to expand sales. They are launching aggressive advertising campaigns and rolling out a host of new products to bring mass marketing to what traditionally has been a mom-and-pop industry. Smaller rivals are fighting back with new products and promotional efforts of their own.

TASTING SUCCESS. Pillsbury, which owns market leader Häagen-Dazs, is now cranking out new sorbet-and-cream flavors. That followed the February introduction of Häagen-Dazs ice cream bars, which are coated with Belgian chocolate. National advertising for the brand began in December. Häagen-Dazs sales, which reached about $175 million for the year ending in May, have more than doubled since Pillsbury acquired the company for $76 million in 1983.

Dart & Kraft bought Frusen Glädjé just a year ago. But it has already tripled the brand's market share. The gains came in part because of a fat advertising budget that uses "enjoy the guilt" as its theme. In one commercial, a woman is eating Frusen Glädjé as her husband comes home. She confesses she has finished the entire container. She looks guilty for a moment, then adds: "And I'd do it again." Thomas Herskovits, president of Kraft's dairy division, says the ads "capture the essence of the indulgent product it is."

Indulgence sells a lot of ice cream these days. While the business has remained flat overall, sales of superpremiums—which contain twice the butterfat of regular ice cream, less air, and generally only natural ingredients—have doubled since 1980. This is now a $1.9 billion market, according to Find/*SVP*, a New York-based research firm. It projects that superpremium sales will grow at double-digit rates through 1990.

Consumers are attracted by the ice creams' taste, quality, and classy image. The products have European-sounding names, although they are as American as apple pie. Häagen-Dazs, which is a made-up name, was created and initially manufactured in the Bronx. Frusen Glädjé, Swedish for frozen dessert, has always been produced domestically. That doesn't seem to bother consumers. They pay an average $2 per pint for superpremiums and about that for a double-dipped cone at the local "gourmet" ice cream parlor. In contrast, a premium ice cream such as Breyer's or Dreyer's sells for about $4 a half gallon.

To ensure that customers can always get their fill of flavors such as Vanilla Swiss Almond and Elberta Peach, Pillsbury and Kraft have built new plants and added the pricey ice creams to their supermarket routes. Herskovits estimates 70% of the nation's supermarkets now carry superpremiums, up from just 45% a year ago. Seeing the success of Pillsbury and Kraft, other packaged-good companies—notably General Mills Inc. and Campbell Soup Co.—are studying the market. The industry is "very open," says Häagen-Dazs President Mark Stevens. "Anybody can launch a new brand or open a store."

Getting started in the business is one thing, but as competition grows more intense, staying in it is something else. "The smaller companies just don't have the supermarket clout and the wherewithal to develop and introduce new products on a large scale like Pillsbury and Kraft," says ice cream expert Arun Kilara, a Pennsylvania State University food-science professor. "Since everyone is looking to get on the superpremium bandwagon, the smaller companies will find it harder and harder to survive."

AMATEUR EXPERTS. Those who do will have to differentiate their products and obtain the necessary capital to compete. One way to do that is by going public, the route taken by Ben & Jerry's Homemade Inc. Ben Cohen and Jerry Greenfield, then both 28, founded the company in 1978. There was no grand design. At the time, Greenfield was a lab technician and Cohen a potter. "We both wanted to quit our jobs, and we both liked to eat," Cohen recalls, adding that they had experience. "Jerry scooped ice cream in the food line at high school, and I drove one of those ice-cream trucks with a bell."

While this would hardly set venture capitalists' hearts aflutter, the Vermont-based company managed to raise a total of $7.25 million in public offerings in 1984 and 1985. The stock now trades at 24—60 times earnings and up 85% from the initial offering price. The new money allowed the company to expand on the East Coast. Ben & Jerry's made $550,000 last year on sales of $9.7 million. Success may stem in part from its anticorporate image: Ben & Jerry's donates 15% of earnings to charity, proclaims that its lowest-paid employee earns at least 20% of the best-paid worker's salary, and shows free films outdoors in many cities where its ice cream is sold.

Cohen argues that large competitors will help his company. "Somebody in Enosburg Falls, Vermont, isn't going to want an ice cream with some foreign-sounding name," he says.

Officials at DoveBar International Inc., a Chicago-based superpremium company, hope their headstart in making ice cream bars—and an innovative new product—will stave off rivals. The privately held company, formed in 1983, sold 184,000 DoveBars—6 oz. of chocolate-coated ice cream on a stick—in 1984 and 7.5 million last year. DoveBar had sales of $5.5 million in 1985. President Louis G. Yaseen won't disclose earnings but says profits are "handsome."

This year, DoveBar projects sales of 35 million units. That includes both DoveBars and its new product, DoveDelight—a 3.25-oz. ice-cream sundae. The company also just launched its first advertising campaign. DoveBar will spend $3.5 million to recall its history humorously. In one ad, Michael L. Stefanos, son of founder Leo Stefanos and now a company executive, explains: "The moment my dad said, 'Son, I've invented the DoveBar,' I knew I wasn't going to grow up to be a veterinarian."

Even strong competitors such as DoveBar and Ben & Jerry's, however, must respond to the big boys. Both companies want to remain independent, but they may be forced to merge with larger companies that have deeper pockets and better distribution networks. Small regionals such as Double Rainbow Gourmet Ice Cream Inc. in San Francisco and Baltimore-based Mellin Foods Co., which makes the Apres brand, may face a similar fate. Many find it hard to break into the supermarket freezer because they lack the needed distribution and ad budgets. And ironically, cutting prices to compete might not help. Part of a super-premium's appeal to consumers is its high price. With Pillsbury and Kraft expecting to grow faster than the market as a whole, the smaller companies may see their market share melt away.

By Paul B. Brown in New York, with Kenneth Dreyfack in Chicago, Alex Beam in Boston, Mary J. Pitzer in Minneapolis, Kimberley Carpenter in Philadelphia, and Joan O'C. Hamilton in San Francisco

McDONNELL DOUGLAS TRIES MORE BUTTER AND FEWER GUNS

AMERICA'S PEACETIME ARSENAL IS NEARLY FULL,
AND DEFENSE ORDERS ARE TAPERING OFF

APRIL 28, 1986, PP. 84–86

Walk through the halls of McDonnell Douglas Corp.'s St. Louis headquarters and pictures overwhelm you. Here, a solitary F-15 heads skyward. There, an F-18 screeches to a halt on a crowded aircraft carrier. Everywhere, the marvels of airborne weaponry—products that strong-willed founder James S. McDonnell created to make his company the free world's largest defense contractor. This is the house that fighter aircraft built in an era when the Cold War was hot and Korea and Vietnam kept order books full.

Times have changed. And no one knows it better than "Mr. Mac's" successors, nephew and Chief Executive Sanford N. McDonnell and son and President John F. McDonnell. The company's 16% annual gain in government sales over the past four years may become just a memory when Washington tackles the budget deficit (chart, page 98). Even if the politicians lose their zeal to pinch pennies, Sandy and John cannot avoid a blunt fact: America is quickly amassing most of the conventional fighters and missiles that it needs for peacetime. And the Pentagon, which is already attacking unjustified charges by contractors, plans to turn up the heat on competition by forcing companies to share contracts.

AT THE PEAK. "With budget concerns and the definite attack on defense contractors, I don't see a repeat of the defense growth we've had in the first years of the Administration," says Sandy McDonnell, 63, with just a hint of the accent that betrays a Little Rock upbringing. John, 48, who grew up in St. Louis, years apart and miles away from his older cousin, agrees on the challenge facing the company: "This military spending cycle is peaking, and we're investing heavily in our commercial businesses while we're still on the upside."

With Sandy focusing on the defense business and John devoting himself to finance and to the key nondefense subsidiaries, they've made a start. Nondefense units piled up losses of about $140 million five years ago but earned an estimated $40 million last year. The company's total profits rose 6.3% last year, to $345.7 million. McDonnell's stock, recently at 88, has been outperforming the market and other aerospace stocks.

Nevertheless, McDonnell Douglas is still inordinately dependent on Uncle Sam's largesse. And the future of the push for more nondefense earnings has problems. The company's line of commercial aircraft, which showed a profit last year for only the fourth time since McDonnell bought Douglas Aircraft Co. in 1967, is facing a major new investment cycle. Efforts outside aerospace have fared even worse, creating a steady drain on the $11.7 billion giant. "McDonnell Douglas is learning other fields surely but slowly, and it's costing them money," says analyst Paul H. Nisbet of Prudential-Bache Securities Inc.

McDonnell's biggest and most embarrassing diversification effort is computer and information services, where the company is building on its own computer timesharing and factory automation units. As recently as 1984 an enthusiastic John McDonnell told *BUSINESS WEEK* that "our target is to have a $4 billion information systems business by 1990 . . . with earnings of about 7% after tax." Instead, losses at McDonnell Douglas

Information Systems Group more than doubled last year, to $109.3 million, on revenues of $1.1 billion.

In hindsight, there's little doubt that McDonnell paid too much for the companies it bought to supplement its own operations. The most glaring example is Tymshare, whose profits were falling just as it sold out to McDonnell in 1984 for $312.7 million. John McDonnell defends the purchase. He argues that Tymshare gives the 10 other computer equipment and data processing units in the subsidiary access to one of the leading data communications networks, Tymnet, which grew almost 30% in 1985. "That we absorbed a $109 million loss in 1985 and McDonnell Douglas' earnings still went up says something about the strength of the corporation," he says.

THE UPDATING GAME. The question is how much longer the company will tolerate such big losses as Pentagon spending growth tapers off. The information services unit has already shelved plans for several new areas, such as providing information systems for supermarkets. Says Information Services Group Executive Officer Robert A. Fischer: "The message for the near term has to be an emphasis on earnings. Nineteen eighty-six is a fairly critical year."

Perhaps the most sobering aspect of McDonnell's information services experience is what caused last year's losses. McDonnell expected fast growth, developed new products, and hired new people to sell them. When the sales failed to materialize, the company waited too long to cut back on personnel and other overhead. Competitors say the episode shows that McDonnell still has a lot to learn about information services and other nondefense businesses.

Sandy McDonnell has certainly worked hard enough at creating a management structure and style that fits a more diversified company. The power-sharing arrangement between the two cousins is a far cry from the days when founder James McDonnell insisted on reviewing every major company decision, even after Sandy was named chief executive officer in 1972. "Mr. Mac was a genius in engineering," says Sandy. "But like anybody who starts a company from scratch, his style was dictatorial."

Sandy, a mechanical engineer by training, prefers a collegial style. "Organizations tend to get old just like people, so you have to have a plan to keep an organization young, flexible, and creative," he says. "One of the keys here is that everyone has something to contribute to the success of the organization, so you've got to listen to the people who work for you."

The flexibility factor in that three-part equation can be seen in the company's commercial aircraft business. Division President James E. Worsham has squeezed a profit out of the operation through the aerospace equivalent of putting new wine into old bottles. Douglas' hot-selling MD-80 twin jet is basically a makeover of its venerable DC-9. By developing a derivative of an existing airframe, Worsham saved more than half of the $2 billion-to-$3 billion development cost of an all-new aircraft. Buyers get a plane that may be more expensive to operate than Boeing's more modern 757, but in many cases the lower price tag for the McDonnell version more than makes up the difference.

Now the company needs an encore. After a buying spree, U. S. airlines have ordered just about all the shorter-range, narrow-bodied airplanes—like the MD-80—that they need. Once again, Worsham is turning to a derivative, the MD-11, an update of Douglas' aging DC-10.

RAISING THE STAKES. The MD-11 still sports three engines, however, putting the $55 million plane at both an operating-cost and a fuel-efficiency disadvantage to newer twin-engine widebodies from Boeing and Airbus Industrie. "I would be surprised if we ever again bought an airplane without just two engines for domestic use," says Wesley G. Kaldahl, a senior vice-president at American Airlines Inc., one of the carriers McDonnell has targeted as a prime prospect. McDonnell's board last July gave Worsham the go-ahead to seek orders for the MD-11, with the catch that he snare big orders from both a major domestic and an international carrier before starting full-scale development of the plane. Douglas executives had hoped to have those orders in hand by spring, but now they have pushed that deadline into the summer.

Scratching the MD-11 would raise the stakes

McDONNELL DOUGLAS' DILEMMA

IT DOES LOTS OF BUSINESS WITH THE PENTAGON...

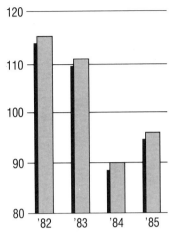

▲ DEFENSE BUSINESS AS PERCENT
OF TOTAL OPERATING EARNINGS*

*EARNINGS FROM COMBAT AIRCRAFT,
AND SPACE SYSTEMS. FIGURES OF MORE THAN
100% REFLECT LOSSES IN OTHER OPERATIONS

DATA: McDONNELL DOUGLAS CORP.

...BUT THE HIGH GROWTH IN DEFENSE SPENDING MAY BE OVER

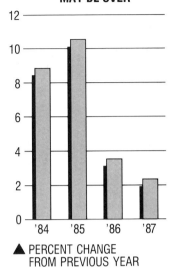

▲ PERCENT CHANGE
FROM PREVIOUS YEAR

DATA: DATA RESOURCES INC.

for a longer-term project. McDonnell has begun initial research on a 110-seat plane powered by new-generation propeller-driven engines that promise fuel savings of up to 45% compared with conventional jet engines. McDonnell has signed up Shanghai Aviation, Italy's Aeritalia, and Sweden's Saab-Scania to share the costs. But Boeing and a consortium of Japanese companies are developing a similar aircraft, raising the possibility that neither plane will garner enough sales to recoup development costs.

The McDonnell cousins have little choice but to push ahead, however. The defense units won't spin off seed money for nondefense businesses any faster in the years ahead. Aside from tighter budget controls, inflation and increasing technological complexity assure that new defense projects will be bigger than their predecessors, but they will also come less frequently.

Meanwhile, the rules that have made defense contracting so lucrative are changing. To introduce price competition to production contracts, the Pentagon has begun forcing more producers to share contracts for some missiles and submarines. It may do the same for advanced fighter planes.

In addition, the government last year reduced its progress payments—which give contractors cash before delivery of a finished product. This move will reduce McDonnell's cash flow by $600 million over the next five years. Finally, Congress seems intent on changing tax rules that allow defense contractors to delay for years the payment of taxes on long-term contracts.

McDonnell can take comfort from avoiding the billing scandals plaguing other defense contractors. It has long prided itself on its scrupulous approach to defense work—buying back spare parts anytime the government says it has been overcharged, for example. But its sterling record is no assurance that it will be favored as the defense-spending pool expands more slowly. Although visitors will probably never find the walls of its headquarters plastered with photos of computer equipment, the company's less glamorous products have never been more important than they are now. *By James E. Ellis in St. Louis*

PART 3

THE MARKETING MIX

The components of a firm's marketing mix vary according to the products, services, and markets. Typically the marketing mix is developed after careful examination of the firm's target market.

Today's products are varied, new and old. And many of the old ones are marketed as "new and improved." Whether it's cars, Paul Newman, or "paper bottles," new products are continually introduced into American markets.

Have you noticed that everyone seems to sell on "price" these days—especially retailers? How long has it been since a consumer paid the full retail price for an electronic product? The same is often true of airline tickets. It seems the huge, super retail warehouses sell everything on the market. Yet to increase sales companies such as K mart have begun to appeal to a more upscale market with shelves full of national brands and higher-quality private labels.

Consumers are asking retailers to carry more varieties of products. Maybe one day fur coats and automobiles will be sold in supermarkets. What is certain is that everyone wants a bargain these days—wants the opportunity to buy at home. Retailers will have to provide the right assortment of products, at the right price, and at the right place, plus plenty of service, if they are going to be in business in the 1990s.

Promotion has become an extremely important ingredient in the marketing mix. Often it takes highly skilled salespeople to sell the product, especially industrial goods. Today's salesforce is likely to consist of well-educated, highly competent (and paid) professionals.

Advertising continues to be an effective tool for selling—especially consumer products. Advertisements are clever, entertaining, and persuasive. And sometimes deceptive, in the view of various complainants who have assumed a watchdog role in response to the Federal Trade Commission's laissez-faire approach.

We can expect the 1990s to have an even higher level of promotional activities. Effective ads, salespeople, displays, coupons, samples, direct mail, and telemarketing will determine whether many companies survive.

The use of promotion by service companies and nonprofit organizations will soar to an unprecedented level. Hospitals, doctors, dentists, banks, universities, cities, states, the Red Cross, churches will use marketing techniques similar to those of IBM and Procter & Gamble.

The following articles provide excellent examples of the use of the marketing mix.

PART 3 ARTICLE SYNOPSES

THE PRODUCT

HOW FORD HIT THE BULL'S-EYE WITH TAURUS	The Taurus is Ford's fastest seller since the Mustang. Behind this success is a break from older sequential design techniques. The Taurus design team incorporated members from all phases of design and production. The team had final responsibility for the car. The Taurus design incorporated the best design features of its foreign competitors. Ford has an order backlog of 100,000 or more.
PAUL NEWMAN IS PACKING 'EM IN AT THE SUPERMARKET	Since going into business as a lark three years ago, Newman has created a $25 million operation that sells salad dressing, popcorn, and spaghetti sauce. His two companies, Newman's Own Inc. and Salad King Inc., which donate all their profits to charity, should earn $4 million this year.
GENERICS GRAB MORE OF THE DRUG ACTION	The $17.5 billion-a-year prescription drug market is yielding an ever-increasing share to generic drugs, which could rise from 6 to 25 percent by 1990. Generics sell for up to 70 percent less than brand-name drugs, and the small firms that specialize in generics are recording earning growth of as much as 166 percent in one year. Some insurance carriers offer lower premiums if patients use generics. Brand-name producers must now develop strategic alternatives to meet the challenge.
"PAPER BOTTLES" ARE COMING ON STRONG	Hellmut F. Kirchdorfer had been sent to the U.S. by Tetra Pak International, a Swedish company, to duplicate Tetra's success in aseptic packaging. Although his sales in the U.S. were a mere $3.5 million, he convinced his bosses to begin building a production plant in Denton, Texas. His bosses

have no reason to regret their decision. Sales in 1983 were $50 million, and the company now claims 5 percent of the packaging market and 20 percent of the fruit drink market.

THE PRICE

ELECTRONICS SUPERSTORES ARE DEVOURING THEIR RIVALS

Volume merchandising and low prices are pulling customers into huge electronic superstores—and smaller retailers are being squeezed out. By 1990 these giants should have 25% of the $81 billion industry. More traditional retailers are beginning to avoid direct competition where possible, especially in selling low-priced equipment. But given cyclical business, these superstores may suffer the same fate as the audio chains that were flourishing in the 1970s.

FARE WARS ARE BECOMING A WAY OF LIFE

Some observers of the airline industry believe pricing policies are getting out of hand. Discounts for domestic airline seats are commonplace, and further fare cutting could seriously erode profits. In the first 10 months of 1985, the average ticket sold for only 56 percent of the full fare, while 86 percent of all tickets went for a discount. The problem is that in order to make even modest profits in the face of intense competition from the newer low-cost airlines, major airlines must keep reducing costs. But if airlines wish to expand, they must hire more workers.

K MART: THE NO. 2 RETAILER STARTS TO MAKE AN UPSCALE MOVE—AT LAST

For years K mart Corp. singlemindedly pursued one strategy: blanket the country with cloned, no-frills discount stores. Now, however, the sleeping giant is on the move. The new strategy is to emphasize growth from productivity gains rather than expanding. K mart is filling its shelves with national brands and higher-quality private labels.

RETAIL

HOW DEPARTMENT STORES PLAN TO GET THE REGISTERS RINGING AGAIN

The department store share of retail sales has slipped 6 percent. Department store executives are looking for new ways to fight back. Some of the strategies include branching out, giving customers more attention, designing premium-priced store brands, and opening glitzy boutiques within their stores. Department stores may be in for a long and difficult haul.

THE NEW SUPER-DEALERS

New marketers called "super-dealers" are appearing in the auto industry. So far only 250 of the

25,000 dealers across the U. S. fit that informal definition. But their numbers and clout are growing. They earn a rough average of $3.5 million in annual profits on $150 million in sales. Experts think these super-dealers may claim 30 percent of all vehicle sales in the U.S. by 1990.

WHOLESALE

HOW OCEAN SPRAY KEEPS REINVENTING THE CRANBERRY

Ocean Spray has been successful in selling cranberry juice to health-conscious Americans. Its success can be attributed to good luck and good planning. The company has aggressively marketed several new products, the newest being a liquid concentrate. However, the concentrate runs a risk of cannibalizing existing products.

CHANNELS

CLOTHING MAKERS GO STRAIGHT TO THE CONSUMER

A new retailing strategy involves selling directly to consumers. Clothing makers like Esprit consider this a double-barreled strategy: opening retail outlets allows them both to create a distinctive, memorable image for consumers and to attract the attention of department stores. The strategy makes excellent sense given the intense competition for retail space.

PHYSICAL DISTRIBUTION

DETROIT TRIES TO LEVEL A MOUNTAIN OF PAPERWORK

Most companies use their computers to move data around internally, but not externally. The auto industry wants to change that. It feels that by making its supply system paperless it could take two days out of the supply pipeline and save $2 billion a year.

SALES MANAGEMENT

WHERE THREE SALES A YEAR MAKE YOU A SUPERSTAR

Zellars West is Cray Research's top salesperson —and he made only three sales in 1985. But the items he sells are supercomputers with a sticker price of up to $20 million apiece. Despite the computer slump, Cray's profits climbed 67 percent to $75.6 million as West was selling his three machines. And though such success attracts competitors like Hitachi and Control Data, Cray retains its market advantage. This is partly due to a superb marketing effort that often sees a salesperson like West take years to close a sale, followed by many more months spent with the customer ensuring a smooth operation. Cray must, of course, target its efforts to those prospects who can afford the product; though engineers and scientists would dearly love a supercomputer, few organizations can indulge their desires.

REBIRTH OF A SALESMAN: WILLY LOMAN GOES ELECTRONIC

Salespeople are going high tech. Heavy expenses of travel, affordable technology, and innovative techniques have made electronic marketing techniques cost-effective. However, electronic sales cannot replace personal contact. Salespeople are shifting to customer support roles.

ADVERTISING

AND NOW, A WITTIER WORD FROM OUR SPONSORS

Advertisers on television are realizing that they have to produce better ads to get viewers' attention. Cable TV, remote control, and VCRs are making it easier to ignore commercials. Advertisers are responding with innovative and sophisticated techniques. They are hiring successful movie directors. The commercials are fun to watch. But there are critics. Some say that the new advertising has nothing to do with the products.

NEW LIFE FOR MADISON AVENUE'S OLD-TIME STARS

Advertisers are bringing back long-abandoned characters and symbols, such as "Mr. Clean." Researchers have found that people still associate the old symbols with the products, even though they may not have seen them for years. The impulse of advertisers for change can throw away major assets, like "Morris" or "Charlie Tuna." However, some of the old characters require image changes to work in a changed society.

DECEPTIVE ADS: THE FTC'S LAISSEZ-FAIRE APPROACH IS BACKFIRING

When Kraft Inc. promoted Cheez Whiz as "real cheese," the Texas and New York Attorneys General investigated the complaint of the Center for Science in the Public Interest that the advertisement was deceptive. More and more complainants are going beyond the traditional petition filed with the Federal Trade Commission, often taking their case to state prosecutors or the National Advertising Division of the Better Business Bureau as well. And while the FTC may go after the more extreme cases of deception, it cannot exact punitive damages, as the courts can.

HOW FORD HIT THE BULL'S EYE WITH TAURUS

A TEAM APPROACH BORROWED FROM JAPAN HAS PRODUCED THE HOTTEST U. S. CAR IN YEARS

JUNE 30, 1986, PP. 69, 70

The most agile and capable sedan Detroit has ever produced

—Car & Driver

. . . scored the highest of any domestic car we've tested

—Consumer Reports

It's been a long time since a car built in Detroit has drawn such rave reviews. But there's no doubt about it: Ford Motor Co.'s new Taurus and its sister, the Mercury Sable, are four-star successes. Customers are snapping them up faster than the company can turn them out. The two cars are Ford's hottest sellers since Lee A. Iacocca's Mustang took the auto world by storm in the mid-1960s.

For Detroit, Ford's success may herald a turning point. It's true that Detroit still suffers from a perception of poor quality and a sense that it's out of step with the customer. That's why the Big Three continue to lose market share to imports from Japan and Europe. But Taurus and Sable demonstrate that the war isn't lost. U. S. carmakers can still build a machine that excites the average American driver.

How did Ford pull it off? Largely by stealing a page from the Japanese. It studied customer wants and needs like never before, made quality the top priority, and streamlined its operations and organization. Top management is so pleased with the outcome that the Taurus approach will be the blueprint for all future development programs.

RADICAL STEPS. The Taurus-Sable project was conceived in the bleak days of 1980, when Detroit was deep in recession. Ford's executives finally grappled with the fact that fuel economy wasn't the only reason consumers were flocking to imports. "It was painfully obvious that we weren't competitive with the rest of the world in quality," says John A. Manoogian, who then was Ford's chief of quality. "It became our No. 1 priority." Adds Lewis C. Veraldi, who headed the Taurus-Sable program: "We decided we had better do something far-reaching—or go out of business."

Veraldi may be engaging in a bit of hyperbole, but there is no question that Taurus and Sable were a huge gamble indeed. When the auto maker realized it needed to take radical steps to lure drivers back into the American fold, it decided that its new cars would replace the company's meat-and-potatoes models, the boxy Ford *LTD* and Mercury Marquis. Selling at the rate of 273,000 units last year, they were among the industry's more popular cars. To make sure Taurus and Sable would succeed, Ford invested a hefty $3 billion—an unprecedented amount for a new-car project.

The first step was to throw out Ford's traditional organizational structure and create Veraldi's group, christened Team Taurus. Normally, the five-year process of creating a new automobile is sequential. First, product planners come up with a general concept. Next, a design team gives it form. Their work is then handed over to engineering, which develops the specifications that are passed on to manufacturing and suppliers. Each unit works in isolation, there is little communication, and no one has overall project responsibility.

TURNING THE TABLES. Team Taurus, however, took a "program management" approach. Representatives from all the various units—planning, design, engineering, and manufacturing—worked together as a group. The team took final responsibility for the vehicle. Because all of the usually disjointed groups were intimately involved from the start, problems were resolved early on, before they caused a crisis. For instance, manufacturing suggested changes in design that resulted in higher productivity or better quality. Chrysler Corp. and General Motors Corp. are similarly moving toward program management. But Ford "hasn't just been talking about it; they've been able to execute it," says William R. Pochiluk Jr., president of Autofacts Inc., a market researcher in Paoli, Pa. "They've really forced *GM* to play catch-up."

After canning the traditional "Detroit-knows-best" attitude, Ford methodically set out to identify the world's best-designed and engineered automotive features, so that as many as possible could be incorporated in Taurus-Sable. Ford engineers turned the tables on the Japanese and did some "reverse engineering" of their own—to learn how the parts were assembled as well as how they were designed.

The company bought a Honda Accord and a Toyota Corolla and "tore them down layer by layer, looking for things we could copy or make better," Veraldi says. All told, engineers combed over 50 comparable midsize cars. They found that the Audi 5000 had the best accelerator-pedal feel. The Toyota Supra grabbed top honors for fuel-gauge accuracy. The award for best tire and jack storage went to the *BMW* 528e. Of the 400 such "best in class" features, Ford claims that 80% are met or exceeded in Taurus-Sable.

At the same time, to determine the customers' preferences, Ford launched its largest series of market studies ever. That led to features such as a net in the trunk that holds grocery bags upright and oil dipsticks painted a bright yellow for fast identification. "Little things like that mean a lot to people," notes Veraldi.

WORKER INPUT. Meanwhile, a five-member "ergonomics group" spent two years scientifically studying ways to make the cars comfortable and easy to operate. They took seats from 12 different cars, stuck them into a Crown Victoria, and conducted 100,000 mi. of driving tests with drivers of all ages and both sexes, who were then quizzed on what they liked and didn't like. The best elements were combined to create the Taurus-Sable seats.

Similarly, dashboard instruments and controls were tested to determine ease of use. People were timed pushing buttons, flipping switches, and pulling levers. It turned out that the quickest and most comfortable way to turn on the headlights was to turn a large round dial mounted on the left side of the steering column. That's how you do it in the new Fords.

Ford also made some distinctly un-Detroit changes in production. It asked assembly-line workers for their advice even before the car was designed, and many of the suggestions that flooded in were used. For example, workers complained they had trouble installing car doors because the body panels were formed in too many different pieces—up to eight to a side. So designers reduced the number of panels to just two. One employee suggested that all bolts have the same-size head. That way, workers wouldn't have to grapple with different wrenches. The change was made. "In the past we hired people for their arms and their legs," says Manoogian. "But we weren't smart enough to make use of their brains."

BULGING BACKLOG. Ford pulled suppliers into the effort too. Typically, an auto maker turns to its suppliers almost as an afterthought. Only when a car's design has been cast in concrete does the manufacturer send out specifications for parts and solicit bids in search of the lowest cost. The companies that are chosen keep the business only until a lower price comes along. Team Taurus, on the other hand, signed long-term contracts with contractors and invited them to participate in product planning. "We never had the supplier input we had on this car," says Veraldi. "Now we'll never do it any other way."

Taurus and Sable have not been completely free of problems. There have already been recalls to correct troubles with the side windows in station wagons and with the clutch in some four-cylinder models. As for overall reliability, it will be a year or two before an accurate track record on repairs emerges.

Still, Ford's bet on Taurus-Sable is paying off—handsomely. With bare-bones models starting at $10,200, more than 130,000 of the midsize sedans and station wagons have been delivered so far, and Ford has a backlog of orders for 100,000 more.

Elated dealers say that customers—some of whom haven't set foot in a domestic producer's showroom for years—are content to wait patiently for two months or more to drive away with a Taurus or Sable.

In fact, transplanting many Japanese principles worked so well for Team Taurus that Ford decided in May to apply management-by-teamwork across the board. It promoted Veraldi to vice-president for car-programs management and gave him the job of spreading the message throughout the company. Ford, it seems, isn't too haughty to say *arigato gozaimasu*—thank you very much.

By Russell Mitchell in Detroit

PAUL NEWMAN IS PACKING 'EM IN AT THE SUPERMARKET

THE SCREEN IDOL'S FOOD COMPANY, STARTED AS A LARK, IS A SURPRISE HIT

NOVEMBER 4, 1985, P. 38

Rome. A warm evening in early fall. At the elegant restaurant Alfredo alla Scrofa, the birthplace of fettucine Alfredo, lovers hold hands across the starched linen tablecloths. From the kitchen appears manager Mario Mozzetti, son of Alfredo, holding a 2-lb. bottle of spaghetti sauce. "The chefs say this sauce is very good," he whispers in a soft Italian accent. "You can present this sauce anywhere." He backs away, bowing. The eye lingers on the bottle of sauce he has left behind—Newman's Own, the creation of actor Paul Newman. Fadeout.

While this may sound like an adman's dream, the praise came after *BUSINESS WEEK* asked Alfredo's for an impromptu tasting. And consumers repeat the plaudits daily. Since going into business as a lark three years ago, Newman has created a $25 million operation that also sells salad dressing and popcorn. His two companies, Newman's Own Inc. and Salad King Inc., which donate all of their profits to charity, should earn $4 million this year.

While the food giants are not exactly trembling, the products cooked up by the movie star have earned their respect. For example, Newman's spaghetti sauce now owns 1.3% of the $770 million market. Says Kathleen MacDonnell, marketing manager at Campbell Soup Co.'s Prego, which has a 30% share: "They're increasing in volume, and that's nothing to blink at."

CLOSE TO HOME. How Newman, 60, manages to do this is enough to drive marketing pros to drink.

His sales philosophy appears on a small banner that hangs above a ping-pong table in corporate headquarters—a three-room suite furnished with patio furniture above a bank in Westport, Conn. The banner reads: " 'If we ever have a plan, we're screwed'—Paul Newman to himself at the Stork Club urinal, 1983."

The company's beginnings are testimony to that statement. After years of receiving Newman's home-bottled products as presents, friends urged him to go commercial. One of them, author A. E. Hotchner, signed on as a partner. Estimates of $500,000 for test marketing didn't daunt the duo: They decided to do without, says Hotchner, author of *Papa Hemingway: A Personal Memoir*.

At first, Newman sold the products to stores near his home in Westport. A chance meeting with a food broker led to nationwide distribution—although the supermarkets had some initial doubts. "Stores [frequently] would not take us until the guy down the block sold a hundred cases," Hotchner, 65, recalls. Media attention and splashy early sales lured the bigger chains. Contracts with regional food companies to make up huge batches of Newman's recipes followed. So did success for his premium-priced products. The salad dressing has a 3% share of the $600 million market, and his gourmet popcorn may own as much as 10% of that $30 million category.

Newman can be fanatical about food. He spent two years searching for the perfect popping corn, an Ohio hybrid. But he leaves day-to-day operations to neighbor Hotchner. The actor explains his products' success simply: "People buy the first bottle because of me. But it's good food—that's why they come back." The experts agree: In a recent taste test, *Consumer Reports* rated Newman's spaghetti sauce No. 3, ahead of Chesebrough-Pond's Inc.'s Ragu, the market leader.

In line with Newman's disdain for modern marketing, his company doesn't advertise and rarely offers coupons. Still, the basic strategy—getting Newman's mug on every label—is perfect. "Those blue eyes cut through the clutter on the shelf," says an envious competitor. Sales have been so good that Hotchner says Beatrice Cos. recently asked about "our availability." (Beatrice has no comment.) The tongue-in-cheek answer: "We're biding our time until we can make an offer to you."

'DIFFERENT RULES.' If Newman and Hotchner—both of whom work without a salary—take anything seriously, it's charity. The company has donated money to 200 groups, including those doing research into cancer and Alzheimer's disease. Of course, that doesn't hurt business. It appeals to consumers, eliminates the tax man, and insulates the company from criticism. But the tax-free status does cause competitors to grumble. Says John S. Craig, vice-president and director of marketing for the Grocery Products Div. of Kraft Inc.: "It makes it hard to compete when people have an opportunity to play by different rules."

Although Newman claims he's astounded by his success, he doesn't find business difficult. "Introducing new products," he explains, "is like practical joking—you have to retaliate before it's your turn." Coming soon: microwave popcorn. Beyond that, Newman is considering men's toiletries and possibly a commercialized version of the granola-type cereal made by Newman's wife, actress Joanne Woodward.

Does it bother the heartthrob that women now think of the kitchen, instead of the bedroom, when they see his face? "Hell no," Newman says. "It gives me two rooms to operate out of."

By Marilyn A. Harris in Rome and Westport

GENERICS GRAB MORE OF THE DRUG ACTION

BRAND-NAME MAKERS ARE FIGHTING BACK, BUT AS
PATENTS EXPIRE THE BATTLE WILL ESCALATE

MAY 13, 1985, PP. 64, 68

Houston's Ben Taub Hospital has declared war on branded prescription drugs. Since the late 1970s, when it began worrying about how the cost of such products was bloating its budget, the hospital has increased its use of cheaper generics from 30% to 50% of all the prescription drugs it dispenses. In the past year this knocked $700,000 off a $9 million annual drug bill, says Kenneth Stewart, the hospital's pharmacy director. Stewart expects to save an additional $280,000 this year by substituting generics for branded drugs whose patents are expiring.

Experts have long predicted that generics someday would win a healthy share of the $17.5 billion-a-year market for ethical drugs—the formal name for pharmaceuticals that require a prescription. Now it is starting to happen.

Last year sales of generics amounted to about $1 billion, or 6% of the ethical-drug market. This year they could rise to 7%. And some industry experts think their share could be 25% by 1990. "The economic reality is overwhelming," says Hemant K. Shah, an analyst with Mabon, Nugent & Co. "When a product sells for 70% less, it is going to be used."

Since November, when the Drug Price Competition & Patent Term Restoration Act took effect, the Food & Drug Administration has been swamped with 440 applications for generic-sales permits. Many of these should be O. K.'d before yearend under new rules that forgo time-consuming testing and let generics enter the market once their developers prove them chemically equivalent to brand-name drugs already on sale.

Meanwhile, the government's new flat-rate medicare reimbursement program is pushing hospitals into greater use of generics. Health maintenance organizations, unions, and Blue Cross are beginning to demand them, too.

As a result, a handful of small companies that specialize in generics are beginning to record geometric growth. "The tide [for generics] is coming in, and the brand-name companies can't stop it," says Roy McKnight, chairman of Pittsburgh-based Mylan Laboratories Inc., a generic manufacturer with annual sales of $54 million. Mylan's earnings jumped 166% last year, to $12.5 million, and its stock has soared 800% in the past 18 months to $22, or 42 times earnings.

There are still pockets of resistance to generics. Some doctors have more faith in brand-name drugs, or they worry that generics can affect patients differently. And if a doctor does not authorize a switch from a brand-name drug, the pharmacist cannot make it.

But younger physicians are more comfortable with generics, says Shah, because "the medical schools have used their names in teaching for the past 10 years." Moreover, pressure on retail pharmacists to stock more such drugs is coming from insurers, several of whom have written incentives to buy generics into their reimbursement policies. Pharmacists are also being prodded by state governments, such as Connecticut's, which offers a 50¢ bonus to druggists for every generic-drug prescription they are able to substitute when filling prescriptions for medicaid patients.

BONANZA. Patients are feeling the heat, too. In New Jersey, Blue Cross now offers corporations lower premium rates if they can get employees to buy generic drugs instead of brand names. In Michigan, Blue Cross members are not reimbursed for the extra cost of a brand-name drug if a generic equivalent is available, unless their physicians demand the higher-priced brand.

For generic producers, who can bring their drugs to market at a fraction of the patent holder's cost, this promises to be a bonanza. For example, in 1984 Mylan's research and development costs accounted for only $2.7 million, or 9%, of its $28 million in operating costs—well below the roughly 15% typical for brand-name producers. The lower *R&D* cost is helping Mylan sell indomethacin, a generic version of Merck's Indocin, an anti-inflammatory drug, for $10 less per 50 mg. That represents a 23% saving for a one-to-two-month dosage.

Zenith Laboratories Inc., which last fall received Food and Drug Administration approval to market tolazamide, a generic substitute for Tolinase—Upjohn Co.'s big-selling antidiabetic—could similarly show big gains this year. Zenith also sells metronidazole, a generic form of G. D. Searle & Co.'s Flagyl, an intestinal anti-infection agent. Lower *R&D* costs are not Zenith's only advantage over brand-name manufacturers: The company also enjoys lower taxes, because it makes its drugs in Puerto Rico. So does Bolar Pharmaceutical Co., another fast-growing generic producer.

The emerging challenge of the generics is causing major brand-name ethical producers to rethink their strategies. Both prices and profits of brand-name, patented drugs increased more slowly last year than in the past. Moreover, although the *FDA* in 1984 approved 24 original drugs for sale in the U. S., several companies have no new drugs in the pipeline. Since such drugs provide the highest profits, this has led to uncharacteristic cost-cutting. Hoffmann-La Roche Inc., the U. S. unit of the big Swiss drugmaker, dismissed 1,000 of its 8,000 employees late last year, anticipating a dete-

---

Hoffmann-La Roche claims its Valium is unique and wants the FDA to subject substitutes to new tests

---

rioration in profits after its patent on Valium expired in January.

Now the company is fighting to prove that Valium is unique. Arguing that there are "major differences" not apparent in standard blood tests between Valium and two generic competitors, La

Roche wants the *FDA* to use new "site-of-action" tests on the newcomers. "We realize this is the 11th hour, but we don't think the *FDA* is beyond the challenge of evaluating data showing what actually happens" when Valium and its challengers get into the human body, contends Bruce H. Medd, the company's professional and marketing services director.

Similarly, Merck & Co., the largest U. S. prescription drugmaker, has gone on the offensive to protect Aldomet, its antihypertensive drug which has had $200 million in annual sales and came off patent last year. Merck ads in medical journals try to dissuade doctors from prescribing methyldopa, Aldomet's generic substitute, on the ground that it contains a substance that causes allergic reactions in asthma sufferers.

Other companies are pleading their case directly to the public. American Home Products Corp.'s Ayerst Div. is telling consumers that Inderal, its anti-arrhythmic heart drug, which soon faces generic competition, costs the average patient a mere 45¢ per day—not worth the risk of substituting. Still other drugmakers are making their products look distinctive, believing that users will more easily spot a switch and object.

Brand-name producers argue that sales of generics eventually will level off at 20% of the market. "Nothing else in the U. S. marketplace is purchased on a generic basis in significant quantities," reasons Merck's Chairman John J. Horan. But with the new emphasis on reducing medical costs, the brand-name makers could be in for a surprise.

By Christopher S. Eklund in Philadelphia, with bureau reports

'PAPER BOTTLES' ARE COMING ON STRONG

BRIK PAK SOLD $50 MILLION WORTH IN 1983, AND MAJOR COMPETITORS ARE MOVING IN
JANUARY 16, 1984, PP. 56, 57

Two years ago, Hellmut F. Kirchdorfer was steeling himself for what he feared would be a showdown with his bosses at Tetra Pak International. The $1.5 billion Swedish company had converted 40% of the milk sales in Western Europe to its aseptic packaging system, which keeps perishables fresh for five months without refrigeration, and in 1977 had sent Kirchdorfer to the U.S. to duplicate that success.

But all that Brik Pak Inc., the U.S. subsidiary, had to show by the end of 1981 was $3.5 million in sales and a lot of hopeful projections. Kirchdorfer was sure his superiors would question his plans to build a $40 million U.S. production plant and a $10 million research facility to prove that Brik Pak was in the market for the long haul. To his surprise, Tetra Pak's family owners were enthusiastic. "I had my approval in 20 minutes," he recalls.

The cherub-faced West German and his Swedish bosses, Hans and Gad Rausing, have had no cause to regret that decision. Through a canny marketing strategy, Brik Pak sold nearly 1 billion aseptic containers in 1983, worth about $50 million. The company now claims 5% of the fruit juice packaging market, 20% of the fruit drink market, and has begun making inroads in the trickiest area of all—milk sales. Kirchdorfer, confident in his product, has designed the Denton (Tex.) production plant to handle 100% growth in both 1984 and 1985. "We reevaluate our projections every third month and increase them," he boasts.

PORTABLE PRODUCTS. Another measure of Brik Pak's success is that it is no longer the lonely apostle of aseptic packaging in the U.S. Combibloc Inc.—a Columbus (Ohio) joint venture of RJR Archer Inc., the packaging arm of R.J. Reynolds Industries Inc., and West Germany's Jagenberg—has already hit the market with Reynolds' Hawaiian Punch. And packagers such as Continental, International Paper, X-Cello, and American Can, among others, are perfecting versions of the process.

The lure of the aseptic "paper bottle" is its cost advantage over cans and bottles. The Brik Pak and Combibloc method sandwiches aluminum foil between laminates of paperboard and plastic to create an air-tight container. The 1-liter aseptic boxes cost about half as much as cans and 30% as much as bottles.

Although some of those savings are surrendered because of the more complicated filling process (both the container and the contents must be sterilized), Schotland Business Research Inc., of Princeton, N.J., estimates that the cost of packaging juice concentrate in 8-oz. Brik Pak boxes is 18% cheaper than filling conventional paper and metal cans. And, since aseptic goods are subjected to a briefer heating during sterilization than canned goods, their flavors are truer, and—a major saving—they do not require refrigerated shipment or storage.

LUNCH-BOX HIT. Indeed, it is the convenience factor that has fueled Brik Pak's success. Its 250-milliliter (8.4 oz.) box, complete wth drinking straw, has turned out to be a natural choice for snacks and lunch boxes— opening new markets for manufacturers. "The kinds of products we offer suddenly became portable," says John S. Llewellyn, senior vice-president of Ocean Spray Cranberries Inc. The Massachusetts-based cooperative became the first in the fruit juice category to feature paper bottles: Its early ad campaign starred the package rather than the product. The TV spots touted the cost, convenience, and "uncanny" taste. Now that the package is a hit, the product takes top billing. The latest ads—geared to families—show Dad sipping the juice in his office, the kids slurping away at school, and Mom saying: "Now wherever they go, I know they will be drinking something good for them." Ocean Spray's revenues from aseptics ran about 7% of its $417 million sales last year.

The story is similar at Coca-Cola Co. Foods Div., where aseptic packaging has increased Hi-C's volume by almost 20%. "And that gain has been almost completely incremental," notes Clint E. Owens, the senior vice-president for marketing. The company believes aseptics will grab a third of the fruit drink segment.

Aseptics may also expand markets by opening up new distribution channels. For example, Squirt & Co., a soft drink maker, has moved into the fruit juice segment with a Brik Pak package. It has formed a cooperative that has begun offering licenses to soft drink bottlers in order to form a national delivery system. In some parts of the country, soft drink bottlers are already stocking aseptic boxes next to soda in supermarkets and are placing custom vending machines in schools and other institutions.

But cracking other major markets may be tough. Dairy producers are showing the most resistance. Many do not believe that consumers will accept months-old, unrefrigerated milk—and pay a premium for it.

STUBBORN CONSUMERS? But a few dairies are starting to experiment with the idea. For the past year, Dairymen Inc. has been packing 1% of its Savannah (Ga.) milk production in half-pint aseptic Brik Paks for the lunch-box trade and in 1-quart boxes for emergency home use. "Aseptics allow milk to compete with other convenience drinks," says J. Lawrence Johnson, vice-president for market development at Dairymen. "We look at it as a way to get incremental business." Still, Johnson finds that "the U.S. consumer is pretty satisfied with the milk available now," and sees aseptics growing to only 3% of the milk market.

Brik Pak's Kirchdorfer disagrees strenuously. He insists aseptic packaging will replace traditional plastic milk gallons and gable-top paper half-gallons. To those who say consumer habits will not change, he retorts: "I have seen some amazing changes here. Who would have imagined that Americans would be pumping their own gas?" He ticks off the reasons why dairies and grocers will adopt the new packages: Producers could adopt more normal manufacturing schedules, avoiding the weekend rushes, because the product would not be perishable; and there would be better efficiency and less waste in milk distribution. He even believes aseptics will improve the consumption of milk—on the decline for 10 years—since people would always have it handy on shelves.

SODA AND WINE. So confident is Kirchdorfer of the milk market that Brik Pak will introduce a resealable half-gallon package in 1985 to compete directly with paperboard and plastic. Within 10 years, he predicts, aseptics will account for 45% of milk sales. "The retail trade will take milk out of their coolers as soon as there is an acceptable alternative," he says.

Brik Pak also has its sights set on other liquids. Though aseptic boxes lack the rigidity to hold carbonated beverages—thereby missing out on the huge soft drink market—Brik Pak claims such a casing is possible and is working on one. And it is close to introducing a strawless version of its single-serving box for wine.

Combibloc is taking a different route by going after processors of semisolid or particulate foods, such as yogurts, puddings, sauces, or soups. (The ultrahigh temperature sterilization process limits the size of food particles that can be packaged.)

Assessing the potential of these markets, Arthur M. Stupay, an analyst with Prescott, Ball & Turben, states that "aseptic processing will be the predominant method in the 1980s." To get there, however, Stupay says that a family of materials, including coextruded plastics, must be developed. But Brik Pak, which with its Swedish parent claims no less than 95% of the world's aseptic packaging market, will move cautiously. "We have decided to stay in a narrow sector, liquids only," says Kirchdorfer. "If you try to dance at too many weddings, you will end up without a bride."

ELECTRONICS SUPERSTORES ARE DEVOURING THEIR RIVALS

HUGE AD BUDGETS, VOLUME BUYING, AND
ONE-STOP SHOPPING GIVE GIANTS AN EDGE
JUNE 24, 1985, PP. 84, 85

Despite the $50 million in sales his 12-store Videoland chain in Dallas recorded last year, Trevor Glanger knew he was in trouble. With small stores, he could carry only merchandise that sold quickly. This limited his stock to items that are heavily discounted, such as television sets and videocassette recorders. To make matters worse, Highland Superstores Inc. had already entered the Dallas market with its supermarket-size outlets, and another major out-of-town chain, Federated Group Inc., hovered in the wings. "There is limited life for the small retailer," says Glanger, who ended up selling his chain to Federated late last year.

Glanger's experience is not unique. The proliferation of low-cost consumer electronics products during the past five years has created a new type of retail outlet: the electronics superstore. These stores keep prices low, thanks to volume purchasing through co-ops. They also have huge ad budgets, and they offer the convenience of one-stop shopping. As a result, the companies that run them are changing the face of consumer electronics retailing, one of the fastest-growing segments of the industry.

'THE RACE IS ON.' The huge stores—some sprawling over an acre—offer almost every electronic gizmo, from projection *TV*s and *TV*s with stereo sound to telephones and microwave ovens. A bit like Toys 'R' Us for adults, electronics superstores are steadily forcing mom-and-pop competitors to close or sell out. Moreover, they are taking sales away from the mass-merchant discounters, catalog showrooms, and department stores. The chains, which accounted for only 2%

of the $22 billion in retail consumer electronics sales in 1980, now own 10% of the market. They are expected to grab up to 25% of the projected $81 billion industry by 1990, according to analyst Barry Bryant of Goldman, Sachs & Co.

The superstore chains—companies such as Federated on the West Coast, Audio/Video Affiliates in the Midwest, and Circuit City Stores in the Southeast—were once content to stay close to home. But now they are storming major metropolitan areas nationwide to tap what's expected to be a $34 billion retail market for consumer electronics this year. They are trying to establish position before the market cools. "The race is on for real estate," observes Terrence L. Foran, national director of retail consulting for Touche Ross & Co.

A rash of stock offerings is funding this expansion. Since 1983, seven companies have gone public. In one of the biggest deals so far, Highland, a 33-store chain operating primarily in the upper Midwest, raised $103.6 million on May 9 by selling 5.6 million shares at 18½. The stock recently traded at 21. While some observers are concerned that superstore owners are just taking advantage of the booming market to cash out, investors have not been disappointed. For example, Crazy Eddie Inc., the New York-based consumer electronics chain, went public last September at 8. It recently traded at 29. Analysts project that the 25% sales and earnings gains that most chains have maintained over the last five years will continue for the foreseeable future.

Traditional retailers are taking note. In March, Tandy Corp.—which sells more private-label consumer electronics gear than anyone else through

FEDERATED IS TAKING ITS 'SHOW' ON THE ROAD

Unshaven and wild-eyed, Fred Rated—the television pitchman for Federated Group Inc.—picks up an ax and bludgeons another television set. Standing amid the rubble, he yells: "Federated smashes prices."

The ad campaign—showing products destroyed by a chain saw, a sledgehammer, and even a steamroller—has paid off handsomely for the 43-store chain that is the prototype of the coming wave of discount consumer-electronics superstores. In the past five years, sales of this City of Commerce (Calif.) retailer climbed at 41% annually, while net income rose 58% per year. Its shares, which recently traded at 22, have almost tripled in price since the company went public in late 1983. And analysts say Federated's rapid growth will continue: They project a sales increase of nearly 80%, to $410 million, in the fiscal year ending February, 1986. And earnings should hit $1.55 a share, up 32%.

Aggressive expansion will fuel that growth. Last year, Federated opened stores in Texas and Arizona, and it is eying locations in Nevada, New Mexico, Oklahoma, and Louisiana. "We've come up with a format that can quickly establish us in any market," asserts Wilfred Schwartz, 57, Federated's chairman and founder. The format calls for 25,000-plus-sq.-ft.stores that look spacious and uncluttered although they are stocked with a mind-boggling array of 9,000 items. Customers are encouraged to touch and play with the merchandise. "We're running a show," says Gary R. Tobey, Federated's senior vice-president for sales and marketing.

But Federated's real secret is product mix. It sells fast-moving items—such as *TV*s and *VCR*s—at close to cost. That means some 40% of Federated's products generate just 20% of its income. This strategy reinforces the company's low-price image and encourages customers to return. To boost gross margins, which at 29.4% are among the industry's best, Federated links commissions to profits, not sales, and uses a sophisticated point-of-sale computer system to control inventory.

SLICK STORES. Still, Federated faces threats. Circuit City Stores Inc. is preparing to invade its lucrative Southern California market, and it is already fighting Highland Superstores Inc. for control of Texas. Federated's broad inventory makes it vulnerable to any sales slowdown. With unusually slick stores, Federated also risks being perceived as having high prices. Nevertheless, analysts are high on Federated. It has a strong balance sheet, one of the best management teams in the industry, and plenty of room to grow, says Jeffrey B. Logsdon of Crowell, Weedon & Co. No wonder the chairman is doing a little soft-shoe in the latest annual report. Says Schwartz: "Federated sells pleasure . . . legally."

By Scott Ticer in City of Commerce, Calif.

its 7,679 Radio Shack stores—purchased Scott Appliances, a 24-store electronics and appliance chain operating in the Southeast. Tandy plans to open up to 15 new Scott stores in the next year. "We think these stores are an opportunity for us to share in off-price, name-brand retailing without jeopardizing our private-label business," explains John V. Roach, Tandy's chairman.

Even those retailers that have not hopped on the superstore bandwagon are affected. The superstores, with their wide variety of merchandise, are forcing them to specialize. The 85-store Pacific Stereo chain now concentrates exclusively on video products and home and car stereos. Independent retailers have done well by selling items geared to the connoisseur. This takes them out of competition with the superstores that concentrate on low-priced items.

The aggressive expansion of the superstores means that eventually the major chains will be forced to go head-to-head. Highland, for example, is moving away from its Detroit base and during the next two years plans to add 22 stores in Texas and Chicago, where it will compete against Federated and strong independents. And Circuit City Stores Inc. will spend $50 million in the next two years to open 15 superstores in Southern California, a market dominated by Federated.

DISTANT SHAKEOUT. "Federated doesn't own the Los Angeles market," says Alan L. Wurtzel, Circuit City chairman. "There's room for more than one." Still, observers say that most metropolitan areas can't support more than two or three superstore chains, which is why the rush to open stores is now on.

Since most major markets have yet to be tapped, the inevitable shakeout appears to be years away. There are, however, strong indications that the demand for consumer electronics is beginning to drop. Factory shipments are slowing dramatically. Those shipments, which doubled from $10.9 billion in 1980 to $23 billion last year, are expected to rise only 2.6% this year, according to the Electronic Industries Assn. Also, the industry may be unusually dependent on sales of just one product—*VCR*s. Look at Circuit City, the chain with the highest sales. Revenues of the Richmond (Va.)- based company have grown at an annual compound rate of 41% over the past four years, while earnings have climbed 65% annually. But *VCR*s accounted for 5% of sales in 1981, and 26% last year. Says analyst Bryant: "When all is said and done, it's a cyclical business."

Indeed, many manufacturers look at soaring consumer electronics sales and draw parallels to the 1970s' stereo boom, which gave rise to several large but now defunct audio specialty chains, such as Custom Hi-Fi in the Southwest. They believe many of the superstore chains will also run into trouble when sales start to slip.

The increases in sales and earnings that come with opening more stores can hide a multitude of problems. That's why the real test for the superstores probably won't come until the expansion stops several years from now. Then the chains will have to prove they can manage as well as they can grow.

By Scott Ticer in Los Angeles, with Kimberley Carpenter in Philadelphia and Paul B. Brown in New York

FARE WARS ARE BECOMING A WAY OF LIFE

JANUARY 13, 1986, P. 120

'The next time somebody buys a full-fare ticket from New York to Florida, we ought to give him a free airplane," jokes John W. Nelson, a senior vice-president at Eastern Air Lines Inc. But the pre-Christmas price war in which Eastern and other domestic lines dropped some fares from the Northeast to Florida to $49 is no laughing matter. The airlines are poised for a fare battle this year that will erode profits and imperil some carriers' survival.

Roughly 86% of domestic airline seats sold in the first 10 months of 1985 went at a discount, with the average ticket selling for only about 56% of full fare, according to the Air Transport Assn. With seat capacity expected to grow this year at nearly double the anticipated 4% to 5% increase in passenger traffic, the industry may be turning discounting into a way of life.

LEAST LOSS. "Some of the pricing that's going on today is absolutely irrational. You can go broke attempting to control market share with such tactics," warns the marketing chief of one major regional airline. Reacting to the competition, agrees American Airlines Inc.'s Senior Vice-President Thomas G. Plaskett, has deteriorated into a " 'how-do-you-lose-the-least-revenue' strategy."

The dilemma stems from two factors: big differences in the operating costs of established airlines and newer, low-cost, nonunion carriers, and the seemingly insatiable desire of practically every airline to expand, no matter what the consequences. The industry will add about 9% more seats this year, even though only about 61% of its available seats were filled in 1985. The only way to make even modest profits in this environment is to keep cutting costs.

As has been the case for most of this decade, labor will get the closest scrutiny. Most big airlines have negotiated two-tier wage scales that pay new workers lower salaries than previously hired ones. These pacts will finally start to show results in 1986 as airlines hire more workers to expand. United Air Lines Inc., for instance, will complete the training of 1,250 new pilots by July 31. By late 1987, says United's Chairman Richard J. Ferris,

---

The average ticket sold for 56% of full fare in the first 10 months of 1985, and 86% of tickets went at a discount

---

the company's second-tier wages will lower the pilot costs of a newly staffed Boeing 727 by 30%.

It's true that the costs of discount carriers are rising as their work forces mature and they buy costly new aircraft for their fleets. For example, in the third quarter of 1985 the operating costs per seat mile of People Express rose 9.6%, compared with declines at American, Delta, Eastern, Northwest, and Pan Am. Even so, People's 5.38¢-per-mi. operating costs were at least 20% lower than those of 10 of the 12 major U. S. carriers.

One bright spot for all airlines in 1986 will be fuel costs, which account for roughly 20% of operating expenses. Jet-fuel prices threatened to rise last fall after an 18-month decline. But the recent collapse of *OPEC*'s price floor on crude oil seems certain to cut airline bills—at least through the first half of the year. Because a 1¢ drop in jet fuel prices saves the industry about $100 million a year, declining fuel costs may serve as a buffer against profit-paring fare skirmishes this winter in several Florida markets as well as in Hawaii, Denver, and Houston.

Airline strategists vow to avoid full-scale price warfare such as occurred in 1982-83, when flyers could buy tickets between many major cities in the U. S. for only $99. "Despite what the alarmists have predicted in the past two years, the industry has shown fairly consistent ability to control the spread of fare wars," says A. B. Magary, senior vice-president of Republic Airlines Inc.

Still, it won't be possible to postpone price-cutting indefinitely—especially as the low-cost carriers expand geographically. Continental Airlines Corp.'s low coast-to-coast fares have started a ripple effect in other markets that feed the same long-haul traffic. People Express' pending acquisition of Frontier Airlines Inc. could have the same effect throughout the West.

Moreover, in an effort to balance the negative profit impact of increasingly price-sensitive markets such as Denver and Texas, the major airlines are crowding into the nation's few remaining high-fare areas, such as the Southeast. American will open new hubs in Nashville and Raleigh-Durham, N. C., this year, while United is opening one at Washington's Dulles International Airport. This could lead to fare-cutting in the Southeast, which now is dominated by Delta and Eastern in Atlanta and by Piedmont Aviation in Charlotte, N. C.

Even more worrisome is the growing use of discounted fares for corporations—the last stronghold of full-fare travel—to fill seats on selected routes. Continental, Republic, and Delta are testing such contracts. Eastern's Nelson estimates that a 10% cut in the $30 billion in fares corporations pay the 12 major airlines annually would wipe out those carriers' profits—only $726 million in the first nine months of 1985. "Corporate contracts would be abysmal for the industry," he says.

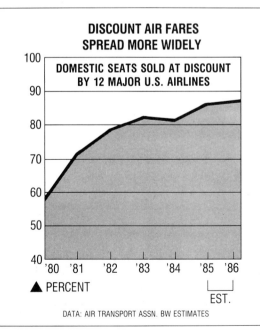

DISCOUNT AIR FARES SPREAD MORE WIDELY

DOMESTIC SEATS SOLD AT DISCOUNT BY 12 MAJOR U.S. AIRLINES

▲ PERCENT

EST.

DATA: AIR TRANSPORT ASSN. BW ESTIMATES

While the major airlines will fight hard to stanch corporate discounts, they have little choice but to accept the basic challenge driving the industry in 1986 and beyond. "With the growth of the [lower-cost] carriers, over time we will gradually be forced into a simplified, lower-revenue pricing structure," says Wesley G. Kaldahl, a senior vice-president at American. "The struggle will be getting costs down to survive in that environment."

By James E. Ellis in Chicago

K MART: THE NO. 2 RETAILER STARTS TO MAKE AN UPSCALE MOVE—AT LAST

JUNE 4, 1984, PP. 50, 51

After decades of wearing the same plain suit, the emperor of mass merchandise discounters is trying on some new clothes. For years, K mart Corp. single-mindedly pursued one strategy: blanket the country with cloned, no-frills discount stores. But by the early 1980s—with a K mart within reach of 80% of the population and one out of two adult Americans shopping in K marts monthly—the Troy (Mich.) chain had no more room to expand.

Just as important, the formula—so bold when the old S. S. Kresge Co. launched it and produced growth of 20% a year through the 1970s—had grown stale. Consumer preferences were shifting upward, but K mart was slow to notice. Meanwhile, aggressive regional discounters, such as Wal-Mart Stores Inc. and Dayton-Hudson Corp.'s Target Stores division, had moved quickly. They freshened up their stores, brought in name brands, and stressed value over price. K mart's sales started to flatten, and earnings slumped.

Now, however, the sleeping giant is on the move as strategies Bernard M. Fauber put into place when he took over as chairman in 1980 start to click. Short-term, Fauber is emphasizing growth from productivity gains rather than from expanding the 2,161-unit chain. To sell more goods to its existing customer base, he is taking K mart upscale, filling its shelves with national brands and higher-quality private labels. He is installing snappier displays and modern fixtures. Through 1988, Fauber expects the No. 2 retailer—behind Sears, Roebuck & Co.—to garner sales gains of 5% to 6% a year, outpacing the anticipated 4% annual rise in the $522 billion mass merchandise market.

UP FROM THE STOCKROOM. But by 1990 or so, Fauber thinks this strategy will play out. So K mart is launching separate off-price and discount specialty chains and is browsing for acquisitions. "The fact that K mart needed to change was recognized by a lot of people in the company," says Fred E. Wintzer Jr., a vice-president at Shearson Lehman/American Express Inc.

The changes are just now having an impact. Revenues remained nearly flat in 1981 and 1982 (chart, page 119). But in the year ended Jan. 25, sales climbed 11%, to $18.6 billion, while earnings leaped 88%, to $492 million. With a helping hand from the resurgent economy, sales reached a record $4.2 billion in the first quarter of 1984, while profits hit $58 million, 30% above a year earlier. Immodestly, Fauber says 60% of the turnaround reflects K mart's own efforts.

The 61-year-old former stockroom clerk, who has spent his entire working life with the company, is aiming to attract more affluent customers, who regularly pop into K mart for low-price items such as toothpaste. By updating K mart, he hopes to keep them in the store longer and get them to spend more money on a wider mix of goods, especially higher-margin apparel.

When the refurbishing is complete in late 1986, K mart's endless rows of metal pipe racks will be history. Departments will be clearly delineated, and the merchandise mix will change. Floor coverings, lamps and furniture, and—in some stores—automotive services are on the decline. On the upswing are sporting goods, leisure products, and electronics. Already name brands such as Levi's and Wrangler make up 15% of the apparel stock, compared with 100% private labels just a few years ago.

Last year, K mart installed 715 home electronic centers—complete with computers, software, and video-game cartridges—and will add 750 more this year. Several hundred bed and bath areas are being updated, and 650 "Kitchen Korners" are being put in. This year 125 do-it-yourself home improvement centers will open. Through 1986, K mart plans to spend $450 million on such projects and millions more in store enhancements.

'ONE MORE NEED.' Taking a cue from Sears, K mart is also tackling financial services. But instead of buying a brokerage house, as Sears did, K mart is seeding its own operation. It is testing insurance centers in 48 Texas and Florida stores. Eight are selling money market funds and certificates of deposit. By 1985, nearly 100 stores will sell insurance, with expansion through the South slated for 1985. "We're trying to take care of one more consumer need so he doesn't go to the competition," says Robert E. Brewer, executive vice-president of finance.

But to reorient the company successfully, Fauber must lift productivity. Instead of the average of 160 stores K mart opened annually in the 1970s, Fauber plans only a few dozen new units each year. That means K mart will have to squeeze more than the $155 in sales from each square foot of space that it pulled in last year—a mere 12% rise over 1979 and far behind the $172 of Target. By 1988, Fauber predicts, K mart's fresh approach will kick sales up 29% on a square-foot basis, to $200.

K mart's upscale move will require deft execution. As Fauber tries to lure shoppers who have deeper pockets, he must be careful not to alienate the traditional customer who is attracted by low prices. "W. T. Grant [now defunct] confused customers because it couldn't figure out what it was trying to do," warns one competitor. "That's exactly the kind of problem K mart has to avoid." Fauber hopes that by broadening the assortment within product categories to give consumers a range of price, quality, and fashion, he can retain the loyalty of existing clientele while attracting bigger spenders.

GROUND-FLOOR MOVES. Long-term, however, K mart knows gains from these changes will dry up. To keep up momentum, it is adding stores that stretch beyond the traditional K mart. Because increasing the company's enormous sales base will take years, Fauber is striking out in many directions, hoping to get in on the ground floor. Armed with $1 billion in cash and burdened by only $711 million in long-term debt—12.6% of total capital—K mart can afford acquisitions. And Fauber plans to speed up purchases, paying particular attention to retailing, where he will able to tap the company's expertise in management and real estate.

Already familiar with discounting, K mart sees potential in off-price apparel retailing, where seconds and overruns sell at 20% to 70% below standard prices. Analysts expect this $6 billion market to grow by 25% a year through 1990.

The company's biggest venture so far is an off-price apparel chain called Designer Depot. From its one-store beginning in 1982, Designer Depot has grown to 29 units in eight states. This year, K mart plans to open 30 of the carpeted stores, which carry prestigious labels such as Gloria Vanderbilt and Calvin Klein at large discounts. It hopes to reach 100 stores by 1986.

Accents, another experiment, is an offprice gift and housewares store located in an affluent suburb near Troy. Garment Rack, an outlet for lower-quality merchandise, opened in November, and this fall, K mart will open two discount home improvement centers in the Chicago suburbs. These two warehouse stores could each generate upwards of $20 million in sales a year. Fauber hints that discount automotive parts could be the next experiment, and analysts note that there is room for products such as toys, sporting goods, hardware, and jewelry.

TOO CAUTIOUS? Last year, K mart bought Bishop Buffets Inc., a growing cafeteria chain in the West and Midwest with 30 outlets. In 1980 it acquired Furr's Cafeterias Inc., which now has 117 units, and wants more cafeterias. "They make so much sense," Fauber says in a voice tinged with his native Virginia. "The average check is

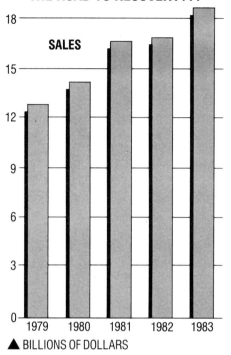

K MART SALES ARE ON THE ROAD TO RECOVERY...

SALES

▲ BILLIONS OF DOLLARS

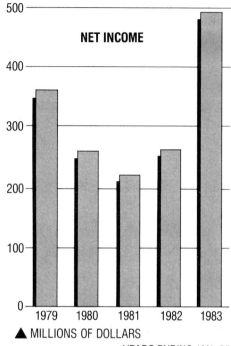

...AND EARNINGS ARE SWINGING UP SHARPLY

NET INCOME

▲ MILLIONS OF DOLLARS

DATA: K MART CORP.

YEARS ENDING JAN. 25

$3.85. Where else can you get a well-balanced full meal for that price?"

Fauber talks expansively of a host of other prospects, including discount books, sit-down restaurants, and deep-discount drugs. But some critics believe K mart is erring on the side of caution.

Two deals—a takeover of Associated Hosts Inc., an $88 million restaurant and hotel operation, and a joint venture with Hechinger Co., a home improvement retailer—fell apart soon after being announced. Fauber says he would have bought Walden Book Co. from Carter Hawley Hale Stores Inc. in the latter's tussle with Limited Inc., but the plum was never offered. "Management is not being terribly bold, though they are somewhat imaginative," says Jay A. Levine, a Chicago-based retail consultant.

Moving a ponderous giant such as K mart takes time. By the end of 1983, all ventures outside of its basic business still amounted to only $575 million, a mere 3% of sales.

HOW DEPARTMENT STORES PLAN TO GET THE REGISTERS RINGING AGAIN

THEY'RE REDISCOVERING SERVICE AND ADDING HIGH-QUALITY PRIVATE-LABEL BRANDS

NOVEMBER 18, 1985, PP. 66, 67

Ever since the early 1970s, department stores have been outflanked by savvy competitors whose specialty shops and discount barns have delivered more and better goods for the money. Traditional merchants have tried to retaliate by cutting overhead to provide lower prices, retreating from weak product lines such as appliances and toys, and seeking sales growth by building stores in the Sunbelt.

But they're still losing ground. Although retail sales have almost tripled since 1975, to $1.4 trillion, the department store share has slipped 6%. Specialty stores have passed them in profitability, and discounters are closing in fast (chart, page 121).

Department store executives are searching for new ways to fight back. Some, following Dayton Hudson Corp.'s lead, are branching out. Associated Dry Goods has gone into off-price apparel with Loehmann's. Federated is trying to duplicate the success of *DH*'s Mervyn's with a new value-oriented softgoods store called MainStreet.

To regain their waning power, department store executives are also turning to the past for answers. After years of cutting service to reduce costs, many think that giving customers more attention might bring the defectors back. As a result, they are copying specialty store techniques, such as designing premium-priced store brands and opening glitzy boutiques within their stores.

But can old-line merchants create a distinctive new image that will draw shoppers? The problem, according to New York retail consultant Walter K. Levy, is that "everybody is carrying the same bloody things."

PROTECTING MARGINS. Private labels may be one answer. Department stores have long used private-label merchandise as a lower-cost alternative to national brands, but today they are doing more than just slapping the store name on a cheap sweater or towel. They are hiring designers to create distinctive looks that can be targeted to specific customers.

This strategy, used so successfully by fast-growing clothing chains such as The Limited and The Gap, allows department stores to protect margins and offer exclusive goods. "If they do it well, if they have the right level of fashion, color, and styling, the private label becomes a preferred brand among shoppers," notes Daniel J. Sweeney, executive vice-president of Management Horizons, the retail consulting division of Price Waterhouse.

Dayton Hudson is a case in point. About three years ago, the Minneapolis-based company introduced the "Boundary Waters" line of casual clothes. Designed in-house, it was named for a nature preserve in northern Minnesota. It even had a symbol: a little duck called "Matthew Mallard." Sales reached $40 million in two years, so Dayton's has expanded the line to more than 200 items, ranging from candy to stationery. Since then, the company has spun off other labels, including Stork Club infant wear and Ice high-fashion designs.

It does little good, however, to carry dozens of labels that mean nothing to customers. Macy's, which at one time had about 100 private labels, realized that and is now spending millions to produce fewer, more identifiable lines. There's also a limit to how much private-label merchandise

THE LEADING DEPARTMENT STORES...

	1985 sales* (millions)	Return on assets**
Federated	$10,300	6.7%
Dayton Hudson	8,925	6.7
May Dept. Stores	5,200	6.8
Assoc. Dry Goods	4,500	5.8
R.H. Macy	4,368***	8.4***
Allied	4,250	6.3
Carter Hawley Hale	4,080	2.9
Mercantile	1,870	8.6
Dillard	1,600	7.2
Carson Pirie Scott	1,320	3.9

*Estimated for retail year ending Jan. 31, 1986
**For the 12 months ended July 31, 1985
***Actual figures based on fiscal year ended Aug. 3

***AND HOW THEY'RE LOSING GROUND

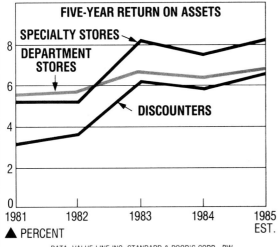

FIVE-YEAR RETURN ON ASSETS

SPECIALTY STORES
DEPARTMENT STORES
DISCOUNTERS

▲ PERCENT

DATA: VALUE LINE INC, STANDARD & POOR'S CORP., BW

department stores can offer, since consumers still expect them to stock a large selection of national brands.

'GUM-CHEWING PEOPLE.' Improving service may also help the industry. Service was traditionally a department store's strongest asset. But over the years, many cut corners by doing away with salespeople. Before long, customers couldn't get answers to questions, find help in the dressing rooms, or reach a cash register without a long wait. "Why go to a department store and pay high prices only to be offended by the seeming lack of concern for service," asks Robert G. Nesbit, senior partner and retail specialist for Korn/Ferry International, an executive search firm.

Department stores have little choice but to do better. Noting that many want to raise sales above the industry average of $132 per sq. ft., Paul Nebenzahl, publisher of the retail newsletter *Here, There & Everywhere*, insists: "They can't do $200 by having gum-chewing people standing behind a cash register. Someone has to pick up the phone and tell a customer a shoe size is in."

Old-liners are spurred on by the success of such service-oriented companies as Nordstrom Inc. Sales at the Seattle-based apparel retailer have doubled to more than $1 billion in the past five years. By paying well and promoting from within, Nordstrom has recruited an eager staff who will stop at nothing to ring up a sale. "When the blouse I wanted wasn't in stock, the clerk volunteered to get one from another store and drop it by my house," says one customer.

To match that kind of service, department stores such as Carter Hawley Hale Stores Inc. are experimenting with commissioned salespeople. Perhaps the ultimate in service comes from Carson Pirie Scott & Co.'s Corporate Level shops in Chicago. Here, a customer can buy a wardrobe, get a haircut, and drop off the dry cleaning.

But good service is costly. To afford it, stores must cut expenses elsewhere. They can't depend on gross margins of 35% to 40% when much of the competition gets by on less than 30%.

That's why many chains are consolidating operations. Last year, *DH* joined its Dayton's stores in Minneapolis with the Hudson's division in Detroit. It also sold two remote regional chains in the Southwest to Dillard Department Stores Inc. Such moves eliminate overlap and improve distribution. By combining its three Joske's units in Texas, Allied hopes to save $6 million a year.

Department stores are also centralizing purchasing to gain clout with vendors. Central buying has long been used by national chains such as J. C. Penney Co., but department stores shied away from it for fear of being unresponsive to local preferences. Now, since mass-media exposure creates nationwide fashion trends, regional differences have faded.

Leanness is one of Mercantile Stores Co.'s strengths. The Wilmington (Del.) company, with 12 divisions extending as far as Denver, keeps only token local buying staffs and does more than half its buying from New York. Such efficiency helped it post 1984 operating profits that were 10.3% of sales, above the 9.5% industry average.

Department stores want to increase store productivity, too. May Department Stores Co. in St. Louis is altering one-third of its 30 million sq. ft. of retail space. Last month it opened a 275,000-sq.-ft. Hecht's in Washington, D. C. The new store is only 40% as large as the old one the company closed several blocks away, but Hecht's expects it to generate at least twice as much business because the layout does not waste space. Ten years ago, Allied Stores Corp. allocated about 70% of its store space for selling and 30% for stockrooms and handling. Today, thanks to regional distribution centers, the ratio is 87% to 13%, says Chairman Thomas M. Macioce.

With consumers buying more than $45 billion worth of goods through the mail—150% more than 10 years ago—department stores are placing greater emphasis on catalogs. They can use catalogs to drum up new business, as Saks Fifth Avenue did when it mailed 125,000 "Folios" to San Antonio residents just prior to opening a store there Nov. 2. Orders placed through the catalog make it the company's third-largest "store."

TALENT SEARCH. All this requires creative management—something the industry hasn't always enjoyed. Department stores found it tough to attract top graduates because the pay was low and work schedules included nights and weekends. The business was also dominated by buyers rather than marketers. This is changing, as companies put more emphasis on recruiting and keeping talent. But old cultures die hard.

Department stores do have strengths they can capitalize on. They have well-known names, reputations for value, and some of the best retail locations. An aging population means there are more typical department store shoppers these days—over-30 adults with steady incomes. And by 1995,

eight million more women will be working. Department stores are well-positioned to serve their needs for fashion and convenience.

Still, they face a long, difficult transition. It requires investments that often pay off too slowly to please Wall Street. This very dilemma prompted Edward S. Finkelstein and his fellow executives at R. H. Macy & Co. to propose a $3.6 billion leveraged buyout. "It became clear that a private Macy's in the next five to 10 years would be a much more energized, exciting Macy's than a public one," Finkelstein says.

Public or private, however, department stores must grope with similar challenges. "We're in an era where strategic thinking is important," Levy says. "Department stores must be first to maximize a trend rather than react to it." How well they do that will determine whether department stores can outmaneuver the competition for a change.

By Amy Dunkin in New York, with bureau reports

THE NEW SUPER-DEALERS
THEY'RE CHANGING THE WAY AUTO MAKERS SELL CARS—AND HOW YOU BUY THEM
JUNE 2, 1986, PP. 60-64, 66

It happened by accident. Michael L. Dever, a junior at the University of Cincinnati back in 1964, was running out of money for his education just as he wrecked his 1959 Renault Dauphine. Searching for a way to solve both problems, Dever figured he'd try selling cars to pay for more schooling—and drive home a demonstrator model when he needed wheels.

Dever liked the work so much that he stayed with it after graduating. By 1972 he was ready to spend $15,000 to become co-owner of a Toyota Motor Corp. franchise. More dealerships followed, and Dever set up a separate holding company, Automanage Inc., to control them. Today his $360 million empire includes 13 auto dealerships, a motorcycle store, a car-leasing company, real estate operations, and, next year, a $35 million hotel/retail complex with room for eight dealerships. "We're still buying," says the 43-year-old entrepreneur. "This isn't a business that a small operator can survive in anymore."

CORNER GROCERIES. Dever is at the forefront of a transformation in the $260 billion auto-retailing industry that will affect everyone from the companies that make the cars in Detroit and abroad to the 15 million Americans who buy a car or truck each year. Each of these new marketers, called super-dealers or mega-dealers in the industry, sells upward of a dozen different brands of cars, made by different manufacturers, at up to 30 locations. Just the land the dealer's lots sit on may be worth $100 million or more.

So far, only about 250 of the 25,000 dealers across the U.S fit that informal definition, earning a rough average of $3.5 million in annual profits on $150 million in sales. But their numbers and clout are growing. The super-dealers will make 15% of all vehicle sales in the U.S. this year, and experts think they could claim 30% by 1990. "The day of the Ma and Pa operation is about over," declares Robert E. Crabtree, who runs his 12 dealerships from Crabtree Automotive Inc., in New Rochelle, N.Y. "If you're going to be a chain operator, you might as well be a big one."

Crabtree and nine other dealers may lift even the super-dealer approach to a new plateau. They are thinking of forming a publicly owned corporation with annual sales of at least $6 billion and 80 outlets that would market 200,000 vehicles a year in more than 20 states. Their latest meeting to discuss the plan was in Atlanta on May 15-16. A final decision is still three months away.

Other dealers may take a similar step, and Wall Street is watching closely. "I think it will happen. After all, we have fast-food franchises that have gone public," says Ronald A. Glantz, auto analyst for Montgomery Securities in San Francisco, whose company is advising at least one super-dealer interested in it.

The big losers will be the neighborhood dealers that sell one or two car brands. Industry experts are already comparing them with the corner groceries driven out by the supermarkets after World War II. Over the next 10 years the spread of super-dealers may trim the number of single-dealership owners by one-third, to 12,000, according to J.D. Power & Associates of Westlake Village, Calif. Power, which does market research for auto makers and dealers, last year organized a consulting group called the SuperDealer Roundtable for about 100 multi-franchisers.

"Anybody selling [cars] the way he was even five years ago is facing problems," declares J. Alan Spitzer, a member of Power's group and executive vice-president of Spitzer Management Inc., in Elyria, Ohio. His company controls 21 auto showrooms and 35 mostly auto-related corporations in Ohio and Florida. Compared with traditional dealers, says Glenn R. "Pete" Lassiter, vice-president for research and development at Nichols, Campbell & Morrow Inc., an auto-dealer consultant based in Kansas City, Mo., "megadealers think more in terms of finance than operations, and of control rather than ownership."

A prime example is the family-run Potamkin group, a loose conglomerate that needs double-sized business cards just to list its 32 dealerships in New Jersey, Florida, Georgia, Pennsylvania, and New York. Last year, Victor Potamkin and his sons, Robert and Alan, sold nearly 40,000 new cars and trucks as well as 26,000 used vehicles. Anticipated 1986 revenues: $800 million. The Potamkins won't discuss earnings. Their still-expanding chain handles all models made by American Motors, Ford, and Chrysler, plus Cadillac, Chevrolet, Isuzu, Hyundai, Subaru, Toyota, Mitsubishi, and Volkswagen. Not bad for a business that started nearly 40 years ago when Victor Potamkin opened a single Lincoln-Mercury dealership in Philadelphia.

As their numbers increase, companies such as Potamkin will exert unprecedented influence on the auto market—in ways that will both please and disturb carmakers. On the plus side, they are already streamlining the distribution of cars and are improving service. These are changes that Detroit, in particular, has wanted for years but couldn't make because of state franchising laws and intransigent dealers. On the negative side, however, the auto makers will lose power to force dealers to sell any old car they happen to make. Says Donald L. Keithley, vice-president of dealer services at J.D. Power: "The megadealers [already] are picking which franchises they want to represent, and some will be left out in the cold."

From the formation of the franchise system 80 years ago until quite recently, that was impossible. Dealer fortunes depended on auto makers' unilateral decisions on everything from car design to pricing. If cars were ugly, poorly made, or too expensive, the auto makers'

RICK HENDRICK JUST KEEPS REPEATING HIMSELF

Whenever J. R. "Rick" Hendrick III buys an auto dealership, he doesn't worry about what computer system to install or which management method to try. The 36-year-old super-dealer simply duplicates what he used the last time. "You've got to run all [your] stores the same," he declares. "We're trying to do it like McDonald's."

Not all megadealers use Hendrick's homogenized approach, but it works for him. His Charlotte (N. C.)-based *JRH* Inc. holding company, formed in 1976, now owns a controlling interest in 22 dealerships in eight states: Annual revenues, about $400 million. With an estimated net worth of more than $100 million, Hendrick ranks—financially, at least—far ahead of most Detroit auto executives.

JRH sells more than a dozen brands of domestic and imported cars and trucks—from Honda's new Acura models to Chevrolets, Mercedes, and Volvos. And more acquisitions are on the way, though Hendrick claims he may take a breather next year. "I never intended to have this many franchises," he shrugs. "The deals just came along."

So did the people to staff Hendrick's fast-growing company. His former banker is now his financial vice-president, and applications for employment flood in from salespeople seeking better career opportunities. "We get general managers from other [dealers] who are ready to start as salesmen," he marvels.

> Dealers who don't offer good service and repair are 'the first down the tube when things get tough.'

'A GOOD NAME.' Hendrick shops for available franchises or foundering outlets in metropolitan markets. Then he installs a general manager to handle day-to-day operations and implement a management philosophy that emphasizes careful cost controls and consistent service rather than flashy promotions and cut-rate deals. He monitors performance of his dealerships daily through computerized sales reports. *JRH* also uses computers to keep tabs on used cars, making sure they're sold within 60 days, before they lose too much

answer was "Tough. You sell what we make." But now "we are seeing a big power shift away from the manufacturers toward the distribution chain," says Harvard business school professor Thomas V. Bonoma. Because super-dealers carry several car brands, they can afford to drop a producer whose quality or prices are uncompetitive. "The tables have turned," declares Todd W. Hoffman, 32, vice-president for operations at Hoffman Enterprises Inc., a family-run chain of 10 auto dealerships in the Hartford area. "Now the dealer isn't so beholden to the manufacturers."

The Big Three are taking notice. "Instead of three manufacturers peddling their wares through nine dealerships in town, it's 25 or 30 manufacturers fighting for shelf space in seven or eight dealerships," says Bennett E. Bidwell, vice-chairman of Chrysler Corp.

"It's like ladies' night at the dance hall. [The megadealers] are asking the manufacturers to dance, and the manufacturers had better dance good."

TUNED UP. On balance, the shift to megadealers will be good for consumers. It's true that there may be fewer car showrooms, and they may be farther apart. But the dealers with the best economies of scale can cut a lot of fat from current marketing costs—and theoretically pass the savings on to car buyers. A report released last year by Booz, Allen & Hamilton Inc. concludes that the present dealer system "does not adequately serve the needs of the manufacturer, dealer, or consumer." Booz Allen figures that $3,400, or 30% of the price of the average 1986 car, is tacked on after it leaves the factory. Aside from a pretax profit of $1,500 for the average dealer, that $3,400 includes $1,070 for resale value. Hendrick meets quarterly with general managers, who earn between $100,000 and $200,000, to compare performance and discuss market trends, cost controls, and new sales ideas.

JRH showrooms operate independently, and they don't share a single company name. But they use the same telephone system, inventory controls, sales techniques, and accounting methods. Even Hendrick's basic building is the same—modified only in exterior trim to mesh with local architectural tastes. "We used brick in Tennessee and stucco in Charlotte," Hendrick says, "but I've built that same building eight times."

The young tycoon aims for high sales volume, of course. But he insists on a strong parts-and-service operation, too. Thus, each *JRH* dealership sets aside $2,500 to $10,000 per month to pay for "good will" repairs or free rental cars for customers with a persistent complaint. "If you spend $75,000 a month in advertising to get people in to buy a car," Hendrick says, "I don't think it's out of line to spend one-tenth that amount in the back shop to maintain a good name." Besides, he adds, strong service helps keep dealerships profitable when sales slump. He disdains high-volume, low-margin operations that ignore demands for service after a sale. "They're the first down the tube when things get tough," he contends. "People don't forget—and they don't come back."

Hendrick's dedication to cars started early. As an 8-year-old Virginia farm boy, he attended auto races with his father, a stock-car driver. Six years later he purchased his first auto for $250, a '31 Chevrolet, and started entering it in drag races even before he was licensed to drive on public roads. Not long after, he was earning tidy sums buying, repairing, and reselling old cars on his own. Hired by a successful dealer in Raleigh, N. C., to operate a used-car lot, Hendrick abandoned his plans to attend college and get a degree in engineering. His experience on the car lot taught him useful business skills, and he purchased his first dealership in 1975.

Success has led Hendrick deeper into racing. He employs a 100-member staff and budgets $4 million a year to campaign 22 stock, drag, and road-racing Chevies. Among them: the Monte Carlo *SS* that Geoff Bodine drove to victory in last February's *NASCAR* Daytona 500.

Like many megadealers, Hendrick has thought about taking his company public. "When you see some of the [financial] numbers," he notes, "you'd be crazy not to consider it." But he'll probably wait awhile because of his concern that the rules for public companies may not be adaptable to the almost daily ups and downs of car retailing—or to his independent style. "Most [megadealers] have built it all themselves," he says, "and they don't want to accept a board telling them what to do."

By William J. Hampton in Detroit

advertising and marketing, $470 for the car's delivery from the manufacturer, and $360 for marketing overhead and field sales costs. The report estimates that perhaps $800 could be cut from the total with more efficient retailing methods.

Super-dealers also should help improve service, a common complaint of buyers (poll, page 128). Many already pamper their customers with such amenities as extended hours, door-to-door limousine service, inspectors to double-check repairs, computerized service records, longer warranties on repair work, and free car washes. Eloy Renfrow, president of Renfrow Auto Center Inc. in Santa Maria, Calif., backs up the 11 brands sold from his five-showroom "motor mall" with 80 service bays open six days, or 75 hours, a week. He and his controller show up at 7 a.m. to handle service calls until the mall's switchboard opens at 8 a.m. "We keep enough people so we don't have to turn down anybody who needs fast service," says Renfrow.

There's no single dealer who typifies the new breed. Renfrow consolidated his operations into five showrooms in a 15-acre mall to cut costs. San Francisco super-dealer Martin L. Swig went a step further, gathering sales and service for 10 car brands under one roof. The result, dubbed the San Francisco Autocenter Inc., is open seven days a week. Auto makers normally aren't thrilled about selling competing brands in the same facility, though none prohibits it. Swig convinced manufacturers that high land costs in San Francisco left him no choice, so he sells Chryslers, Toyotas, Rolls-Royces, and Saabs side by side. It sounds like all these brands would cut into each other's sales. But, says Har-

SEVEN OF THE LARGEST SUPER-DEALERS

Dealer	Headquarters	1986 sales* $ Million	Vehicles	No. of brands	No. of outlets	States
POTAMKIN	New York, Philadelphia, Miami	$800	66,000	14	33	5
ROSENTHAL (Geneva Mgt. Inc.)	Arlington, Va.	$430	30,000	11	11	3
HENDRICK (JRH Inc.)	Charlotte, N. C.	$400	41,400	13	22	8
HOLMAN (Holman Enterprises)	Pennsauken, N. J.	$375	22,600	7	11	2
DEVER (Automanage Inc.)	Cincinnati	$360	35,000	11	13	4
FRINK (Bob Frink Mgt. Inc.)	Sacramento	$325	24,000	14	11	4
TONKIN (Ron Tonkin Dealership Group)	Portland, Ore.	$100	18,000	13	8	1

*Estimate   Total sales include new and used cars and trucks   DATA: NICHOLS, CAMPBELL & MORROW INC.

vard's Bonoma, "the dealer is drawing in a new layer of customers and spreading out his fixed costs."

At the other end of the spectrum is Frederick A. Lavery Jr., a 47-year-old Porsche-Audi dealer in Birmingham, Mich. Lavery and two partners in New Jersey and California have set up a corporation called U.S. Autogroup Ltd. through which they hope to create a chain of perhaps 60 dealerships. The company wants no more than two outlets in each of 30 metropolitan markets, thus blanketing 15 regional economies. "We're hedging our bets," says Lavery, "and that means operating coast to coast, with several marques."

DIFFERENT TALENTS. Many multi-franchise operators don't bother to identify their ownership with a common name, especially when their showrooms are sprinkled over several cities or states. Others, such as Potamkin, display the group name on every location. Some insist on owning each of their auto dealerships entirely. Others think it's better to turn over as much as 50% of the equity to on-site general managers who handle day-to-day operations. Many megadealers centralize their chain's basic functions—such things as administration, advertising, payroll, and parts ordering. But some still encourage each showroom to handle such matters. "There's no one way that's been proven yet," says J.D. Power's Keithley. "The book is still being written."

There are plenty of one-showroom dealers who know how to run their business efficiently. But controlling a network requires different talents. One per-

son usually can't run two dealerships. So super-dealers eager to grow must find or develop competent managers for every new outlet they add. Many, in fact, say this dictates the pace of their growth.

Super-dealers also take a corporate view of their business. They typically rely on a chief financial officer to monitor each dealership on a daily basis, diverting cash from one to another as needed. Their central staff also includes a parts-and-service executive who visits each showroom to coordinate operations and other managers to handle leasing, insurance, equipment, purchases, architectural work, advertising, and extended warranty business.

Cincinnati super-dealer Michael Dever uses an International Business Machines Corp. 4331 mainframe computer in the basement of his townhouse headquarters to monitor service records, parts inventories, parts ordering, and daily sales at each of his 13 dealerships. Dever, who employs about 1,000 people, meets monthly with his top 20 executives and confers with individual staffers almost every day. Only one of Dever's showrooms—a Cadillac-Oldsmobile outlet in nearby Fairfield, Ohio—handles domestic brands. He concedes that some manufacturers grumble about his chain operation, but he soothes them with high sales volumes and by pointing out that his holding company provides only centralized services. "I don't sell cars, the general managers do," he says. "I'm an investor rather than a dealer."

Although a few big dealerships have been around

for decades, the super-dealer movement really took root in 1979. U.S. auto sales were plummeting at about the same time consumers discovered the better quality of imported cars. To protect their sales volume, dealers of domestic brands added import franchises, and they're still doing it. "If General Motors was going to be partners with Japanese and Korean companies, we thought we should do the same," says Robert Potamkin, 40, who along with his brother is a graduate of University of Pennsylvania's Wharton School.

IMPORT APPEAL. Dealers that diversified into imports made a startling discovery: There's a lot more money in selling foreign cars. Several super-dealers told BUSINESS WEEK that it costs twice as much to sell 1,000 U.S.-made cars as to sell 1,000 Japanese cars. The higher quality of imports means they come back for warranty repairs less often. One result: a smaller staff of mechanics for dealers to maintain. Japanese product lines are simpler, reducing the number of spare parts a dealer has to stock. And a chronic shortage of imports adds up to less need for lot space—and faster turnover, often at list prices.

Statistics compiled by *Automotive News,* an industry trade magazine, show that U.S. Honda Motor Co. outlets averaged 640 sales per dealership last year, compared with 331 for Chevrolet, 295 for Ford, 124 for Chrysler, and only 87 for American Motors. One East Coast super-dealer who sells 20,000 cars annually estimates that the return on investment at one of his import franchises is 300%, compared with 80% at one selling domestic cars only.

Ironically, it was a restrictive General Motors Corp. policy banning its dealers from acquiring more than one GM outlet in the same market that drove many super-dealers to imports. One was Ronald B. Tonkin, whose dealerships are all within a few miles of Ron Tonkin Dealership Group, his Portland(Ore.) headquarters. "When they wouldn't let us grow," says Tonkin, "we went to the people who would." Now, Tonkin—like many super-dealers—carries many more imported than domestic brands. GM has since eased its restrictions, but the damage has been done—to the benefit of overseas carmakers, especially the Japanese. National Automobile Dealers Assn. figures show that about 33% of all U.S. auto dealers now have franchises that sell both foreign and domestic cars, up from 20% a decade ago.

Other super-dealers picked up franchises cheaply during the auto sales slump that began in 1980. J.R. "Rick" Hendrick III, for one, grew from two to eight dealerships in the downturn (page 124). Now he owns 22 outlets in eight states and counts among the 15 employees at his Charlotte (N.C.) headquarters four auditors, a financial officer, two certified public accountants, in addition to an executive in charge of operations.

No domestic or foreign auto maker is happy about the idea of dealers calling the shots on car design and pricing. Yet the emergence of the super-dealer may be just what the industry needs to update its retailing techniques. "A lot of people agree there should be changes," says Paul F. Anderson, a senior vice-president and author of the Booz Allen auto-distribution study. "But you get blank stares when you ask what should be done."

GETTING SATISFACTION. As complaints over U.S. car quality have mounted in recent years, all domestic manufacturers have deluged dealers with ideas for improving service. They also rank them on a "customer satisfaction index," or CSI, compiled from questionnaires filled in by recent car buyers. How a dealer scores is compared with others selling the same car brand. Manufacturers penalize poor performers by refusing to give them new franchises—or threatening to withdraw their present one.

Detroit can go only so far, however. Some dealers see buyer surveys as an attempt by manufacturers to

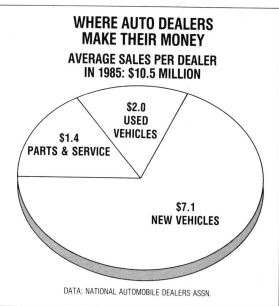

WHERE AUTO DEALERS MAKE THEIR MONEY
AVERAGE SALES PER DEALER IN 1985: $10.5 MILLION

$1.4 PARTS & SERVICE

$2.0 USED VEHICLES

$7.1 NEW VEHICLES

DATA: NATIONAL AUTOMOBILE DEALERS ASSN.

BW/HARRIS POLL: DEALERSHIPS SHOULD BE SMALL—AND MORE RELIABLE

Super-dealers may be in their future, but most Americans would rather buy their cars from an auto dealer who sells only one or two makes. As for service, they complain that dealers don't get repair work done right the first time. What do they think about the people who sell cars? You guessed it: They've got to be watched like a hawk.

Q People go to different places to get basic service for their cars—gas stations, auto dealers, independent garages, tire dealers, and specialty shops like Sears and Midas. In the following categories, who do you think does the best job?

A

	Gas stations	Auto dealers	Garages	Tire dealers	Specialty retailers	None	Not sure
Quality of service	7%	32%	28%	10%	15%	3%	5%
Value for the money	10%	21%	31%	7%	19%	2%	10%
Being honest	9%	25%	32%	7%	13%	6%	8%
Caring about customers	9%	29%	32%	10%	12%	2%	6%

Q As far as auto dealers go, which do you prefer to buy a new car from—one who carries as many as six or more different makes or one who carries only one or two makes?

A
6 or more	**26%**
1 or 2	**61%**
Makes no difference	**10%**
Not sure	**3%**

Q Do you agree or disagree that an auto dealer who carries six or more makes is likely to have the customer's interest at heart more than the manufacturer's?

A
Agree	**38%**
Disagree	**47%**
Not sure	**15%**

Q If you had to choose, which type of car dealer do you think it is better to do business with—a dealer who carries domestic cars or one who carries foreign cars?

A
Domestic	**69%**
Foreign	**17%**
Not sure	**14%**

Q Let me read you four things people say are areas where auto dealers should do better than they do now. Tell me which one is most important to you?

A
Getting the work right the first time	**60%**
Doing better on completing work when promised	**10%**
Keeping within the original cost estimate	**14%**
More willing to tell you when you don't need something done	**16%**

Q Finally, would you describe the salespeople who work for most auto dealers as thoroughly reliable to deal with, the same as most other salespeople, or types you have to watch like a hawk?

A
Thoroughly reliable	**22%**
Same as most others	**25%**
Have to watch like a hawk	**48%**
Not sure	**5%**

Edited by Stuart Jackson

Telephone survey of 631 adults in households that have bought a new car within the past five years. The poll was conducted May 16-20 by Louis Harris & Associates Inc. for BUSINESS WEEK. Overall results should be accurate to within five percentage points.

meddle in their affairs. "They say, 'I can't be that bad,' " notes Donald W. Hudler, general director of sales operations for GM's Customer Sales & Service Staff. Improving the relationship between carmakers and dealers isn't easy, concedes Joseph A. Kordick, general manager of Ford Motor Co.'s Parts and Service Div. "These are cultural issues, and boy, are they hard to deal with."

Carmakers also are hamstrung by a web of state franchise laws pushed through by dealers over the years to protect their profitability. These laws restrict how many franchises a manufacturer can grant in a single market, make it hard to rearrange dealerships when populations shift, and even regulate the auto maker's ability to choose franchisees. Only new car companies setting up sales outlets for the first time can really try something different—selling cars through Sears, Roebuck & Co. stores, for example. So far, however, none of the newest manufacturers from South Korea, Eastern Europe, or Japan have dared upset the status quo.

One reason is Porsche's spectacular failure to revamp its retailing system in 1984. The West German carmaker announced that it was dropping Volkswagen as its U.S. distributor and would sell Porsches itself. In doing so, the company figured it qualified as a "new" distributor with the right to overhaul its franchise system. Outraged Porsche dealers filed $2 billion in lawsuits against the company. Faced with going broke while fighting in one state court after another, Porsche caved in and decided to keep its conventional distribution system. "You had to laugh—or leave the country," sighs John A. Cook, president of Porsche Cars North America Inc.

BETTER THAN AVERAGE. Whiffs of a similar reaction have forced GM to soft-pedal plans for a nontraditional distribution scheme for its new Saturn Corp. subsidiary, which won't start selling cars until about 1990. Saturn was set up as a separate company in part to qualify it as a new manufacturer unfettered by franchise laws. Reports last year that Saturn officials were thinking of doing without dealers surfaced as New Jersey adopted a law that forces manufacturers to sell vehicles only through franchised dealers. The law, prompted by Porsche's ill-fated experiment, is currently being studied by a number of other states. Concerned GM officials have since hinted that they may stick with the conventional dealer system.

The super-dealers may be the way around such problems for Detroit. They are results-oriented and know they can grow only by providing better-than-average customer service. They are accustomed to looking for the best practices in each of their outlets and applying them throughout their chains. That doesn't guarantee that super-dealer service will be better than that provided by the best of the small dealers, but it does help make it better than the average. Like any auto dealer, if the super-dealer "doesn't take care of his reputation, his reputation will take care of him," warns Portland's Tonkin. "He's got to provide good service, or he's not going to have enough business to survive."

That is precisely the point manufacturers have been trying to make to their legions of single-showroom dealers. Many have gotten the message and are trying to improve. The rise of super-dealers gives them no long-term alternative, just as it leaves the producers little choice but to build better products. The consumer wins on both counts.

By William J. Hampton in Detroit

HOW OCEAN SPRAY KEEPS REINVENTING THE CRANBERRY

CLEVER MARKETING, A LITTLE LUCK, AND THE LATEST PACKAGING TECHNOLOGY KEEP SALES FIGURES SWEET

DECEMBER 2, 1985, P. 142

The perfect breakfast? Waffles with a Cran-Orange topping. Lunch? Shish kebab with a cranberry glaze. And at the end of the day, why not relax with Cranberry Sangria, a concoction of cranberry juice and wine?

Executives at Ocean Spray Cranberries Inc. recently offered these serving suggestions to the nation's restaurateurs. Offbeat? Of course. But the menu options show how far Ocean Spray marketers will go to promote the little red berry once served only at Thanksgiving.

Its efforts are paying off handsomely. Ocean Spray has done well in pitching cranberry juice as the drink of choice for increasingly health-conscious Americans. On top of that, Ocean Spray is aggressive in adapting new packaging technologies. Ocean Spray, a Massachusetts growers' co-operative that operates out of a refurbished clam factory in Plymouth, has been growing fast. Sales, which were $542 million in the year ended Aug. 31, have increased an average 18% annually for the past decade.

How the 800-member co-op does so well is a study in serendipity—and clever planning. The good luck started about a decade ago, when Americans began searching for beverages with more nutrition than soda pop. Ocean Spray drinks, which have on average 30% fruit juice, were a logical choice. The co-op nurtured its image with the advertising slogan: "It's good for you, America."

Ocean Spray was also careful not to jeopardize its opportunity. The co-op avoided the competitive orange juice market, dominated by Coca-Cola Co.'s Minute Maid and Beatrice Cos.' Tropicana.

Instead, it worked to create a line of beverages based on its core product, Cranberry Juice Cocktail. While some products—such as Cran-Prune—failed, most succeeded. The Ocean Spray line now includes seven drinks, everything from Cranapple to Cran-Raspberry.

HAVE A GUAVA. With its basic line secure, Ocean Spray could capitalize on its growing brand-name recognition. In 1976 the company began selling grapefruit juice, and in 1982 it added apple juice. Packaging advances such as "paper bottles" added to Ocean Spray's healthy image and helped get its juices into the nation's lunchboxes. New-product development is venturesome, too: Ocean Spray began selling a guava-based drink in August.

To keep up this pace, Ocean Spray is launching its boldest and costliest marketing scheme ever—and true to form, it is trying something new: Ocean Spray Liquid Concentrate. The product, a syrup positioned to compete in the $2.9 billion frozen-concentrate market, requires no refrigeration. It also contains no artificial preservatives, because it comes in aseptic containers—the same rectangular paper bottles Ocean Spray pioneered in the U. S. four years ago.

Ocean Spray ads stress convenience and price, which may be a winning formula. The syrup—available in such flavors as Cranapple and Pink Grapefruit Cocktail—is 10% cheaper per glass than frozen concentrate and 30% less than bottled drinks. Further, customers don't have to thaw Liquid Concentrate. To get things off to a good start, the co-op will spend $10 million on advertising.

CANNIBALIZING. There is a danger, of course,

that all the promotion might backfire. Liquid Concentrate could "cannibalize existing Ocean Spray products," says Tropicana Products Inc. President Spencer J. Volk. This has already happened with juice flavors. When Ocean Spray introduced Cran-Raspberry last year, sales of the new product quickly topped $50 million. But demand for Cranapple and Cran-Grape suffered.

Now both brands have revived, after reformulation and a dose of advertising. That helps explain why Ocean Spray executives are confident about Liquid Concentrate. An early, five-city test is likewise comforting: Supermarket sales of all Ocean Spray products climbed 15% after the concentrate appeared.

With that in mind—along with the prospect of several new flavors, including a Cran-blueberry—President Harold Thorkilsen expects that Ocean Spray will hit $1 billion in sales by 1990. The 60-year-old Thorkilsen, who worked in Ocean Spray's cranberry bogs near Plymouth while attending Massachusetts Institute of Technology, worries about spreading his good brand name too thin. But Ocean Spray has proven before that it can turn one successful product into many—even if it is working with the unheralded cranberry.

By Barbara Buell
in Plymouth, Mass.

CLOTHING MAKERS GO STRAIGHT TO THE CONSUMER

APRIL 29, 1985, PP. 114, 115

In Hong Kong's bustling Causeway Bay district, at a glittering clothing store that resembles a high-tech discotheque, pretty, young saleswomen in oversized cotton shirts greet shoppers with unfailing exuberance. Esprit de Corp, which owns the store, makes sure they all look hip and unselfconscious. "If she's dull, she's not part of the Esprit life," says store manager Evelyn Cheah.

On trendy Melrose Avenue in Los Angeles, customers at L. A. Gear's two-level showcase browse to the beat of throbbing rock music in rooms splashed with neon light. "The store is our image," says Robert Y. Greenberg, founder of the fast-growing apparel chain.

PROVING A POINT. What's unusual is that Esprit and L. A. Gear aren't retailers. Instead, they are among the growing number of clothing manufacturers that are opening retail outlets to deliver their sales pitch directly to consumers. Taking a cue from fashion designers such as Yves Saint Laurent and Giorgio Armani, these makers of less

> The strategy is aggressive: Open retail outlets that build a strong image and draw department stores' attention

pricy garments think they can build sales—both in their own shops and in department stores. "We want to show how our goods can be displayed and prove we can move more fashion merchandise than the chains believe we can," says Roger Kase, president of Esprit's retail division.

San Francisco-based Esprit, which has parlayed its breezy, colorful fashions into a worldwide empire and expects sales of $800 million this year, is one of the most aggressive users of the new retailing strategy. After trying out the concept in its Hong Kong store, which cost $3.8 million to open in 1983, privately held Esprit recently plowed more than $10 million into a dramatic 30,000-sq.-ft. outlet in Los Angeles. It opened another store in New Orleans and plans at least eight more.

Other manufacturers are moving fast, too. Murjani International will open two stores in September that will feature a new line of clothes carrying the Coca-Cola label (BW—Apr. 8), and Chairman Mohan B. Murjani talks about having hundreds more. Also on the retail bandwagon are Copenhagen-based In-Wear/Matinique, Eileen West of San Francisco, and Los Angeles sportswear makers Guess? and Cherokee.

The push to open stores reflects the fierce competition in the industry. Retailers want the most revenue per square foot, and they increasingly rely either on big names such as Calvin Klein and Liz Claiborne or on private labels. That hurts small manufacturers.

Apparel makers also complain that department stores have cut back on sales help in an effort to boost margins. "It's hard to do well in a store where there is no sales staff and little money for visual presentation," says an executive of one leading designer's company. To get the attention of the chains and to build the right image with consumers, "we have to become a self-promoting resource," one manufacturer says. That often means opening stores.

A good example is Eileen West, which recruited local socialites to model its new collection at the

A DESIGNER WHO FOUND HAPPINESS AT J.C. PENNEY

While other designers fight for floor space in department stores, Lee Wright has secured an exclusive home in 500 J. C. Penney Co. outlets. For two years the 36-year-old former actor has been an integral part of Penney's plans to become a high-fashion retailer. Starting with a signature line of men's clothing, Wright has branched out into shoes, home furnishings, and, most recently, women's wear. His clothes, which often feature soft colors and fabrics with unusual weaves or textures, appeal primarily to people under 40.

So far, both Penney's and Wright are pleased with their partnership. Last year, before the women's line was introduced, Penney's sold $75 million worth of Wright's designs. Prices range from less than $50 for a sweater or pair of slacks to $250 for a man's suit. The idea is to appeal to higher-income, fashion-conscious customers who shop at Penney's for sheets and perhaps children's apparel but normally don't buy their own clothes there.

Wright, who won the coveted Coty fashion award in 1979 and the Cutty Sark trophy for outstanding menswear design in 1981, fit naturally into Penney's strategy. "He had the appropriate design credentials and was the perfect marketing tool for Penney's," says J. Hicks Lanier, chairman of Oxford Industries Inc., which manufactures Wright's clothes for the chain. The personable Wright both models and helps write scripts for Penney's *TV* commercials and magazine ads.

The designer, who gets paid through an undisclosed royalty arrangement with Oxford, admits he has profited handsomely. Thanks to Penney's, he has also reached the major leagues of American fashion—a leap few designers can make independently. "Today, to promote a designer and get into major selling, it's like putting on a Broadway show. You're talking about an immense amount of money, maybe $4 million to $5 million to start," says New York menswear designer Garrick Anderson, who is trying to raise money to expand.

IN STRIDE. Despite Penney's offer, Wright resisted the idea of working for a mass marketer. His experience was at the couture end of the business. Following a stint as a design assistant for Bill Blass Menswear, Wright began, in the mid-1970s, to create his own line of expensive Italian-made men's clothes that were sold to department and specialty stores. He feared that becoming closely tied to a chain store would hurt his image. "My whole life had been about creating a prominent position in the industry," he says.

Whatever his initial doubts, Wright now takes his success in stride. "From a philosophical point of view, I asked myself whether I was really making a difference selling $600 suits when I could be selling something progressive to millions of people," he says. "It was an opportunity to make a much bigger difference." And he doesn't have to beg for space in department stores.

By Amy Dunkin in New York

opening of a San Francisco outlet last November. The store—which uses wood, granite, and other natural materials to complement a line of simple, low-key garments—is the prototype for what the company expects will be a chain of franchised outlets. President Laney Thornton, the youngest son of the late Charles B. "Tex" Thornton, founder of Litton Industries Inc., hopes that the stores and a growing catalog operation will establish an image for the Eileen West label that will give him clout with chain-store buyers.

DESTINY. He is not alone. "We realize we need more control over the ultimate point of sale," says Barry Miguel, a spokesman for Alexander Julian Inc. in New York. Perry Ellis America, a new division of Levi Strauss & Co. that is selling casual sportswear with the designer's label, began by building a model of the retail look it was after.

Then it sold only to retailers willing to copy the model within their stores. "We believe strongly in creating our own destiny," explains Robert C. Siegel, president of Perry Ellis America. "You can't do that by selling to a store and walking away."

Esprit is taking similarly gutsy steps to establish its own identity. President Doug Tompkins, who freely criticizes the treatment most retailers give his products, has reduced the number of U.S. stores carrying Esprit from 4,000 to about 2,000 and plans to cut it further. "Department stores are famous for cramming a lot of stuff together so that you lose the personality of each line," notes Jerard L. Less, vice-president of Colton Bernard Inc., a leading apparel industry consulting firm. "Esprit will do business only with those merchants that will establish a partnership and follow the direction they set." To take that independent stance, manufacturers have to have a hot line and the ability to sell through their own stores.

Esprit is not the first manufacturer to try retailing. As early as the 1920s, some men's clothing manufacturers like Hart, Schaffner & Marx owned retail outlets. Then as now, it is not easy to be in both businesses. Manufacturing and retailing "are two different worlds," warns Brian J. Minnihan, an apparel consultant at accounting firm Laventhol & Horwath's San Francisco office. A few apparel makers that recently tested the retailing business backed away. Levi Strauss liquidated its chain of about 70 close-out stores in 1980 to concentrate on manufacturing. And Los Angeles sportswear maker Jag of Beverly Hills Inc., which at one time had 20 stores, now has just two.

One problem for would-be retailers is finding a broad enough line of merchandise to fill a store. "If your range is too narrow," says one manufacturer, "people won't come in." Here again, Esprit is at the head of the pack with a fast-growing lineup of shoes and apparel for children and young adults, as well as adolescents. But some competitors believe Esprit may have gone too far. "Each store has to have its target customer," says W. Jay Carothers, a director of Hong Kong-based apparel maker Mast Industries (Far East) Ltd. "What Esprit is trying to do sounds a bit like a department store."

Perhaps the biggest danger in the move into retailing is that manufacturers risk alienating their traditional outlet—the department store. But for now, since the number of stores owned by the manufacturers is small, retailers do not feel threatened. "We don't look at any of it as competition," says a spokeswoman for Macy's California, a division of R. H. Macy & Co. "We are selling image, and anything that helps their image only helps our business."

By John W. Wilson in San Francisco, with Teresa Carson in Los Angeles, Dorinda Elliott in Hong Kong, and Amy Dunkin in New York

DETROIT TRIES TO LEVEL A MOUNTAIN OF PAPERWORK

ALL-ELECTRONIC COMMUNICATION WITH SUPPLIERS COULD SAVE $200 A CAR BY 1988

AUGUST 26, 1985, PP. 94, 96

Imagine a company equipped with plenty of telephones but no outside lines. That would be fine for internal communications, but useless for dealing with the outside world. Yet most companies use their computers just that way, relying on the equipment to move information around internally. When it comes to shipping heaps of data to each other, most fall back on a traditional method: the mailman.

Nowhere has the resulting blizzard of cross-country paperwork piled up deeper than between auto makers and their 25,000 suppliers. Experts say the billions of bills, orders, and requests generated each year add at least $200 to the cost of each U. S.-made car and truck. Put another way, the U. S. auto industry is wasting $2 billion a year to shuffle paper around. But that won't be the case much longer. Detroit has an ambitious goal: to eliminate virtually all intercompany paperwork by 1988.

This project is being orchestrated by a voluntary committee representing the Big Three auto makers plus American Motors Corp. and about 300 large suppliers. Organized in 1981, the Automotive Industry Action Group *(AIAG)* is setting up standard forms and instructions for transmitting the forms among companies. "If a supplier is not prepared to communicate electronically" in three years, warns Thomas M. Hummer, chairman of the *AIAG*'s communications team, "he's probably not going to be able to bid on Big Four [automotive] business."

U. N. STANDARD. Cost-cutting is the obsession behind this enormous project. Detroit will try al-most anything to offset Japan's average $2,500-per-car cost advantage. So committed is General Motors Corp. to cleaning up its information-handling mess that it bought Electronic Data Systems Corp. *(EDS)* last year for $2.5 billion.

Detroit's effort reflects the thinking in numerous industries around the world. Last year, for example, nine European auto makers formed the Organization for Data Exchange by Teletransmission in Europe *(ODETTE)*. Using U. N.-approved standards, *ODETTE* is trying to come up with a single communications system for manufacturers, suppliers, customs authorities, and shipping agents across Europe. Europe's chemical, electronics, shipbuilding, and steel industries will soon follow the lead of autos, says Alfredo Sarich, director of Euromatica, a Brussels consultant. He adds that the U. N. standard is the first step toward saving $15 billion a year worldwide by reducing paperwork in international trade.

In the U. S., the grocery industry launched an electronic document transmission system two years ago to link manufacturers such as Kraft Inc. and Procter & Gamble Co. with supermarkets and other retailers. It is saving an estimated $300 million a year. Trade groups in the chemical and aluminum industries are making plans to convert to electronic systems, too. And the American National Standards Institute is working on the next step: standards that will let companies in different industries communicate electronically.

HODGEPODGE. The auto industry will give the idea its biggest push. Its supplier base extends into almost every major industry—steel, chemicals, rubber, textiles, electronics. Says Richard C. Norris, a consultant at Arthur D. Little Inc.: "It's going to dramatically increase the operating efficiency, time responsiveness, and productivity of U. S. industry."

Carmakers need all the help they can get. Consider the current method for ordering parts: First, an auto or components maker punches information into its in-house computers to decide how many parts it needs and where they should be delivered. The next step is getting the data to suppliers. *GM*, for example, might repunch the information and send it to its destination over telex lines. Or the company might bundle up the paper forms and mail them. Either way, the data is keypunched one more time—this time into the computer of a supplier that must keep its own inventory-control records.

The *AIAG* says this tedious process adds errors to about 5% of auto documents. Transmitting the information electronically could cut errors to 1%, the *AIAG* predicts—and nearly wipe out postage and telex costs in the bargain.

Some auto suppliers have been taking a communications shortcut for years by setting up their own direct computer linkups. But the process isn't easy. Each carmaker—and some of the divisions within each company—has its own idiosyncratic electronic formats. This leaves suppliers facing a software hodgepodge. "We've got more than 100 different program modules," groans Thomas P. Zelinsky, director of materials control for Rockwell International Corp.'s automotive operations. Creating standard industry formats "would bring maybe an 80% reduction in our document transfer workload," he says.

'FAT AND SASSY.' The trick is getting everyone to use the same standards. Earlier this year, the *AIAG* unveiled telecommunications standards to ease electronic communication among companies. Now it wants to reduce the hundreds of forms companies use to order, ship, and confirm goods to about 18. So far it has completed two, an invoice and a shipping schedule. It expects to finish most of the others—from bills of lading to purchase order acknowledgments—in 1986.

The *AIAG* estimates that its system will require only a microcomputer and a few software packages, so that even mom-and-pop suppliers can hook up for as little as $10,000. Larger companies won't have to alter their mini or mainframe hardware, but they will have to come up with a software that can translate the new standards. One such program for mainframe computers costs $15,000. Companies will decide among themselves whether to communicate directly or through electronic mailboxes provided by third-party companies.

> Carmakers predict that going paperless will 'trim a minimum of two days out of the supply pipeline'

The new systems are certain to produce broad changes in everything from staff size to inventory control. Peter C. Van Hull, an auto consultant for Arthur Andersen & Co., says that electronic communication systems will account for up to a quarter of the 5% decline in auto employment his firm expects each year through 1990. Lower-paid clerical workers will be the primary victims.

Moreover, the systems eventually could help carmakers save much more than the targeted $200 per vehicle by letting them operate more efficient just-in-time systems. These reduce inventory costs by having parts delivered to assembly plants just as they're needed. With mail, "there's a 7-to-10-day lag from the time a part is ordered until it is received," says the *AIAG*'s Hummer. With a paperless operation, "we can trim a minimum of two days out of the supply pipeline." Notes Charles E. Richards, a systems development supervisor for Ford Motor Co.: "You really couldn't do just-in-time between Ford and its suppliers without electronic communication."

If electronic interchange makes so much sense, why didn't the industry convert to it years ago? For one thing, microcomputers have only recently become cheap enough to allow data interchange to extend to the bottom of the supplier chain. But a much more telling reason may be the one offered by James R. Oravec, an *AIAG* member and a systems manager for *EDS*: "Everyone was pretty fat and sassy at one point," he says. "Now the Japanese have forced us to look at other ways to make our industry more profitable."

By Russell Mitchell in Detroit, with Peter J. Heywood in London

WHERE THREE SALES A YEAR MAKE YOU A SUPERSTAR

FEBRUARY 17, 1986, PP. 76, 77

If Zellars C. West were a car salesman, he might have to think about another line of work. He made only three sales last year. But West doesn't push Pontiacs: He works for Cray Research Inc. selling the Porsches of the computer industry, fast and powerful supercomputers with a sticker shock to match—up to $20 million apiece. These are huge machines used for such complex jobs as weather forecasting, oil exploration, and automotive design. So even though West's numbers sound puny, they make him a superstar. When 45 of his peers from Cray gather in Hawaii on Feb. 12 for their annual sales meeting, West will be honored as a top company salesman.

Cray isn't doing badly itself. The three machines West sold last year contributed $33 million in sales to the Minneapolis-based company, whose profits climbed 67% last year, to $75.6 million, on a 66% revenue jump, to $380.2 million. Company shares split at 90 in August and are already back above 60. And that's while many computer makers have been mired in a slump. Cray's performance reflects the supercomputer business in general. Overall worldwide sales were only $450 million last year. But there are 179 supercomputers in use today, far above the 80-machine limit that Cray foresaw when it entered the market in the mid-1970s.

All this has vaulted West, a Pittsburgh-based district manager whose territory covers New Jersey, Pennsylvania, and Ohio, into the ranks of the world's elite salespeople. It has also attracted competitors. Cray still holds a 64% share of the worldwide supercomputer market. But others, notably Japanese companies such as Fujitsu, Hitachi, and *NEC*, are turning up the heat.

TOP OF THE HEAP. U. S. contenders are springing up, as well. *ETA* Systems Inc., which is 90% owned by Control Data Corp., has sold three of its new supercomputers—six times faster than the highest-powered Cray but priced about the same. Other companies—among them Alliant, Convex, Sequent, and Floating Point Systems—are developing "Baby Crays"—a lower-cost class of so-

FIVE YEARS TO A SUPERCOMPUTER SALE	
1981	
April	Salesman West first visits General Electric's R&D center in Schenectady
June	GE's computer programs are tested on Cray computers
September	20 GE scientists and managers hear informal Cray presentation
1982	
April	Cray analyzes GE divisions to see which most needs its machine
1983	
September	West makes two-hour presentation for most likely prospect, GE's Evendale (Ohio) aircraft engine manufacturing facility
1984	
October	West briefs 50 Evendale employees on Cray applications
1985	
January	GE approaches West with inquiries into specific Cray model
August	West arranges two-day seminar on Cray's potential uses
September	GE signs letter of intent to buy a $9.5 million Cray X-MP/28
1986	
February	Anticipated signing of purchase agreement

called minisupercomputers. International Business Machines Corp. is also after the low end of Cray's market, with add-ons for its 3090 mainframe, popularly known as Sierra. All the same, Jeffry Canin, senior technology analyst for Hambrecht & Quist Inc., is betting on Cray's future: "We don't expect it to lose its dominant position anytime soon."

West seems firmly planted on the top of his heap, too. Like other sellers of big-ticket items, he gets a base salary—about $60,000. But he also works on commission—about 0.4% of the total sale. That sounds small, but the numbers add up. Although West won't disclose his income with bonuses, Cray says its top salespeople earn $250,000 a year—nearly as much as some of Cray's top executives and far more than the $43,000 or so pulled down by the average computer salesperson in the U. S.

West has to earn his pay. In nine years with the 14-year-old company, he has locked up sales on just nine machines. That's still better than most of his peers. Some Cray salespeople go 2½ years without making a sale. "There's a lot of pressure," West concedes.

EVEN SWEETER. At 57, he's been selling computers for nearly 30 years. Although his training at Pennsylvania State University was in industrial relations, West signed on with the Univac division of Remington-Rand in 1956 and moved on to Honeywell four years later. After joining Control Data in 1966, he began selling multimillion dollar systems. West, who says he foresaw Control Da-

---

West says his clients are mostly engineers and scientists, '10 times smarter than me'

---

ta's current financial troubles even back then, took a 50% cut in pay to join Cray at $50,000 a year in 1977. Covering the entire Northeast, he had no secretary, no office, and little marketing support— "nothing behind me but my rear," he recalls with a grin.

After just three months on the job, West stunned corporate headquarters by landing an $8.5 million contract. What made it even sweeter was that top Cray executives, including current Chairman John A. Rollwagen, insisted that the customer, *AT&T* Bell Laboratories in Murray Hill, N. J., was a poor prospect. To prove the Cray machine's capabilities, West had flown to Minneapolis and test-run some of Bell's programs without his boss's knowledge.

Despite such coups, West has never thought of himself as a hotshot. A Brooks Brothers-style dresser, he still lives in the split-level, three-bedroom home he bought 19 years ago in a small community 35 mi. east of Pittsburgh. Among his few indulgences are collections of toy soldiers, Oriental ivory, and American Western art.

Neither he nor Cray tries to woo customers with expensive lunches, dinners, or tickets to theaters and sporting events. When Bell Labs recently bought its second Cray, for $10 million, West arranged a small party that featured a cake shaped like a cylindrical Cray computer. Traditionally, when Cray ships a machine, it sends along a case of beer. That's about as fancy as it gets.

West also soft-pedals the hard sell. He says his clients are mostly engineers and scientists—"10 times smarter than me"—who respond best to a "subdued" approach. "He doesn't bother us a whole lot when we don't want to be bothered," says James R. Kasdorf, manager of engineering computer services at Westinghouse Electric Corp., which has bought two Crays from West. Kasdorf says he and his staff are so tuned in to the small— and gossipy—supercomputer world that "there's little selling" to do.

Even West concedes that Cray machines almost sell themselves. "I don't fool myself that people are buying because of my tremendous good looks," he chuckles. Adds Marcelo A. Gumucio, Cray's executive vice-president for marketing: "We're not trying to sell a product. We're trying to establish a relationship. It's a little like a marriage."

'ADMINISTRIVIA.' West's biggest challenge is identifying prospects with big enough dowries. Lots of engineers and scientists want Crays. But many don't have the money and management support to buy one. Once West finds a plum, his next step is getting an insider to champion the effort. From then on, he tries to provide anything needed to induce a decision. A recent deal with General Electric Co. took nearly five years (chart, page 139). Once the contract is signed, Cray spends up to a year installing the computer and making sure it works.

The extra effort wins accolades. "Cray has marvelous marketing," says Rick J. Martin, an analyst for Sanford C. Bernstein & Co. "They spend months and months with a customer. It's an absolutely first-class operation."

The company also wins praise for being well managed, thanks mainly to what's known as the Cray style. Cray emphasizes small management groups and shuns what Edward A. Masi, its Eastern region general manager, calls "administrivia." It also promotes decentralized decision-making: Cray's four domestic regions are run as if they were independent subsidiaries, answerable to their own boards of directors. The Cray style seems to pay off where it counts. The company keeps debt low and earns 20% or more on equity.

Yet it remains a technological explorer, spending 15% of revenues on research and development, compared with 7% to 10% at places such as *IBM*. Two teams, one led by company founder Seymour R. Cray and another by designer Steve S. Chen, are now using separate approaches to develop the next generation of Cray machines. Cray's group is using exotic materials such as gallium arsenide to make a superfast chip. Chen's is working on a machine with as many as 64 separate processors instead of the four used on a Cray *X-MP*.

In general, things couldn't look much better for Cray—or for West. The company will probably deliver 40 systems this year, up from 28 in 1985, and analysts believe that should generate record-breaking revenues of $520 million. West is planning to outdo himself, too, by making $45 million worth of those sales. Maybe Willy Loman was right when he said in *Death of a Salesman* that selling is "the greatest career a man could want." Even if it does take five years to close a deal.

By Patrick Houston in Pittsburgh, with Gordon Bock in New York

REBIRTH OF A SALESMAN: WILLY LOMAN GOES ELECTRONIC

FEBRUARY 27, 1984, PP. 103, 104

"Old Dave, he'd go up to his room, put on his green velvet slippers—I'll never forget—and pick up his phone and call the buyers, and without ever leaving his room, at the age of 84, he made his living. And when I saw that, I realized that selling was the greatest career a man could want."
—Willy Loman in *Death of a Salesman*

Truth is, old Dave was on the right track. Telephones were the predecessors of the computers, videocassette recorders, automatic dialers, and other electronic tools that sales staffs are beginning to use—devices that are causing dramatic changes in the way goods and services are sold. Some salespeople have already traded in their bulky sample cases for videodisc players or compact portable computers to display their wares, and many have given up traveling altogether to spend eight hours on the phone talking to customers hundreds—perhaps thousands—of miles away.

The driving force behind the change has been a corporate emphasis on productivity. Top executives are pressuring sales and marketing managers to boost sales without increasing personnel. To meet corporate demands, sales managers have turned to such cost-effective techniques as electronic marketing because of the following factors:
High expenses. The cost of keeping a salesperson on the road has risen dramatically. By some esti-

mates, travel expenses—car rental or mileage, hotels, and meals—are higher than a salesperson's wages (chart, page 143).

Affordable technology. The price tag on much of the technology used in telemarketing, teleconferencing, and computerized sales has been slashed,

---

The sample case gives way to video—a tool that's lowering the high costs of selling
sale

---

making sophisticated electronic marketing possible, even for small companies.

Innovative techniques. In many industries, tough competition, combined with the recent recession, is encouraging innovation in sales techniques. The search for that "something extra" is leading many to the drama of high tech. Some sales managers admit that sending salespeople on the road with portable personal computers is a bit of showmanship. "The ability to interact in a sales meeting is an attention-getting device," says Karl M. Sooder, vice-president for marketing at Barq's Inc., a soft-drink manufacturer in New Orleans. "It's much better than flopping an old printout on the bottler's desk."

Theatrics aside, video presentations can quickly and precisely show off a complicated product's assets. "One of the problems in technical sales," says Thomas E. Bird, president of Gould Inc.'s medical products division in Oxnard, Calif., "is that some salesmen do not exactly convey the message the inventor and manufacturer had in mind when the product was designed."

To get Gould's message across, Bird decided on video support for a sales effort on a new product, a disposable transducer that translates blood pressure into readable electronic impulses. Gould produced two videotapes—a six-minute sales presentation and a nine-minute user-training film—costing $200,000. Salespeople were equipped with videorecorders—an additional $75,000 investment—to take on calls. "Video tells a concise,

clear version of our story. It gives a more professional approach to our sales effort," says Bird.

But does it work? Gould targeted its competitors' customers and maintains that it captured 45% of the $75 million transducer market in less than a year. By the end of nine months, the company reported sales of more than 25,000 units per month. "We're seeing significant penetration where we weren't able to penetrate before," Bird says.

A video presentation during a sales call is certainly not new. General Motors Corp. and Ford Motor Co. were pioneers in the use of videodiscs and telephone networks in the late 1970s—moves that revolutionized their sales operation. At least 70% of Chevrolet's sales managers and 55% of Ford's now use videodiscs as a sales tool. But according to a Ford survey, the discs are more useful in training Ford's own salespeople than in selling. Salespeople say they like training with the discs because they assimilate more, are able to pay more attention to it, it's an easier way to get information, and the discs get the point across more vividly. They said as sales tools, however, the discs were inconvenient to use.

Nevertheless, some smaller companies are finding success in the limited use of video to help make a sale. Foxboro Co., the Foxboro (Mass.) maker of industrial measurement devices, installed a broadcast-quality video facility to produce promotional pieces and customer-education programs that could be used either as in-house training guides or for outside selling.

Henry L. Berman, Foxboro's manager of video services, calls the promotional films "infomercials" and says they can be helpful to employee and customer alike, because the company's product line is difficult to visualize. Phillip G. Scott, senior product specialist, uses them to familiarize the sales force with new products, eliminating the need for extensive traveling.

ACTING ABILITIES. "All that traveling got very expensive," Scott says. "You can save a lot of money and time doing it this way." Yet he says video presentations are no replacement for personal contact. "Sure, you can show a customer a tape, but I'd be fooling myself if I thought the customer was going to stand up and give the

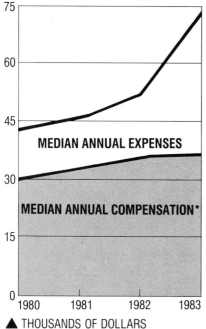

WHAT IT COSTS TO SELL INDUSTRIAL PRODUCTS ON THE ROAD

MEDIAN ANNUAL EXPENSES

MEDIAN ANNUAL COMPENSATION*

75
60
45
30
15
0

1980   1981   1982   1983

▲ THOUSANDS OF DOLLARS
PER SALES REPRESENTATIVE
*SALARY PLUS BONUS OR COMMISSION
DATA: EXECUTIVE COMPENSATION SERVICE INC.

salesman a sales order because of the tape I made," Scott adds. "It's just one part of the [sales] puzzle."

Moreover, salespeople have found that customers can get bored or distracted when looking at a video presentation. "Viewers tend to zero in on the speaker's acting abilities, because it's film," says David R. Fernald, vice-president for marketing at Datapoint Corp., a San Antonio manufacturer of office-automation equipment. "And sometimes that leads to criticisms that the speaker didn't move his arms enough or something like that."

Despite the alternatives, the telephone remains the most reliable and inexpensive tool in the work of the business-to-business sales force. Telemarketing ranges from perfunctory order-taking to an active sales program. In most cases, it consists of a small number of incoming Wide-Area Telecom-

munications Service (WATS) lines attended by operators. When sales prospects call for information about a product or service, the operator determines the extent of the interest and whether or not a salesperson should call on the new prospect. If so, information about the caller is passed on to the sales office.

An increasing number of companies, however, are setting up inside sales forces that actively solicit business from existing and potential customers. Selling by phone "inserts the salesperson into the customer decision-making process in a timely fashion," says Merrill R. Tutton, sales vice-president at AT&T Communications, one of the primary beneficiaries of the telemarketing phenomenon. "An inside salesperson is just like an outside salesperson without wheels." He says telemarketing can be helpful in four areas: order processing, customer services such as technical-assistance hotlines, sales support, and account management, or providing data to the sales force and top management.

Telemarketing has become so popular that some companies are taking their salespeople off the road and bringing them back to headquarters, where they are retrained to sell by phone. At Louisiana Oil & Tire Co., all 10 of the traveling salespeople were brought inside and put at a bank of phones. Since then the company's phone bill has increased by $6,000 a month, but other sales expenses have declined by $15,000 a month. More important, says Gregory B. Martin, sales manager, is that sales have doubled.

SHIFTING ROLES. Telemarketing works, says Emmett G. Cobb, a former Louisiana Oil & Tire executive, because customers are too busy with their own work to spend much time with salespeople. "Today, customers say, 'Give me the product, give me the price, and see you later, alligator.'"

Cobb's informal assessment of the marketplace is backed by research. According to a study of trends in the wholesale-distribution industry conducted by Arthur Andersen & Co., customers say personal contact with a salesperson is becoming less important to them than contact with a capable inside sales force. The study says that by 1990, half of a company's sales force will be inside and that the role of the outside salesperson will shift toward promotion and customer instruction and away from field sales.

"The salesperson will become more of a trainer, a technical adviser and consultant as opposed to an order-taker," says Steven B. Zimmerman, a partner at Arthur Andersen. Murray Roman, chairman of Campaign Communication Institute of America Inc., operator of telephone marketing programs, agrees. "The future is for the sales specialist rather than the sales rep," Roman says. "The salesman will become more technical and more specialized. The one who can be replaced by a telephone is not a specialist."

'PAPERLESS ORDERING.' In fact, technology has made what was a primary function of the salesperson, order-taking, almost obsolete. As more and more companies buy sophisticated mainframe computers, which are capable of "talking" to each other, "paperless ordering" is becoming common. Customers of American Hospital Supply Corp. in Evanston, Ill., can enter purchase orders into their computer, have it contact American Hospital's mainframe, find out instantly what is available and when it can be shipped, and place the order automatically. Called analytical systems automated purchasing *(ASAP)*, it frees the company's 3,100 sales reps to "detail high-tech products. We didn't want order-takers for salespeople," says Gail S. Gulinson, director of hospitals systems. "We said, 'Let's make our salesforce more productive,' and they are."

Companies are reluctant to say that these new tactics can or will ultimately eliminate the need for an outside sales force. Even businesses using sophisticated electronic marketing techniques have kept their salespeople, but they have given them different duties, such as those at Louisiana Oil & Tire. But Campaign Communication's Roman warns against taking the good outside salesperson off the road and putting him on the phone. "The personality skills that make for a successful salesman make for a lousy telemarketer," he says. "A salesman uses the way he dresses, the way he acts, everything, to sell." Still, Roman agrees that the days of the Willy Lomans are numbered. "You don't need Murray Roman to tell you what is happening; Arthur Miller said it better."

Advertising

AND NOW, A WITTIER WORD FROM OUR SPONSORS

ADVERTISERS ARE VYING FOR VIEWERS WITH GLITZY, CREATIVE COMMERCIALS

MARCH 24, 1986, PP. 90, 91, 94

You'd never know it's a detergent commercial. There are no kids spilling ice cream or catsup all over themselves, no close-ups of dirt that lifts out in seconds. Instead, the pulsating beat of the popular '60s song *High-Heeled Sneakers* sets the tone for Colgate-Palmolive Co.'s new Fresh Start ad, in which a young housewife scrambles to get ready for a night on the town with her husband. The 30-second message ends with the line, "Concentrated Fresh Start—because there's more to life than laundry."

No doubt Colgate has known that all along, but it's the first time the consumer-products giant has said so—and the unorthodox commercial has won raves from viewers.

The Fresh Start commercial is not the only one turning viewers' heads these days. A new spot for Gillette's Right Guard deodorant forgoes the usual shots of hardworking Americans, offering instead a fanciful barroom scene where a cyclops woos a sultry blonde. Then there are the dramatic *Sports Illustrated* ads that zero in on a baseball player sharing his thoughts as he steps up to bat.

Not all of today's commercials are so innovative, but a revolution is taking place nonetheless. The usual stand-up pitchmen and annoying jingles are giving way to ads that often are as entertaining as the shows they finance.

A growing number of commercials softly cajole rather than hammer home their selling points. Some are packaged like the music-video programming created by *MTV* Networks Inc. Others are glossy mini-epics or futuristic flights of fantasy. But this creative renaissance is firmly rooted in reality: Advertisers now realize that viewers are no longer a captive audience. To keep people tuned in, they must produce better ads.

ZIPPING AND ZAPPING. Before cable *TV* and videorecorders, this wasn't necessary. The three networks dominated the medium. If viewers bothered to get up and change channels during a commercial break, all they were likely to find were other commercials. Today they have many more options. Some 45% of U. S. homes get cable *TV*, and 20% have sets equipped with remote-control units that make it easy to zip around the dial.

About one-third of all homes have *VCR*s, and more than one-half are expected to have such machines by 1990. Users can record *TV* programs and "zap" through the commercials by hitting the fast-forward button when they play back tapes. The research on zipping and zapping is still preliminary. But Jane Fuller, senior vice-president and media director at Jordan, Case, Taylor & McGrath Inc., a New York ad agency, believes advertisers are "in for a rude awakening" when they see final results. She predicts that by the year 2000 about 60% of all television viewers will be tuning out ads.

This is dire news to the companies that spent $21 billion on *TV* commercials last year—especially when they face advertising costs that are increasing much faster than inflation. So is a recent study by *Advertising Age*: Half the people surveyed couldn't recall any specific ad. And companies can only wonder what will happen as commercial clutter increases. If 15-second ads become the norm, as many predict, the number of commercials would double. According to Ronald B. Kaatz, senior vice-president at J. Walter Thompson *USA*, research shows the more commercials consumers see, the less they like them.

Given all this, it's no wonder that "more advertisers are willing to take risks in terms of creativity," says Dick Draper, advertising director for *AT&T* Information Systems. "If people don't watch your ads, you've thrown your money away."

DANCING CARS. Chanel No. 5's 1979 "Share the Fantasy" spot probably paved the way for today's creative revolution. The ad, directed by Ridley Scott (box), showed a swimsuit-clad woman sitting by a pool. As a man appeared at the far end of the pool and swam toward her, an ethereal female voice whispered: "I am made of blue sky and golden light, and I will feel this way forever." The viewer never knew whether the man was meant to be real or merely part of the woman's fantasy.

Other companies, such as Ford Motor Co.'s Lincoln-Mercury Div., soon jumped aboard the new-wave bandwagon. A 1980 Mercury Lynx commercial, showing a mountain lion stalking a Mercury in the desert, was a startling departure from traditional automobile advertising. Mercury's current Sable ad, while less surreal, is no less innovative. Set to '60s hits such as *Do You Want to Dance?*, the ad by Young & Rubicam is edited so that the car's movement seems dancelike. Sable now has a three-month order backlog—and Thomas B. Ryan Jr., national advertising manager for Lincoln-Mercury, credits the ad with helping make the car an immediate success.

One thing that distinguishes the Sable commercial and other new campaigns is their highly sophisticated cinematography—most evident in such mini-epics as Apple Computer Inc.'s much-publicized extravaganza, reminiscent of George Orwell's *1984*, used to introduce its Macintosh computer. This isn't surprising, since many directors of today's commercials are also successful movie directors: Adrian Lyne (*Flashdance*), Hugh Hudson (*Chariots of Fire*), and Ridley Scott (*Alien*).

THE MTV LOOK. The moviemakers' influence can be seen especially in the ad industry's use of elaborate, expensive special effects. Pepsi went all out on a *Close Encounters of the Third Kind* parody, and Timex's current ad for its new Atlantis 100

sports watch cost a cool million to produce. The ad takes viewers beneath the Red Sea, where eerie lighting reveals scuba divers uncovering a 60-ft.-long replica of the watch.

The *MTV* look is also much in evidence. General Foods Corp.'s Kool-Aid ads once showed thirsty kids on skateboards. No more: Today's ads are filled with rapid-fire images of the animated "Kool-Aid man" breaking through walls into an executive-filled boardroom and of a boy flying in a biplane with a parrot perched on his shoulder.

Even commercials for traditionally staid advertisers are showing new spark. Metropolitan Life Insurance Co. features characters from the *Peanuts* comic strip to sell insurance. American Telephone & Telegraph Co., another company that used to stick closely to institutional messages, has turned to the Swiss mime troupe Mummenschanz to illustrate how it can link different telecommunications systems.

Whatever the creative execution, advertisers are trying to capture viewers' attention by rebelling against old formulas. "In the 1970s, a lot of advertising insulted viewers' intelligence," says Jay Schulberg, creative head at Ogilvy & Mather-New York. "Too many ads had artificial people saying artificial things in artificial circumstances."

John Ferrell, creative director at Young & Rubicam New York, says the volatile economy in the decade following the oil embargo made advertisers conservative. They wanted "safe" campaigns. "The *MBA*s took control, and no one cared if there was a real creative idea," Ferrell says. As companies tried to reduce advertising to a science, commercials became loaded with product mentions, facts, and demonstrations. Compare that kind of ad with Pizza Hut's current campaign, which shows celebrities talking about how they like to eat pizza. Pizza Hut isn't even mentioned until the final frame.

The bottom line: ads that are fun to watch. "In the past, advertising took itself too seriously," says Ferrell. "It may be a life-and-death matter to a client, but it's usually not to a consumer."

The danger in the new advertising, however, is that companies may be exchanging one formula for another. Many ads made in the style of music videos, for example, look alike. J. Roy Grace, who

HOW THE MAN WHO MADE *ALIEN* INVADED MADISON AVENUE

Ridley Scott has taken the Pepsi Challenge, and Coke thinks he's it: The hottest new-wave director on Madison Avenue recently directed commercials for both—yes, both—soft-drink companies.

How did Scott become so popular that the two main combatants in the cola wars turned to him for firepower? It started in 1979 with his ground-breaking "Share the Fantasy" commercials for Chanel No. 5, which created a sensuous haze between dreams and reality. And his *1984*-inspired Apple Computer commercial was the most talked-about ad of that year—even though it ran only once.

Still, the British filmmaker seems surprised at the suggestion that he has helped inspire a new look in American *TV* advertising. "If that's what they think, you've made my day," says Scott, sitting in the shadow of a giant *TV* screen, in his stylish black-and-white office in London's Soho district.

ARTISTIC EDGE. Scott began directing television commercials in London in 1967 at the request of an ad agency executive who had used Scott as a free-lance set designer. But Scott didn't abandon advertising when he moved up to feature films such as *Alien, Blade Runner,* and *The Duellists.* "If you're a filmmaker and you're not filmmaking, that's a fallow period," says Scott. "It's like being an athlete. If you're not running around the track, you're losing your edge."

To Scott, directing commercials is just as artistically fulfilling as doing a movie. "It is like doing a pocket version of a feature film," he explains. "The advantage with advertising is you don't have to live with something for months on end." Another advantage is the pay. Scott says it can take anywhere from 1 to 10 days to film a commercial, and he reportedly gets paid $10,000 a day.

Scott won't discuss his fees, but he will offer an explanation for the new wave of advertising: economics. Innovation is "closely tied up with how much money is being spent," he says. When he arrived in New York 15 years ago, the country was at the brink of a recession and at the tail end of an era of great advertising. "Now," he says, "some of the best creative thinking is coming out of the U. S. again."

As for his influence on American advertising, Scott says: "I think any top-of-the-line director, certainly if he's been [at the top] over a period, is bound to be an influence on the group that follows." And Scott has been around long enough to call himself an "old fogey." Says he: "I just stagger along. Whether I like it or not, I'm one of the Establishment." But it is an Establishment he helped create.

By Barbara Rosen in London

---

created highly acclaimed Avis and Volkswagen commercials at Doyle Dane Bernbach Inc. in the 1960s, sees a problem with the new ads, which, he says, often have nothing to do with the product. They're just "hollow gloss," says Grace, who now heads Grace & Rothschild, a New York ad agency. He doubts that the new breed of advertising is boosting sales.

Nonetheless, a recent study by the Ogilvy Center for Research & Development found that people who like a commercial are twice as likely to be persuaded by it than those who feel lukewarm toward it. But no matter what the research shows,

ultimately, only advertisers' earnings will prove whether the new approach is working.

DEATH OF A SALESMAN. At least one unconventional ad campaign is on its way out because of poor results. Last November, Burger King put $40 million behind its effort to promote the nerdy-looking Herb, the only person in America who has never tasted a Whopper. Although the campaign increased viewer awareness of Burger King, sales were "disappointing," according to an executive at Pillsbury Co., which owns Burger King. The campaign will end this month.

Even great ads can suffer if poor ones surround

them. If the first commercial during a station break is a dud, viewers are likely to switch the channel, missing the messages that follow. To overcome that problem, companies such as Alcoa, American Cyanamid, and *IBM* have taken to running short programming with their commercials. During sports telecasts, for example, American Cyanamid Co. shows footage of a great sports achievement and follows it with a commercial for Old Spice. Says Jim Gibbs, director of advertising services for consumer products at Cyanamid: "Because we have attached programming, somebody is going to see our ads."

Holdout advertisers may have little choice but to join the creative revolution. "It's important [that] the industry as a whole elevates the quality of its work," says Diane Rothschild of Grace & Rothschild. "If that doesn't happen, people may tune out advertising altogether."

By Christine Dugas in New York

NEW LIFE FOR MADISON AVENUE'S OLD-TIME STARS

APRIL 1, 1985, PP. 94, 95

What 25-year-old star is better known than Vice-President George Bush, even though he hasn't been seen on television in 10 years? Hint: He's bald, muscular, and wears a single earring.

Answer: Mr. Clean, the genie who has graced the bottle of Procter & Gamble Co.'s household cleaner of the same name since 1959. Despite his long sabbatical from *TV*, Mr. Clean was identified and described by 93% of consumers in a recent *P&G* poll. In contrast, a *People* magazine poll showed that only 56% of shoppers knew who George Bush was. With that kind of popularity, it's no wonder that Mr. Clean is making a comeback. He stars as "The Man Behind the Shine" in a new ad campaign.

P&G is not alone in returning to tried-and-true advertising. Philip Morris Inc.'s Seven-Up Co., for example, is again calling its lemon-lime-flavored soft drink the "Uncola," a description the company abandoned in the mid-1970s. And Switzer Clark, a division of Leaf Inc., recently brought the character of Choo Choo Charlie back to life in ads for Good & Plenty candy. The boy engineer hadn't run the Good & Plenty train since 1974.

The resuscitation of characters and themes of yore is surprising in the world of Madison Avenue, where everything is supposed to be new and improved. But the images that flickered across *TV* screens in the 1960s occupy a unique place in the hearts and minds of baby boomers who grew up in front of the tube. In contrast, much of today's advertising "says the same thing, and it's all disappearing in people's minds," explains John R. McKee, group creative director at Tatham-Laird & Kudner, *P&G*'s agency for Mr. Clean. And so some marketers are striking a nostalgic chord to distinguish themselves from the competition.

SINGING ALONG. Seven-Up is a good example. The company experienced strong sales gains two years ago when it began promoting its soda as a caffeine-free alternative. That success, however, brought similar campaigns from Coca-Cola's Sprite and Pepsi's Slice. By going back to the Uncola pitch, "what we're really trying to do is point out that, despite these other no-caffeine products, there's still only one Uncola," says Charles W. Schmid, Seven-Up's executive vice-president. "It's a unique, strong symbol to separate us from the competition." Company research showed that even after 10 years two-thirds of consumers still call Seven-Up the Uncola.

Similarly, Switzer Clark found that plenty of consumers between the ages of 18 and 35 remembered Choo Choo Charlie and could still sing the Good & Plenty jingle. "The awareness level just broke the bank," says Robert P. Zabel, president of the Midwest division of N. W. Ayer & Son Inc., Switzer's ad agency. When the company decided to revitalize its candy brand, it turned to the black-and-white television cartoon that first ran in 1959. The new ad features footage from the old cartoon interspersed with color scenes of baby boomers singing along with the jingle. (Opening couplet: "Once upon a time there was an engi-

Pond's Inc.'s Vaseline Intensive Care. Both products claimed to be the best hand lotion available, and both inundated a court with expert testimony. A federal district judge found much of the testimony incomprehensible and ordered both companies to refrain from making such claims. More

---

'The FTC is no longer even a cop on the beat,' says one lawyer. 'It's doing virtually nothing'

---

recently, American Home Products Corp. has sued Johnson & Johnson for its claims in Tylenol ads that ibuprofen-based analgesics—including *AHP*'s Advil—cause stomach irritation. *J&J*,which denies the allegations, has filed a countersuit.

Advertisers are no happier about a barrage of enforcement efforts by states such as New York, Texas, Massachusetts, and California. New York State Attorney General Robert Abrams challenged Coca-Cola Co. when a consumer complained that diet Coke ads proclaimed, "Now with NutraSweet," even though the product also contained saccharin. Last year, Coca-Cola agreed to change the ads to "NutraSweet blend." Currently, both Texas and New York are investigating Kraft Inc.'s Cheez Whiz ads (table, page 150).

A few advertisers are even getting sued directly by consumers. A California class action against General Foods Corp. claims that ads for some of its sugared cereals were deceptive and preyed on the "unique susceptibility of children." One advertisement for Honeycomb cereal, the plaintiffs allege, showed that after eating the cereal, children had the power to lift large playhouses. They are asking for $25 million in damages.

BAD OLD DAYS. Advertisers would rather such matters be handled by the *NAD*, established in 1971. It evaluates more than 100 complaints annually. But critics complain that it lacks muscle. Cases are kept confidential until resolved, no fines are imposed, and ad changes can only be requested—not ordered. "I usually agree with [the *NAD*'s] decisions, but by the time they get around to making them, the ad probably has been dropped," says Herschel Elkins, senior assistant attorney general of California.

With such challenges coming from all directions, some advertisers may even long for the days of a tougher *FTC*. "We don't want the *FTC* to be like [it was under] Pertschuk," says Douglas J. Wood, an attorney with Hall, Dickler, Lawler, Kent & Friedman, a firm specializing in advertising cases. "But today, the *FTC* is no longer even a cop on the beat. It's doing virtually nothing."

By Christine Dugas in New York, with Paula Dwyer in Washington

PART 4

MARKETING IN SPECIAL FIELDS

The marketing of services and products by profit and nonprofit organizations is big business. Everyone, from Motel 6 to Harvard University, is striving to market what they are selling (or attempting to exchange). Nonprofit organizations want people to use their services, and donate money to help pay the bills for providing their services.

Pressures on American companies to sell outside the U.S. are enormous: international markets are so large and profitable that many American companies generate over half their revenues outside the country. Articles in this part show a side of marketing that many consumers are unaware of. Do you really mean Harvard University practices marketing?

PART 4 ARTICLE SYNOPSES

SERVICE MARKETING

CHEAP DREAMS: THE BUDGET INN BOOM

Motel 6, the pioneer of budget motels is adding amenities, expanding, and increasing its advertising. The company is trying to add business customers to its market of weekend travelers.

    Days Inn introduced the "Supersaver" discounts. It has grown from a regional to a national company. It has used tie-ins with other corporations. However, competition is still strong in the "luxury-budget" market.

A HIGH-POWERED PITCH TO CURE HOSPITALS' ILLS

With the lowest occupancy rates in two decades, hospitals are turning to marketing. They are replacing their old intimidating images with "patient-friendly" images and lower prices. Some are giving their services emotionally charged names to substitute brands for generic services.

Others let the patients tailor their own programs. Even celebrity endorsements are becoming popular.

NONBUSINESS MARKETING

THE BATTLE OF THE B-SCHOOLS IS GETTING BLOODIER

There is an intense competitive struggle between graduate business schools for faculty, students, and respectability. Faculty raids are commonplace. Marketing has become a major consideration. New coursework has been introduced. Although the leading schools are not worried about survival, the bottom end is in danger.

HOSPITAL CHAINS STRUGGLE TO STAY IN THE PINK

Recent changes in government and corporate health plans have substantially reduced hospital occupancy. Hospitals have been forced to cut costs to remain profitable. Hospital firms are likely to increase their moves into alternative services to gain market share. Some hospitals are offering health insurance to compete with health maintenance organizations. Hospital cost cutting is having a strong effect on medical suppliers.

INTERNATIONAL MARKETING

HOW KODAK IS TRYING TO MOVE MOUNT FUJI

Although Kodak is three times the size of Fuji, it holds only 15 percent of the market for consumer color film in Japan. Kodak has created a subsidiary just for Japan, tripling its Japanese staff. Meanwhile, Fuji has increased its assault on overseas markets. Kodak has established relationships with major Japanese corporations and has introduced 20 new products in Japan in the last year.

FIGHTING BACK: IT CAN WORK

Big companies are fighting back against Japanese competition. Several have been successful in halting the Japanese advance. Others have been waiting for external factors to change things. Instead of being merely defenders, the successful companies have become aggressors.

CHEAP DREAMS: THE BUDGET INN BOOM

JULY 14, 1986, PP. 76, 77

A clean room, a comfortable bed, a hot shower, a color TV. That's really all most travelers want. And they don't want to pay an arm and a leg for it. With many full-service hotels priced beyond the reach of ordinary travelers and business people not on expense accounts, economy lodging is booming. These hotels charge 20% to 50% less than the average rates in their areas. They provide bargain accommodations because guests don't get such amenities as fancy lobbies and restaurants.

Economy chains now account for more than 12% of the 2.7 million hotel rooms in the U. S., compared with less than 10% in 1980, says Daniel W. Daniele, a lodging expert at accountants Laventhol & Horwath. And the number of economy inns is up to 3,500 from 1,500 in 1980.

With competition getting tougher, here's how the two economy leaders—Days Inns of America Inc. at the upper end, Motel 6 Inc. at the lower—are trying to tuck more people into bed.

MOTEL 6: WOOING THE FRUGAL BUSINESS CROWD

Willy Loman would be in heaven. Propping up his sore salesman's feet, he could watch the new color *TV* and even call home—now there's a phone on the night table. Sure, the room is small. But it only costs 15 bucks.

Welcome, Willy, to the new Motel 6. The pioneer of spartan lodging gave the world the $6 motel room (hence the name) 25 years ago when it opened its first inn in Santa Barbara, Calif. It now owns 401 properties in 39 states. However, competitors with slightly spiffier rooms—including Econo Lodges of America, Red Roof Inns, and Days Inns—have helped push Motel 6's occupancy down to 59% from 81% in 1981.

Since buyout specialist Kohlberg Kravis Roberts & Co. bought the chain for $881 million last year, Motel 6 Inc. has been adding such amenities as phones and color *TV*s. It is also launching a major marketing push. Except for billboards near its motels, the chain has never advertised. "I find that astonishing," says Joseph W. McCarthy, who worked for Sheraton Corp. and then Quality Inns Inc. before *KKR* hired him in January to be Motel 6's president.

McCarthy, 54, aims to tap a new market: business travelers with limited expenses. These weeknight guests would balance Motel 6's primary clientele—weekend pleasure travelers. The company is also mulling a toll-free reservation system. And it will spend heavily to spruce up run-down rooms.

Remodeling would help: In a recent *Consumer Reports* survey, customers liked Motel 6 least among 14 budget chains. To be fair, its bills are also the smallest. Singles run from $14.95 in Texas to $24.95 in California, or about $5 less than competitors. "Their customers are the sort who ask themselves, 'Do I sleep in my car or at a Motel 6?'" says Henry R. Silverman, chairman of Days Inns of America Inc.

LIKE THE BEETLE. Motel 6 hopes its radio and *TV* ads, to air this fall, will make businessmen feel comfortable about lodging on the cheap. "It's like the *VW* Beetle, which was so practical you felt good about driving it," says Stan Richards, president of Richards Group Inc. in Dallas, Motel 6's ad agency.

Motel 6 also plans to expand faster, aiming to blanket the U. S. before its rivals do. It will build some 30 motels a year—up 50% from recent years. Most will be in the Northeast, where it has few units. Later this month, to help finance expansion, it hopes to raise $270 million by selling 40% of the company to the public.

Motel 6 needs growth. New properties kept its bottom line strong until last year. Then competi-tion and debt on *KKR*'s buyout produced a $20 million pretax loss on sales of $236 million. Still, sources say *KKR* is so sure of growth that it plans to hold its majority interest for the long-term.

Tax-law changes, however, could encourage the building of budget motels, with their fast cash flow, says Saul F. Leonard, a hotel expert for Laventhol & Horwath. That may be bad news for Motel 6. But at least the nation's weary salesmen will have more places to prop their feet.

By Stewart Toy in Los Angeles

A HIGH-POWERED PITCH TO CURE HOSPITALS' ILLS

LOW OCCUPANCY RATES PROMPT A NEW ERA OF MARKETING MANAGERS, HEART-TUGGING ADS, AND FANCY ROOMS
SEPTEMBER 2, 1985, PP. 60, 61

"Complete face lift... was $941, now $675; Breast augmentation... was $504, now $315; Tubal ligation... was $441, now $345."

A few years ago no respectable hospital would have put its name on such a crass sales pitch. But Humana Inc. recently took out ads promoting just such "specials" in local newspapers to drum up business for its Humana Hospital Phoenix.

Welcome to the new gloves-off world of hospital marketing. With occupancy rates at 66%, the lowest in two decades, hospitals are suddenly fighting for patients like product managers clawing for another fraction of the breakfast cereal market. Traditionally, hospitals have been unable "to use the word 'marketing' without gagging," observes Terrence J. Rynne, a health care marketing consultant in Evanston, Ill. Those days are gone.

Indeed, hospitals have seized on marketing with all the fervor—and some of the excesses—of the newly converted. "Today every hospital is trying to hire somebody into a marketing position," says J. Daniel Beckham, president of HealthMarket Inc., a consulting firm in Arlington Heights, Ill.

"The demand for talent is overwhelming. I must get three to four calls a week from headhunters." Those new marketing managers are engaging high-powered advertising agencies, running slick radio and *TV* spots, and plastering their hospitals' messages on billboards, buses, and trains.

One example of the new aggressiveness: A number of hospitals tried to capitalize on President Reagan's recent colonoscopy by offering free colon cancer detection kits and advertising the importance of getting checkups, "no matter what your job."

'PATIENT-FRIENDLY.' Hospital administrators are trying to compensate for a loss of business attributable to a clampdown on health care spending by both the government and employers. They have watched admissions during the first four months of this year fall 6.3%, the biggest drop since 1963. And they can no longer depend on doctors to send them patients. Instead of relying on their physicians' preferences, better-educated consumers are increasingly deciding where they want to stay.

The most successful hospitals are asking the most basic market research question of all—what do consumers want?—and are changing accordingly. The result: Say goodbye to tacky linoleum, disapproving nurses, and hours of waiting. Instead, "patient-friendly hospitals" offer gourmet meals, brass birthing beds, and "hotel" rooms for family members.

Christ Hospital, in Oak Lawn, Ill., is typical of the new breed. It is creating a *VIP* service for well-heeled patients. Those willing to pay a premium of about 20% can recover in rooms decorated with 18th-century-style furniture while dining on specially prepared meals served on fine china. In the evening, they'll find a Godiva chocolate on their turned-down beds. "It's like staying at the Ritz," gushes Carl A. Zimmerman, vice-president for operations at Evangelical Health Systems, the hospital's parent.

For consumers, the new competitive environment means more palatable and cheaper health care. Marketing won't be a cure-all, however, for hospitals' ills. It raises the cost of staying in business at a time when revenues are shrinking. Ultimately, that will speed the consolidation already under way. "Smaller hospitals are finding that the cost of advertising can be enormous," says Steven G. Hillestad, vice-president for marketing at Lifespan Inc., which owns an 800-bed Minneapolis hospital. "So it causes them to rethink whether or not they should be part of a chain."

EMOTION-PACKED. The chains, thanks to economies of scale, have enormous marketing advantages. Dallas-based Republic Health Corp., which owns or manages 90 institutions, credits its aggressive packaged-goods mentality with increasing earnings 420%, to $22.7 million, over the past two years. The product managers of Republic, the Procter & Gamble of hospital companies, work with focus groups and advertising agencies to create promotional packages—often touting low prices—for the surgical procedures and services offered by its hospitals.

The 11 "products"—bearing emotion-packed names such as Gift of Sight for cataract surgery and Miracle Moments for childbirth—will be backed by a $20 million marketing budget this year, almost double what Republic spent last year. An ad for You're Becoming, Republic's cosmetic surgery package, features a negligee-clad woman and will appear in *Cosmopolitan*; a male-targeted version may run in *Playboy*.

"We're trying to substitute brands for generic services," explains Michael J. Haley, senior vice-president for market development and architect of Republic's program. He says hospitals using Gift of Sight have increased the amount of cataract surgery they do by as much as 50%. Republic is

---

After Reagan's cancer surgery, hospitals began promoting checkups 'no matter what your job'

---

now licensing its promotional ideas to unaffiliated hospitals.

CELEBRITY PITCH. Experts consider Humana's multipronged marketing the most advanced in the industry. Using careful research with physicians and patients, a central staff works with the 90 Humana hospitals to remodel and implement a wide range of service products such as cancer screening, senior citizen care, outpatient surgery, and breast diagnostic centers. And Humana works hard to make sure the public knows about the quality of its care. The attention given Humana's Louisville hospital, where William Schroeder's artificial heart was recently implanted, transmitted a "halo" of quality to the entire Humana system, notes Douglas B. Sherlock, a vice-president at Salomon Bros.

Given the chains' built-in advantages, smaller hospitals must work harder to compete. Consider St. Joseph's Hospital, a 261-bed institution in St. Paul, Minn. Located downtown, it serves an aging population. The Minneapolis metropolitan area also has one of the highest *HMO* enrollments in the country—40%—but St. Joseph's gets few *HMO* patients. One result: Obstetrics admissions fell 25% from 1979 to 1983. Jim Thalhuber, the hospital's director of marketing, set out to change that.

"Research showed women felt every baby is unique," he says. "So we asked how we could design a service to help make this event unique." Every mother-to-be now gets a private room and deals primarily with one nurse. Patients can also design their own delivery, choosing to have music played or to have their children present. For husbands who don't want to be in the delivery room, the hospital added a new waiting room that includes lockers, showers, desks, and telephones. Admissions jumped 10% last year.

Baptist Hospital, a 750-bed independent, has committed itself to becoming the low-cost provider in Nashville, even though Nashville is home to Hospital Corp. of America, the nation's largest chain. "We cannot compete dollar for dollar," explains Robert E. Johnson, Baptist's marketing / communications vice-president. So Baptist tries to get the most for its money by airing commercials featuring celebrities such as Dallas Cowboys Coach Tom Landry and country singer Barbara Mandrell, who was hospitalized at Baptist last year after a serious auto accident.

Baptist's real zinger comes from entertainer Jerry Reed. In promoting Baptist's new $15 million medical center, he explains that it was built to keep people out of the hospital. Then Reed looks straight into the camera and says: "Do you think they'd do that if they had to pay a profit to shareholders?"

By Ellyn E. Spragins in Chicago

THE BATTLE OF THE B-SCHOOLS IS GETTING BLOODIER

BIG-NAME SCHOOLS 'COMPETE LIKE CRAZY' FOR TOP-FLIGHT FACULTY AND STUDENTS

MARCH 24, 1986, PP. 61, 64, 66, 67, 70

No peace pipes were smoked. No peace treaties were signed. But when Harvard business school Dean John H. McArthur met the soon-to-be-named dean of Stanford business school, the pair agreed to a truce between the two giants of graduate business education.

A nip-and-tuck race had developed over which school was best. Some polls favored Stanford; others gave Harvard the nod. Stanford's Rene C. McPherson, recovering from a near-fatal auto accident, was on his back in traction, in a Toledo hospital when McArthur visited him in the spring of 1981. McPherson suggested they were largely competing against second- and third-rate diploma mills. "Who's first and who's second and who's 28th is a lot of horse----," he recalls saying.

The pair agreed not to criticize each other publicly. The session cooled down the hostility between the two schools, but it hardly put an end to the great B-school wars. Today a competitive struggle for faculty, students, and respectability rages, and it is more intense than ever. As Stanford's current dean, Robert K. Jaedicke, puts it: "We compete like crazy for students, and we compete like crazy for faculty."

FACULTY RAIDS. The publication of starting salaries for *MBA* graduates has become an annual rite of promotional passage for many business schools. Some prominent schools have hired high-powered public relations outfits to promote them. Others have commissioned sophisticated surveys in hopes of discovering how to win greater market share and esteem. Raids on top-name faculty have become commonplace. And in response to wide-spread criticism, business schools are transforming their curriculums, making education less theoretical and more pragmatic—if not downright trendy.

"The recruiting brochures are getting sexier, and I keep running across more of them," says Jack R. Wentworth, dean of Indiana University's business school. "We now have schools with three business faculty members offering *MBA*s."

Fewer than a third of the more than 650 schools in the U. S. offering the *MBA* degree meet even the minimum standards of accreditation set by the American Assembly of Collegiate Schools of Business *(AACSB)*. "Many of these schools come very close to selling the degree," says Raymond E. Miles, dean of the University of California at Berkeley's B-school. Harvard's McArthur maintains that 97% of the schools that offer the degree admit "virtually anyone who applies."

MARKETING PLOYS. Not surprisingly, an *MBA* no longer carries the cachet it once had. This year a record 71,000 graduates armed with the degree will burst forth from campuses. That's nearly a 30% jump from 1980, more than a threefold rise from 1970, and almost a fifteenfold increase from 1960, when only 4,814 got the degree. And more are on the way: Some 200,000 students now are studying for *MBA*s.

"It's hard to convince myself that the world needs 70,000 or so *MBA*s a year," concedes Jaedicke. "If you look at the growth rate over the past 25 years, you could come to the conclusion that everybody in the U. S. will have an *MBA* degree by the year 2010. But I think we're heading into some sort of shakeout."

BW/HARRIS POLL: HOW EXECUTIVES RATE A B-SCHOOL EDUCATION

Executives give business schools high marks, though they think MBAs know little about the realities of running a company. B-school graduates, they feel, are also prone to job-hopping, and expect to get ahead too fast. Even so, executives are likely to recommend getting an MBA to their children who plan business careers.

Q How would you rate the quality of education most business school graduates receive—excellent, pretty good, only fair, or poor?

A Excellent 11%
Pretty good 70%
Only fair 13%
Poor 1%
Not sure 5%

Q In your own company, in order to get ahead today, how important is it for an executive to have an MBA—very important, somewhat important, not very important, or not important at all?

A Very important 8%
Somewhat important 41%
Not very important 38%
Not important at all 13%

Q Do you yourself have an MBA?

A Have an MBA 23%
Do not have an MBA 77%

Q Since you don't have an MBA, have you ever wished you had one, or hasn't it made much difference?

A Wished I had one............................... 21%
Made little difference..........................77%
Not sure 2%

Q Business schools teach students a lot about management theory but not much about what it takes to run a company.

A Agree 86%
Disagree 10%
Not sure 4%

Q It makes sense for people with MBAs to get higher salaries than people with the same work experience but no degree.

A Agree 33%
Disagree 64%
Not sure 3%

Q Younger employees with MBAs tend to have less loyalty and job-hop a lot more than employees without the degree.

A Agree 63%
Disagree 25%
Not sure 12%

Q Even if merit and abilities are equal, people with MBAs often get promoted faster than people without the degree.

A Agree 56%
Disagree 37%
Not sure 7%

Q Business school graduates tend to be overbearing and abrasive and don't get on well with their colleagues.

A Agree 18%
Disagree 76%
Not sure 6%

Q Business school graduates tend to have unrealistic expectations about how fast they will get ahead in their careers.

A Agree 78%
Disagree 18%
Not sure 4%

Q Do you feel that the starting salary that MBA graduates are getting these days is too high, too low, or about right?

A Too high.. 45%
Too low 0%
About right 45%
Not sure 10%

Q If your son or daughter were planning a career in business, would you advise him or her to get an MBA, or not?

A Would advise to get an MBA.............. 78%
Would not 17%
Not sure 5%

Edited by Stuart Jackson

Survey of 600 senior executives drawn from the BUSINESS WEEK Corporate Scoreboard. Interviews were conducted Feb. 18-25 by Louis Harris & Associates Inc. for BUSINESS WEEK.

The demographics simply do not support the dramatic growth of past years, and many schools already report a falloff in applicants. Schools that lack either strong regional or national identities and are relatively new to the *MBA* game are given slim prospects for survival. "Today the term *MBA* doesn't mean that much," says Dean Russell E. Palmer of the University of Pennsylvania's Wharton School. "Now it's where you get it."

Many others agree with him. "We're going to have a harder time as the enrollment pools shrink," concedes Roy A. Herberger, dean of Southern Methodist University's business school. As a smaller institution with a largely regional reputation, *SMU* still can boast an unusual market advantage: It is virtually alone in granting the *MBA* to students after only one year of study. While many of Herberger's colleagues look askance at such an approach, he believes that more B-schools will begin to offer one-year degrees as the market continues to tighten.

Still, even the elite schools with national reputations are working to ensure that they'll remain in the upper tier when the fallout begins. The struggle for increased recognition has compelled some B-schools to turn to aggressive marketing. The University of Virginia's admissions office offers potential students a toll-free telephone number: 800-*UVA-MBA*-1. New York University's business school has hired the former managing editor of *The Charlotte Observer* in North Carolina as its director of public affairs.

Schools are also taking a lesson from Madison Avenue in product differentiation. Wharton, long known for research in finance, has made a major effort in international business under its two-year-old Joseph H. Lauder Institute. Wharton wants to teach future managers how to deal with global competition. Duke University's Fuqua business school has bet much of its future on information technology. Students use computers in 75% of their required courses and check out floppy disks from the school library.

A spate of schools are conducting research and introducing courses in such hot areas as entrepreneurship, leadership, operations management, and technology as a management tool. The race to get faculty to teach these and other courses has exacerbated a faculty shortage caused largely by the *MBA* explosion.

'MATINEE IDOLS.' Aggressive deans, seeking to propel their schools into the top 10 or to secure their current ranking, are in some cases offering to double and triple the salaries of "matinee-idol" faculty from other schools to lure them away. "The schools are looking for stars and will pay big premiums for them," explains a Stanford official.

Wharton's Palmer has been among the most active deans in bidding up salaries by luring already tenured, professorial "stars" such as Robert H. Litzenberger from Stanford, David F. Larcker from Northwestern, and Ian C. MacMillan from *NYU*. In the past 2½ years, Palmer has recruited 58 new faculty members, a third of Wharton's total, and has committed $20 million toward building a new executive education facility to open next year.

"When Wharton hired two tenured professors in accounting from Northwestern last year, it raised some salaries and eyebrows," says Gilbert R. Whitaker Jr., dean of the University of Michigan's business school. "Now there are raids going on all over the place. The best schools are all looking at the same handful of people."

Palmer's self-styled "Plan for Preeminence" seems to be paying off. A poll of corporate recruiters last year ranked Wharton ahead of Harvard, Chicago, and Stanford—traditionally considered the three best B-schools. In *BUSINESS WEEK*'s recent poll of senior executives, Wharton placed third.

ON THE STUMP. Other big winners include Dean Thomas F. Keller of Duke University's Fuqua school and Dean Donald P. Jacobs of Northwestern University's Kellogg school. Both deans have significantly enhanced the image of their institutions by bringing aboard new faculty and taking risks with new curriculums. And neither of them is shy of publicity. "They caught on early to the value of effective public relations and have not been reticent about getting out to tell their stories," says Charles W. Hickman, an *AACSB* official.

Keller's expansionist strategy has more than doubled Fuqua's enrollment since 1980, to 460 graduate students. But that growth has forced him

20 LEADING BUSINESS SCHOOLS—
BY THE NUMBERS

School	Budget (millions)	Specialties and characteristics	Annual tuition	Applicants accepted
CALIFORNIA (Berkeley)	$12	A leader in organizational theory and finance; among best MBA education values	$5,222	27%
CARNEGIE–MELLON	9*	Highest faculty/student ratio, 1-to-2.6; known for its quantitative approach	10,600	39
CHICAGO	25	Highly regarded for its expertise in economics, finance, and accounting	11,400	30*
COLUMBIA	27	Blends theory and practice; 300 executives lectured on campus last year	11,280	29
CORNELL (Johnson)	9	Known for expertise in accounting and finance; claims low dropout rate of only 2%	11,100	48
DARTMOUTH (Amos Tuck)	4	First graduate business school in 1900; small classes and teamwork	11,000	23
DUKE (Fuqua)	9	A leader in information technology; 43% of students enter Fuqua direct from college	11,400	67
HARVARD	100	Boasts best teaching faculty; pioneered case-study approach to problem-solving	10,750	18
INDIANA	7	Lowest annual tuition for a leading school; claims its graduates don't job-hop	5,043	34
MIT (Sloan)	16	Known for finance and economics; has largest foreign student group (29% of total)	11,200	29
MICHIGAN	22**	Blends analytical and practical; auto companies heavy recruiters	9,200	53
NEW YORK UNIVERSITY	23	Has lowest faculty/student ratio at 1-to-16; offers more than 250 electives	10,308	44
NORTHWESTERN (Kellogg)	18	Has one of the largest executive education programs; a leader in marketing	11,295	23
PENNSYLVANIA (Wharton)	25	Known for outstanding finance work, now putting major focus on international business	11,565	29
ROCHESTER	9	Emphasizes analytical approach; small classes and economics expertise	10,500	53
STANFORD	20	Often cited by deans as the best school for combining theory with practice	11,100	9
TEXAS (Austin)	11**	Growing emphasis on such hot topics as entrepreneurship and technology	11,000	41
UCLA	12	Respected for combining theory and practice; a leader in financial theory	5,252	24
VIRGINIA (Darden)	5	Offers a Harvard-like regimen, stressing communications skills and teamwork	7,440	43
YALE	9	Admits only those with work experience; largest female student group (46% of total)	10,350	20

* BW estimate   ** Includes undergraduate business school

Graduate business schools love numbers. Most of the leading schools preach business by quantitative analysis and modeling. That may explain their preoccupation with comparative statistics on their own institutions. The table below contains a slew of them.

Where a student goes will help determine how many offers he gets, how intimate an education he

1985 graduates***	Most common first jobs	Average starting salary	Highest offer	Companies recruiting	Prominent alumni
249	Finance (27%) Consulting (19%)	$36,622	$80,000	160	James Harvey, chmn., TransAmerica
124	Finance (25%) Consulting (20%)	36,500	70,000	140	Gerald Meyers, ex-chmn., AMC
504	Finance (45%) Marketing (14%)	38,500	80,000	234	Steven Rothmeier, CEO, Northwest Air
590	Banking (42%) Accounting (5%)	39,588	49,000	300	Warren Buffett, chmn., Berkshire Hathaway
235	Finance (20%) Consulting (20%)	36,525	65,000	150	I. MacAllister Booth, chmn., Polaroid
141	Finance (22%) Consulting (19%)	42,620	62,500	150	Owen Butler, chmn., P&G
212	Banking (24%) Marketing (20%)	36,118	62,500	135	David Bagwell, pres., Crow Development
780	Consulting (31%) Finance (28%)	44,500*	75,000	342	James Burke, CEO, Johnson & Johnson
332	Finance (28%) Marketing (18%)	31,500	61,000	300	Harold Poling, pres., Ford Motor
193	Consulting (24%) Banking (20%)	42,000	70,000	141	John Reed, CEO, Citicorp
350	Finance (40%) Consulting (8%)	35,000	65,000	330	Roger Smith, chmn., General Motors
362	Banking (34%) Marketing (9%)	37,750	58,000	200	Henry Kaufman, mng. dir., Salomon Bros.
603	Marketing (17%) Consulting (15%)	40,000*	83,000	300	William Smithburg, chmn., Quaker Oats
710	Finance (28%) Marketing (12%)	42,000	75,000	400	John Sculley, CEO, Apple Computer
251	Finance (25%) Accounting (20%)	30,000	55,000	85	Robert Rich Jr., pres., Rich Products
309	Marketing (22%) Finance (21%)	43,500*	85,000	238	Philip Knight, CEO, Nike
343	Banking (29%) Consulting (22%)	30,651	70,000	330	Howard Beasley, CEO, Lone Star Steel
370	Marketing (24%) Finance (19%)	36,700	80,000	200	Laurence Fink, mng. dir., First Boston
206	Finance (32%) Marketing (20%)	40,200	71,000	208	Ronald Trzcinski, pres., Ohio Mattress Co.
150	Banking (25%) Consulting (18%)	40,000	72,000	140	(First graduating class in 1978)

*** Full-time program   DATA: BW

experiences, and how much he initially makes. Three schools (Carnegie-Mellon, Dartmouth, and Virginia) can boast that more companies visit their campus to recruit than they have students to offer.

A Harvard *MBA* still commands the largest average starting salary at $44,500, followed closely by Stanford and Dartmouth. Yet the reported salary offers reflect base pay only. Both Harvard and Stanford say that a few select graduates garner compensation of more than $100,000 in their first year out after the addition of bonuses and other payments.

Numbers, of course, can mislead. At Yale, where the average starting salary is $40,000, one student reported making only $19,000 after choosing to enter the nonprofit arena. The Stanford graduate who reported getting the highest starting salary—$85,000 base, a $15,000 sign-on bonus, payments for incidental expenses, and a cut of the action in financial deals—brought to his "first job" five years of financial experience along with his *MBA*.

The most selective school by far is Stanford, which accepts only 9% of its applicants. Duke, on the other hand, accepts 67% of those who apply—largely a reflection of its strategy to expand its *MBA* program dramatically. Duke's enrollment is up 51% in the past five years, outpacing all the other leading schools, most of which report stable enrollments.

An *MBA* doesn't come cheaply these days. At Wharton, which has the highest annual tuition, the cost exceeds $23,000—and that doesn't include room and board. The least expensive? Indiana, where tuition is 50% less.

Harvard easily can boast the greatest number of prominent alumni. Examples: Texas Air's Frank Lorenzo, People Express' Donald Burr, *RCA*'s Thornton Bradshaw, American Express' James Robinson, and Ford's Philip Caldwell. That's partly because Harvard's "installed base" of 30,705 alumni exceeds every other school's, and that's more than three times Stanford's output of 9,865 and 10 times Virginia's total. Until last year, Yale's total number of graduates was less than the size of a single Harvard class.

to be far less selective than any of the other leading schools. Fuqua accepts 67% of its applicants vs. Stanford's 9% and Harvard's 18% (table, pages 162-163).

At the same time, academia is undergoing a reexamination of graduate business education itself. Not since 1959, when reviews by both the Ford Foundation and the Carnegie Corp. were highly critical of business education, has there been such introspection. Then, the institutions were attacked for being mere trade schools that lacked the academic rigor of other programs. The result: Business education generally became less vocational and more analytical.

A new round of critics, including some influential B-school professors, argue that business schools are too quantitative and theoretical, that they produce narrow-minded technicians who lack interpersonal and communications skills. Those barbs have driven many educators to add a slew of "soft" courses to their programs. "You are seeing greater concern on such [softer] issues, from people skills to understanding leadership and negotiation," says New York University B-school Dean Richard R. West.

"We want our people well-trained in quantitative methods," says Dean Burton G. Malkiel, of Yale University's school of management. "But the most important thing people can know is how to get along with and motivate others." Yale immediately organizes its new students into small working groups that stress teamwork over individualism. A growing number of schools also are following the lead of Dartmouth and Virginia in requiring students to take oral and written communications courses.

'GOLD-COLLAR.' Even schools that have in the past stressed theory over practice are reaching for greater balance. Consider Carnegie-Mellon University, long a champion of the quantitative approach. Dean Elizabeth Bailey is introducing several "soft" courses: "Crisis Management," taught by former American Motors Corp. Chairman Gerald C. Meyers, is one; "The Gold-Collar Worker," a class that advises students on how best to motivate the growing ranks of "knowledge workers" in service businesses, is another. Bailey also has some faculty members working with major corporations on three-year-long research projects dealing with worker productivity and factory automation—quite a departure from the analytical modeling for which Carnegie-Mellon is known.

"We don't want academics just talking to academics," explains Bailey. "We want to talk to businessmen. Theory has always had the most clout in academia, but the school was ready for this. We're going for more balance. We're making it possible for young people to be in touch with real business."

Similarly, many schools are reaching out to local corporations, trying to link campus research with the executive suite or the shop floor. *MIT*'s Sloan school, another theoretical business haven, has launched a $5 million "Management in the 1990s" research program to examine the impact of technology on management. "It is our reaching out to build bridges with management practice," says Deputy Dean Alvin J. Silk. The University of California at Los Angeles dispatches its second-year *MBA* students in groups to local corporations to act as consultants. Students at Duke use computer data generated from a nearby Westinghouse Electric Corp. plant in an operations management course.

Meantime, the skirmish for students, faculty, and prestige rages on, regardless of the bedside cease-fire negotiated by Harvard and Stanford five years ago. "None of the leading schools are concerned about survival," says J. Clayburn La Force Jr., dean of *UCLA*'s business school. "We're clearly going to survive and do well. But the bottom end of the market is in for a lot of turmoil."

By John A. Byrne in New York

HOSPITAL CHAINS STRUGGLE TO STAY IN THE PINK

JANUARY 14, 1985, P. 112

Upheavals touched off by government and private efforts to control medical costs may reach earthquake proportions this year in the $400 billion health care industry. With occupancy rates in decline, hospital chains are furiously slashing costs to keep earnings on an upward course. Thus, many of the companies that provide medical equipment and supplies are in real pain. For the industry as a whole, predicts Richard K. Eamer, chairman and chief executive of National Medical Enterprises Inc., "there will be rather aggressive marketing in 1985."

After growing at an average rate of 2.3% per year in the late 1970s, admissions to the nation's 6,000 acute-care hospitals flattened out in the early 1980s. Then, last year, as changes in medicare and corporate benefit programs took hold, admissions dropped by 5%, says Randall S. Huyser, an analyst for Montgomery Securities in San Francisco. The dropoff, combined with the trend toward sending patients home earlier, brought the average hospital occupancy rate to just 68% in mid-1984, down from 76% in 1980, according to the American Hospital Assn. *(AHA)*. With admissions expected to fall by an additional 4% this year, the occupancy rate seems set for another decline.

STILL PROSPEROUS. So far the hospitals have managed to adjust their business operations to the emptier beds. The main reason: Since the patients who remain are sicker, their average bill has increased. This has kept revenues growing, albeit at a pace far slower than the 15% annual rate the industry chalked up in the 1970s. "The rate of growth was 4% to 6% in 1984, and I think it will stay that way in 1985," says *AHA* President J. Alexander McMahon.

Meanwhile, cutbacks in staffing, supplies, and purchases of equipment have enabled the major investor-owned hospital chains to keep their profits increasing at a 20% annual clip. The chains are also prospering as a result of medicare's so-called prospective payment system, which has replaced the old cost-based reimbursement system with flat fees for each type of illness. "The reimbursement system has made it possible for hospitals with costs below average to make a profit on medicare business," observes Chairman David A. Jones, of

---

To capture a larger market, the chains may intensify moves into such alternatives as nursing homes

---

Humana Inc., which operates 91 hospitals in 22 states and three foreign countries.

How long such cost-cutting can keep the health care industry robust is unclear, however. "The issue now is to get revenues moving," says analyst Seth H. Shaw of Shearson Lehman/American Express Inc. That effort will become all the more difficult if the Reagan Administration follows through on its threat to freeze medicare payments to hospitals and doctors—a move that could cost hospitals $2 billion in fiscal 1986.

To capture a larger market share, the chains are likely to intensify their moves into such alternative-care businesses as home health services, nursing homes, and urgent-care centers. One hot target may be rehabilitation hospitals for stroke and accident victims. National Medical's Eamer calls this "one of the most rapidly growing, underprovided health care areas in the country."

Another growth opportunity may lie in psychiatric hospitals. For the fiscal year ended last November, San Francisco Community Psychiatric Centers posted an admissions gain of 19.2% in its 21 hospitals. Chairman Robert L. Green attributes that jump to greater awareness of the benefits of psychiatric treatment and to a broadening of referral sources to include employers as well as schools.

FIGHTING BACK. A major problem for the hospitals, however, will be the accelerating growth of health maintenance organizations, which now provide flat-fee medical coverage for some 15 million members. Kaiser Foundation Health Plan Inc., the largest *HMO*, scored one of its best increases in

membership in 1984. This year, it will start up new operations in North Carolina and Georgia.

The chains are fighting back. In 1983, Hospital Corp. of America launched its own medical insurance program, called PriMed, which already has some 250,000 members. PriMed offers cost savings to members who agree to use the chain's physicians and facilities. Other chains are starting up similar schemes. "Changes in the way health care is financed are coming much faster than any of us anticipated," says *HCA* Chief Executive Dr. Thomas F. Frist Jr.

Few know this better than companies that supply to hospitals. At the largest, American Hospital Supply Corp., Chairman Karl D. Bays says he thinks earnings will grow by only 5% in 1985—a far cry from the average annual 15.7% growth *AHSC* had for the past decade. To improve things, Bays is pushing into such new markets as surgical supplies for doctors' offices and emergency clinics. He has also stepped up a move into specialized medical equipment.

But equipment makers are generally finding that the only products passing muster with hospi-

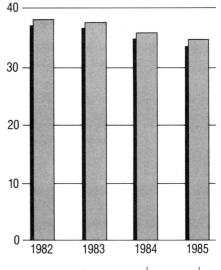

HOSPITAL ADMISSIONS WILL CONTINUE TO FALL

MILLIONS OF PATIENTS

└─EST.─┘

DATA: AMERICAN HOSPITAL ASSN.
MONTGOMERY SECURITIES ESTIMATES

tals these days are those that offer immediate cost-cutting benefits. "Medical equipment is the area most affected by the uncertainties of medicare reimbursement," states David L. Goldsmith, an analyst at San Francisco's Robertson, Colman & Stephens. "Most of the proposals on reimbursing hospitals for their capital costs would penalize those putting in new equipment." As a result, many medical suppliers are stumbling and will continue to do so throughout the year.

By John W. Wilson in San Francisco, with bureau reports

International Marketing

HOW KODAK IS TRYING TO MOVE MOUNT FUJI

DECEMBER 2, 1985, PP. 62, 64

In many countries around the world, photographers shopping for film snap up the familiar yellow boxes made by Eastman Kodak Co. But not in Japan. Although Kodak has sold film there since 1889, for decades it has only been a small player. When photographers in Japan pick up film, they reach for green boxes instead—those bearing the name of Fuji Photo Film Co.

It's an all too familiar tale. Never mind that Rochester (N. Y.)-based Kodak has worldwide sales of $10.6 billion, making it three times the size of Fuji. In Japan, Kodak holds just 15% of the market for consumer color film and paper, while Fuji has a whopping 70%. High tariffs on foreign film helped Fuji, but a slow-moving Kodak also bears much of the blame. With no Japanese sales force of its own and no technical staff to tailor its products to local tastes, sales languished. "We didn't give Japan the attention it deserved," admits Kodak Japan President Albert L. Sieg.

BIGGER CHUNK. But Kodak is working hard to give the story a surprise ending. Over the past 18 months, the company has launched an ambitious effort to tackle Fuji on its home turf. Now the pace is quickening. Kodak recently opened a new technical center for customers and distributors, announced plans to build a Japanese research facility, acquired a 10% stake in a Japanese camera manufacturer, and bought out the Japanese distributor of several important business products. And more deals are on the way.

Kodak's first priority is nabbing a bigger chunk of Japan's $1.5 billion film and paper market—a market second only to that of the U. S. Just as important, Kodak needs to build its Japanese presence to protect its flank. New photographic technology, in both research and manufacturing, comes out of Japan as often as out of America these days. Unless Kodak stays abreast there, it could be vulnerable to inroads from Fuji and other Japanese rivals in the U. S. and around the world. To keep up, Kodak must spend heavily now on research and joint ventures with Japanese companies.

Kodak's drive began in the spring of 1984. The company yanked its Japanese unit from the regional division for Asia, Africa, and Australia and created a new subsidiary just for Japan. When Sieg, former head of Kodak's strategic planning for photography, arrived from Rochester, the message was clear. Japan had been "elevated in status and management attention," Sieg says.

Since then, Kodak Japan has tripled its American and Japanese staff. The promotion and public relations people, who are working overtime to boost Kodak's visibility, may be busiest of all. Kodak Japan now sponsors everything from children's judo championships to *TV* talk shows to an overseas sumo wrestling tournament. And early in 1986 the company will get a listing on the Tokyo Stock Exchange. "Maybe back in the States there's no need to keep pounding the Kodak name, but here, if we don't, we'll be buried by our green-box friends," asserts a Japanese staffer.

Kodak has tripled its staff in Japan, and people are working overtime on publicity

---

Rival Fuji, however, has launched some savvy public-relations assaults of its own. Overseas sales jumped when Fuji outbid Kodak to become the official film for the 1984 Los Angeles Summer Olympics. In the U. S. alone, its share of the $1.1

billion consumer film market climbed from 6% in 1982 to 8% in 1984. William A. Relyea, an analyst at Eberstadt Fleming Inc. in New York, says that most of the gain came from non-Kodak films. Still, stunned by Fuji's coup, Kodak has already spent a bundle for sponsorship of both the 1988 Summer Olympics in Seoul and the Winter Games in Calgary, Alta.

RECENT DEALS. Publicity aside, Kodak still has to contend with Fuji's technical prowess. Fuji gets high marks for quality and has generally matched Kodak in introducing new products, such as high-speed film. It controls more than 250 of Japan's film-processing labs, the largest end-users of photographic paper, against a total of about 150 for Kodak and Konishiroku Photo Industry Co., maker of Fotomat film.

To counter Fuji's strengths, Kodak is betting on its recent series of deals with established Japanese companies. Eastman Kodak President Kay R. Whitmore says the aim is to "build a group of companies" in Japan that can support one another. Kodak Japan President Sieg adds that the moves are designed to give Kodak "an opportunity to learn and understand more about manufacturing in Japan." He cites Kodak's recent $13 million purchase of a 10% stake in Chinon Industries Inc. Chinon will begin making 35-mm cameras that Kodak will sell under its own name in the U. S. and Japan next year. Another Kodak subsidiary, Verbatim Corp., a maker of floppy disks, operates in a joint venture with Mitsubishi Chemical Industries Ltd.

Kodak has also realized, albeit belatedly, that it will need its own marketing and sales staff to succeed in Japan. Until now, the company relied largely on local agents to distribute its products. But on Nov. 13, Kodak announced plans to buy three units of Kusuda Business Machines Co. The Kusuda units sell Kodak's micrographic and business imaging systems in Japan, and the purchase turns marketing control for the products over to Kodak. It also paves the way for Kodak to sell its new $500,000 Information Management System and its Ektaprint Electronic Publishing System (BW—June 10) directly to the Japanese.

In addition, Kodak wants more control over the distribution of its film and paper in Japan, now the province of Nagase & Co. Members of the Nagase family own more than 10% of this company, and they are also sole owners of Far East Laboratories Inc., Kodak's main film processor in Japan. In Rochester, Eastman Kodak Executive Vice-President J. Phillip Samper calls a buyout

---

Kodak is spending heavily to link up with Japanese companies in everything from manufacturing to sales

---

unlikely. But he says Kodak wants to set up a joint venture that "provides us with a management or equity position."

Kodak has also rolled out 20 new products in Japan in the past year. One, a minilab specifically designed for Japanese film processing, should chip away at Fuji's large film labs. That, in turn, would cut into Fuji's photographic-paper sales, concedes Fuji Managing Director Kiyohiro Tokuda. He says Fuji will fight back by offering bigger enlargement sizes than the minilabs.

To help it devise more products and technologies, Kodak plans a new research and development center. The lab, to be staffed by 150 Japanese scientists and technicians, will develop Japanese-language software for Kodak's business products. It will also zero in on electronic imaging, a technology that allows users to display and manipulate pictures or documents on a video screen, thus eliminating chemically processed negatives and paper. Kodak has already unveiled in the U. S. a color video imager, which can make an instant print of any video picture. Soon Japanese consumers will be able to buy it, too.

CUT THE DEMAND. This process is still very new, and no one knows its sales potential. But Kodak cannot afford to be left behind this time. When Japanese companies commercialized videocassette recorders, for example, the new products cut the demand for still pictures. Eventually Kodak settled for a small piece of the action by selling a Matsushita-made 8-mm video camera system.

Kodak hopes that setting up shop in Japan will help it avoid a similar fate in electronic imaging. "They can keep up with fashions and trends better than they can if they're sitting up in Rochester and waiting for Matsushita to call," says Caryn Callahan, an analyst with Merrill Lynch Securities Co. in Tokyo. Kodak has made that mistake in the past and paid for it. This time, Kodak is sitting in Tokyo and waiting for no one.

By James B. Treece in Tokyo, with Barbara Buell in Boston and Jane Sasseen in New York

FIGHTING BACK: IT CAN WORK

SOME COMPANIES ARE FINDING WAYS TO KEEP JAPAN FROM ALWAYS WINNING

AUGUST 26, 1985, PP. 62-68

As any executive facing competition from Japan can attest, fighting back isn't easy. But some Western managers are saying, "enough is enough." And they are starting to produce results that show the task isn't impossible either.

Like born-again capitalists, executives at big companies like 3M (page 175), Motorola, *IBM*, and Philips are rallying to the cause. So are some at smaller companies like Tektronix and Timken, who have few real alternatives. These managers realize that they must act now—or contribute to the loss of the West's industrial base. "We control our own destiny," asserts Frederick P. Stratton Jr., president of Briggs & Stratton Corp., the lawnmower engine maker. Adds C. Fred Fetterolf, president of Aluminum Co. of America: "We have dug in our heels and said, 'no more.' "

It's about time. Relentlessly, Japanese companies have moved into Western markets and swept aside the local suppliers. In microwave ovens, which the U. S. invented, the process took just 15 years (chart, page 172). Japan now produces three-quarters of the world's videocassette recorders, single-lens cameras, and motorcycles. It makes half the world's ships, two-fifths of its *TV*s, and a third of its semiconductors and cars. Japan does lag behind in chemicals, food, and aerospace. It has found the going tricky in telecommunications, computers, and other areas that require service or software. But "if you take manufacturing, the Japanese are winning it all," says James C. Abegglen, former head of Boston Consulting Group Inc.'s Tokyo office, who is now a professor of business at Tokyo's Sophia University.

Maybe not. The game isn't over for Tektronix Inc. For years, Tek supplied two-thirds of the world's oscilloscopes, which test the performance of electronic equipment. Then several Japanese companies jumped into the market, quickly grabbing a 10% share. Now Tek, with new, high-performance scopes and portable models, has halted the erosion. But the company is making sure it measures up in efficiency: It now turns over its inventory an average of six times a year vs. 3.9 in fiscal 1983. And Tek isn't finished. "We want to cut our product [development] turnaround in half," declares Executive Vice-President Willem B. Velsink. "That's what we need to sustain our success against Japan."

Briggs & Stratton was once in similar straits. In 1980 the company found itself besieged by Japanese rivals. So it weathered a three-month strike to cut labor costs, and pushed to improve quality. It is doubling its engineering and product development staff. For the first time, Briggs is advertising to consumers, though it sells only to manufacturers. The chastened company is beginning, only recently, to regain market share.

As such stories illustrate—and more people are coming to see—the lopsided scorecard with Japan may not be entirely attributable to the advantages its companies enjoy. Those pluses are formidable: low wage rates, a strong work ethic, government support, trade barriers, an undervalued currency, low capital costs, and extreme patience in recouping investments. But, instead of looking inward for ways to overcome those factors, Western executives have merely muttered excuses. As a result, Western progress in improving its competitiveness has been worse than slow. "It's glacial," says Walter L. Ames, a former Bain & Co. consultant who now teaches at Brigham Young University.

Instead of acting, too many Western companies have been waiting for the value of the dollar to fall—or for the government to enact protectionist barriers. Many managers even admit it. In a new *BUSINESS WEEK*/Harris Poll of U. S. executives whose companies face Japanese competition, nearly 40% conceded that they do not have a plan to compete with their Asian rivals. And that, of course, says nothing about the quality of the other companies' strategic plans.

"The problems of America are at home," says Michael E. Porter, professor of business policy at Harvard business school. "Yes, we may fight slightly less dirty than they do. And yes, we have trouble getting into their market. But if that were to change overnight, the cold hard truth is, our products are not as good. Someone else has seized the initiative. And yes, their government is helpful in that process, but we don't want our government to play that intrusive role. We're going to succeed based on the degree we make it happen."

A HOLDOUT. The fighters are indeed trying to make success happen. Take the $3 billion U. S. microwave oven market: It's booming, but it's under intense pressure from Japanese and Korean companies. Last fall, General Electric Co., once the market leader, decided to phase out production—and import ovens from the Far East. Will Litton Industries Inc., now the top U. S. producer, capitulate? "No damn way," snaps Wayne L. Bledsoe, president of Litton's microwave unit. Instead, Litton has redesigned its product line to squeeze out labor content and minimize retooling. It is bringing out a new, $399 Micro-Browner oven that keeps meat from turning microwave gray. And it will soon start slapping a "Made in America" sticker on every oven door. So far, the signs are good: Industry sources say Litton has picked up some market share.

The resolve at Timken Co. is just as strong. Most big steel companies have abandoned superclean alloy steels, largely to Japanese competitors. Not Timken. In the midst of the last recession, the company began to shell out $500 million to build an advanced mill that will make better-quality steel for its tapered roller bearings, the antifriction devices Timken invented. And Timken has poured more and more money into modernizing its other

facilities and into research—even during 1982, its worst year ever. Meanwhile, it has swallowed losses to maintain its leading market share in bearings. Says Steven Walleck, a director of McKinsey & Co.: "Timken is doing everything possible to beat the Japanese."

At Motorola Inc., "meeting the Japanese challenge" has become a way of life. The company faces stiff Japanese competition in electronic components, two-way and cellular radio gear, data communications equipment, and computers. It has been boosting productivity and quality, trying to match the Japanese by "practicing the basics," as Chief Executive Robert W. Galvin says. And Galvin is educating his officers—some 150 executives—with special seminars on Asia. Meanwhile, Motorola is increasingly challenging the Japanese around the world, including their home market. It is one of the few U. S. companies that supply a lot of equipment to Nippon Telegraph & Telephone Public Co.

That's not enough for Galvin. Last December he detached eight senior executives from their regular duties to form an "Asia task force." For three months the eight closeted themselves away to determine what else Motorola should do to improve its chances against the Japanese. Galvin will not disclose the panel's recommendations. But, as a result, the company may soon undergo a corporate reorganization. And it may form more alliances with other companies.

Black & Decker Corp. has mobilized, too. In the late 1970s, Japanese companies invaded the professional power tool market, a highly profitable business. By 1980, Makita Electric Works Ltd. alone had won 20% of the world market with its quality, low-priced tools. The new competition rolled back *B&D*'s share of the world market from 20% to 15%.

In response, *B&D* slashed its work force by 40%, pumped $80 million into plant modernization, adopted Japanese manufacturing concepts at home, and began making tools overseas. It followed Makita into home-improvement stores to attract the low end of the professional market. It acquired companies in Switzerland, West Germany, and the U. S. to become a full-line supplier. And it stopped customizing products for every

MICROWAVE OVENS: A MARKET THE U.S. INVENTED—AND THEN LOST

1945 Microwave's cooking ability discovered in Raytheon laboratories in Massachusetts

1947 First microwave oven manufactured by Raytheon for sale to restaurants and hotels

1955 First microwaves for consumer use manufactured by Tappan

1956 General Electric's Hotpoint division introduces a microwave

1967 Raytheon's Amana division introduces the first microwave using standard household circuits

1970 Sales top 100,000 units; Litton enters the consumer market

1977 Last magnetron tube, the heart of microwaves, manufactured in the U.S. by Raytheon. Production shifts to Japan

1978 South Korea starts exporting microwaves to U.S.

1979 Sanyo and Matsushita start manufacturing microwaves in the U.S.

1980 Sharp starts manufacturing microwaves in the U.S.

1983 Sanyo takes market lead, with 19%, from GE. Amana starts importing microwaves from the Far East

1984 Japanese and Korean producers end the year with some 60% of the market

1984 GE decides to phase out U.S. production and buy microwaves from Japan's Matsushita and South Korea's Samsung

1985 Tappan begins importing small microwave ovens from Japan

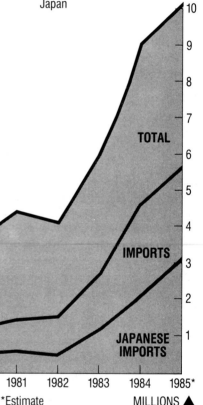

SHIPMENTS TO U.S. STORES

TOTAL

IMPORTS

JAPANESE IMPORTS

1972 1973 1974 1975 1976 1977 1978 1979 1980 1981 1982 1983 1984 1985*

DATA: ASSOCIATION OF HOME APPLIANCE MANUFACTURERS *APPLIANCE* MAGAZINE, BW   *Estimate   MILLIONS ▲

country and started making a few products that could be sold everywhere. Says Alan W. Larson, executive vice-president for *B&D*'s Western hemisphere operations: "We have been working very hard to globalize the range of our products so we can compete with Japan."

B&D says it regained its 20% market share in professional power tools this year. But it hurt. The company had to meet Japanese prices, eroding its profits. "We will never again see the profits of the early 1980s," moans an executive.

In some cases, fighting back is causing even more wrenching changes. At Chaparral Steel Co., management has already substantially overhauled a steel minimill that was built only in 1975. "We probably have the most modern plant in the world," boasts President Gordon E. Forward. That is one reason Chaparral produces steel at 1.8 man-hours per ton vs. 2.3 for Japanese competitors.

Just as important, Chaparral practices egalitarianism to improve output and quality. "We consider everyone to be line [workers]. There are no staff positions per se," says Forward. The company has no customer service representatives, for example. It sends production managers out to answer customer complaints. "You ought to see how motivated they are to fix the problem when they come

---

'We're simply not making the capital investments needed to stay the course'

---

back," says Forward. And while Chaparral's hefty borrowings for investment pushed it $4.8 million into the red in 1984, the company is expected to earn a modest profit this year.

Against the odds, these companies are risking huge sums of money to compete. But the risks of not fighting back would appear to be even greater. Many Western companies have simply ceded business to the Japanese, particularly in tough, high-volume markets where their production efficiencies are difficult to overcome. That happened in consumer electronics. It happened in small cars, textiles, and machine tools.

Now it may be happening in semiconductors. Most chipmakers are giving up in commodity memory products known as dynamic random access memories. Instead, they are concentrating on specialized and customized chips. Charles E. Sporck, president and chief executive of National Semiconductor Corp., says there is little choice in the matter: "At current price levels, it's difficult to see a return in dynamic *RAM*s. That makes the decision pretty straightforward."

MEMORY GAME. The danger in such retreats is easy to see. "First you move the industrial part to the Far East," says C. J. van der Klugt, vice-chairman of Philips, the consumer electronics company. "Then the development of the product goes there, because each dollar you pay to the overseas supplier is 10¢ you're giving him to develop new devices, new concepts, to compete against you." Japanese dominance in chip memories, for example, could eventually give them a permanent advantage in all chips, as well as in products that use semiconductors. Thus, even without the prospect of profits, European companies such as Siemens, Philips, and Thomson Group are investing heavily to stay in the memory game.

The erosion of technical knowhow has already tripped up U. S. consumer electronics companies. The Japanese first won a foothold in radios. Gradually, they took the lead in audio technology. Then the ability to develop audio and related products shifted to Japan. Eventually the U. S. forfeited production capability. As a result, the U. S. was shut out of the videocassette recorder business: American companies simply cannot make the high-precision recording and playback heads in large quantities at reasonable cost. And it would cost too much to try.

Western executives see the problem. Admits Sporck: "Long-term, we have to be reasonably competitive with the Japanese, which means to some extent we are going to have to meet their competition in the commodity area." Executives polled by *BUSINESS WEEK* agree that retreating into niches is "not a viable long-term strategy." Rather, 67% said "American companies should fight it out at all levels of the market."

But, apparently, many cannot figure out a way to win in a fight that is stacked in favor of their Eastern rivals. Even putting aside the cultural differences that help the Japanese, competing is difficult because of Japan's lower cost of capital. Interest rates in Japan can be as little as half what Western companies pay. "The numbers are scary," concludes John J. Murphy, chairman of Dresser Industries Inc.

That edge can be insurmountable in itself, but Westerners—and Wall Street—make it worse because they emphasize short-term results. The Japanese "are under much less pressure for quarterly earnings," says Edson W. Spencer, chairman of Honeywell Inc. Edoardo Pieruzzi, a 3M Co. vice-president, is more blunt: "The Japanese are in business for the year 2010, and Western companies are in business for next quarter's profit report."

Taken together, costly capital and the pressure to perform sooner rather than later make Western companies cautious about investing. "We're simply not making the capital investments needed to stay the course," says Sophia University's Abegglen. As evidence, he cites a study comparing U. S. and Japanese chemical and electronics companies. The Japanese companies, on average, turned in aftertax profits that were only about half those of the American companies. And Japanese companies paid out less in dividends. But they took on much more debt and have been growing a third faster than their U. S. counterparts.

Short-term orientation and high interest rates are lethal for another reason. Compared to Japanese rivals, Western companies, with less room to maneuver financially, are less willing to cut prices to keep customers. In *BUSINESS WEEK*'s survey, half the executives said that cutting prices would help them compete against Japan. But only 2% said they would be likely to do so. That limits their staying power in the marketplace.

Underlying all these factors lurks a stunning difference between Japanese and Westerners: A survey by Booz, Allen & Hamilton Inc. shows that Japanese executives most want to make their companies the global leader in an industry. On the other hand, Western managers—particularly Americans—place the most emphasis on increasing shareholder value. In *BUSINESS WEEK*'s survey of executives, U. S. managers placed industry leadership fourth on their list of corporate objectives, after shareholder wealth, technological innovation, and sales and earnings growth.

ACROSS THE BOARD. That difference between East and West bolsters the Japanese ability to compete. To become industry leaders, Japanese companies build international distribution systems and brand-name recognition. Then they leverage the name by diversifying into related products. Honda Motor Co., for example, started in motorcycles, moved into cars, and now makes everything from rototillers to lawnmowers—and supplies their key component, gasoline engines, in competition with Briggs & Stratton. With risk spread geographically and over a broad product line, Honda can more easily absorb profit squeezes in key markets. By and large, even Western companies that manufacture overseas haven't learned this lesson.

The past few years have spotlighted the need for Western companies to compete across the board with the Japanese. The U. S. trade deficit with Japan has more than doubled since 1982. It may reach $50 billion this year. In part, the increase is the result of a strong dollar, but only in part. And the figure leaves out the damage inflicted in U. S. export markets and on European companies.

Clearly, most Western efforts to date—largely cost-cutting drives—haven't been enough to stop the Japanese juggernaut. Ford Motor Co., for example, has wrung out about $300 in costs from its compact Escort in the past four years. But it is only voluntary import quotas that have kept Japanese manufacturers from increasing their market share in cars.

Technology isn't the entire answer, either. It is changing quickly, and the Japanese are coming on strong in many key areas, such as fiber optics. "If you look at the levels of technology in Japan, they are competitive," says Richard C. Alberding, an executive vice-president at Hewlett-Packard Co. Besides, advances can be copied so rapidly these days that many technological advantages do not last long in the marketplace.

FAR HORIZONS. To get ahead, Western companies are going to have to make an all-out effort. And they are going to have to compete globally, even in Japan, if only to tap into Japanese developments. Eastman Kodak Co. is moving in that direction. It started selling film in Japan 95 years ago, but only recently moved 30 research and marketing people to Tokyo. The company, under worldwide attack by Fuji Photo Film Co., is gearing up for a bigger push in film on Fuji's turf. And the new staff will help Kodak keep tabs on developments in electronic imaging products there.

Most important, Western companies must learn to compete with longer, broader horizons in mind. "We've been caught in a perpetual follower position because we've never understood the long-term strategic intentions of [Japanese] competitors," says Gary Hamel, a lecturer at London Business School. Most Western companies, he says, haven't even begun to think about what the Japanese will be doing in 1990.

A few of the best companies are now. Cummins Engine Co. faces no Japanese competition in its heavy-truck engines—now. But with the threat ever-present, Cummins is keeping a tight grip on costs, introducing new technology, and improving quality. Its warranty expenses, for example, were down from a peak of 4.5% of net sales in 1978 to only 2% in 1984, despite several product launches in the last three years.

The major-appliance industry offers other examples. Besides microwaves, the Japanese have made inroads mainly in room air conditioners. But Sanyo and Matsushita are taking initial steps to get into the highly competitive U. S. market. Partly in response, Whirlpool Corp. is working hard to keep ahead with product innovations and to increase productivity and quality.

And General Electric, after backing out of several areas hit hard by Japanese rivals in recent years, appears to be drawing the line in major appliances. *GE* has been spending an average of $200 million a year investing in appliances. Part of its program is a new materials-handling scheme, inspired by Japan.

SMALL CHANCE. Some of the companies waging campaigns against Japanese competition may not be successful. Motorola tried to fight back in dynamic *RAM*s, but it has only recently begun shipping the latest generation of such chips, a year after most Japanese competitors. Texas Instruments Inc. is sticking it out in the same market, with plants both in Japan and the U. S. But it's been painful: Earnings fell dramatically in the first quarter, and *TI* lost $3.9 million when sales dropped 16%, to $1.2 billion, in the second quarter.

General Motors Corp. is pouring $5 billion into its Saturn project to beat back Japan in the small-car market and is trying all sorts of management techniques to beat the Japanese at their own game. But outsiders give the world's biggest car company little chance of outdoing its Asian rivals in small cars. Even Litton's Bledsoe may have to eat his words: Although his division is making more money these days than it used to, Litton Industries—determined to concentrate on its defense and electronics operations—has considered selling the microwave unit. There's no telling what a new owner might do, or who it might be.

One thing is certain, however: Competition with Japan is only going to get more virulent. The efforts Western companies are making may not be enough, but they are a start toward reclaiming lost industrial ground.

By Judith H. Dobrzynski in New York and Thane Peterson in Paris, with Larry Armstrong in Tokyo and bureau reports

HOW 3M IS TRYING TO OUT-JAPANESE THE JAPANESE

Donald J. Patrican, national sales manager for Hitachi Maxell Ltd.'s U.S. subsidiary, remembers well his initiation into the recording-tape business. It was 1970, and he was a regional sales manager making a call near Boston. As he pitched his audio tapes, the store manager hefted a tape deck onto the counter, loaded it with a 3M Scotch Brand cassette, and launched into a lecture on Scotch's superiority. Back then, "3M was the tape you sold against," says Patrican.

Within five years, Japanese producers such as Maxell and TDK Corp. had stolen much of 3M Co.'s 30% market share. And by 1982, 3M, which had pioneered the development of magnetic recording tape, had virtually walked away from the market.

'GIGABUCKS.' Now 3M is engaged in another tape war with the Japanese. This time the prize is the booming videotape market. And this time 3M is the aggressor, bent on knocking the Japanese from their dominant position the Japanese way—with innovations, efficient manufacturing, and aggressive price-cutting. The battle even extends to Japan, where 3M claims a 10% market share and vows to be No. 1. "We have every intention of doing to them on their turf what they are doing to us here," says George L. Hegg, the group vice-president in charge of 3M's "memory technology" products, such as tapes and computer floppy disks.

3M believes the Japanese thought they could drive the company out of tapes again, mainly by slashing prices. Instead, they found a 3M that "clearly would go one better than anyone in the business," says John H. Hollands, president of Sony Tapes Sales Co. 3M, which posted $7.7 billion in sales last year, is pouring a lot of money into the battle. The St. Paul (Minn.) company has given Hegg's group some $420 million, or 22% of its total capital budget, since 1982. And Hegg says future spending will amount to "gigabucks." Says Koyo Yokoi, national sales director for TDK's U.S. subsidiary: "I have never seen an effort of this magnitude."

Why is 3M fighting so fiercely? For one, the potential market for videotape alone is expected to be $7 billion by 1990. The entire memory media market could reach $15 billion by then, and 3M believes that becoming the brand leader in videocassettes will help establish it as a leader in other memory media. More broadly, 3M Chairman Lewis W. Lehr wants to make the company less dependent on highly cyclical industrial markets by producing more consumer goods, and Hegg's group fits that bill.

The outspoken Hegg "is the right guy to stay on top of this wild tiger we're riding," says Edoardo Pieruzzi, vice-president of the audio/video products unit. Before he was named head of the Memory Technologies Group in 1983, Hegg, a 54-year-old chemical engineer, spent 6 years in Japan.

Hegg is spending his funds to upgrade and increase capacity at existing facilities. He wants to build brand loyalty by offering premium videotapes—the new Scotch brand, EXG, exceeds the quality of a 3M tape ranked No. 1 by *Consumer Reports*. He'll also capitalize on the company's wide distribution system, which puts its videocassettes into all the logical outlets, from office-supply vendors to discount houses. The Japanese, 3M says, cannot match that.

At the same time, 3M has spared no expense in marketing. It is advertising its cassettes during top sporting events. It unveiled snappy new packaging for them. And it is mailing a raft of circulars to those who claimed refunds in its long-running rebate campaign.

So far, the company seems to be winning. Laurence B. Lueck, president of Magnetic Media Information Services, a Chicago consulting firm, says 3M is the leading branded producer in the U.S., with a 19% share, up from 5% in 1980. Worldwide, 3M claims a respectable 13% of the market. And Lueck believes that the Japanese are getting "demoralized and disillusioned" in the market for ½-in. videotape.

"IT MUST HURT.' Because price-cutting is rampant, though, 3M's fight is taking a toll on profits. Harry A. Hammerly, vice-president for finance, says 3M makes a "small profit" in memory media. But the company cited price competition as a main reason for its 13% earnings dip in the second quarter. All told, 3M's Electronics & Information Technologies Sector, which includes Hegg's group, has seen earnings decline 46% since 1980, to $163 million, on a 22% increase in sales, to $2.4 billion.

Thus, 3M has departed from its historic practice of refusing to fund ventures that do not measure up to its standard for returns. And Lueck, for one, thinks 3M "still has five tough years ahead of it." Is it worth it? Insiders say that even a lot of people within the company ask that question.

But perhaps tantalized by the profits audio tapes deliver to the Japanese, Hegg insists 3M won't give up. "'Surrender' is not in my dictionary," he says. "We are positioning everything with the long term in mind." Says Lueck: "For one of the first times, a company is looking longer than just one quarter. I have to salute them, but it must hurt," 3M can only hope that it hurts its Japanese rivals more.

By Patrick Houston in Minneapolis

PART 5

CAREERS
IN MARKETING

It is never too soon to begin thinking about your career. No matter what your major or type of organization you work for, chances are you will be involved in marketing its products and services.

Most people have not fully realized the many excellent career opportunities available in marketing. Whenever and wherever any organization wants to influence its sales, it requires a marketing person. Oh sure, you may become an accountant, a banker, or a candlestick maker, yet all three of these occupations employ people to create revenue. Many of you reading this book will go directly into marketing.

The three excellent articles in Part 5 are intended to get you thinking about your career early in your college years. Actually, when you are looking for a job, you are marketing yourself. You (the product), your appearance (the package), your salary (the price), the job location (place), your résumé (advertising), your interview (personal selling)—all involve the marketing of your product: "you"!

PART 5 ARTICLE SYNOPSES

THE WIDE WORLD OF MARKETING	Any businessperson must understand and apply marketing concepts to stay in business. Marketing has many different aspects, requiring diverse training. Marketing positions may entail sales, brand management, advertising, research, consulting, and much more. Marketing is becoming important even in industries where it has traditionally held low priority. This article describes many of marketing's career opportunities.
WHEN TO START LOOKING FOR A JOB	It takes six months to secure the first position. Many companies recruit heavily during the fall term because of training programs beginning

soon after graduation. The first part of the job search is developing career awareness. Working part time or summer at a company where you'd like permanent employment can be helpful. Informational interviews are good for making contacts and getting inside information. Résumé campaigns should be carefully targeted and begun early. Average or inexperienced students shouldn't be discouraged.

THE HIRING PROCESS—HOW IT WORKS

Different companies may use vastly different recruitment methods. Although on-campus interviews are a good way to make contacts with some companies, other companies will be missed. One should understand the jobs applied for. Networking is a valuable technique. Want ads are also useful. Sending résumés "cold" is ineffective. Communication skills are extremely important to most prospective employers.

THE WIDE WORLD OF MARKETING

THIS FASCINATING FIELD OFFERS MANY INTERESTING JOBS AND ABOVE-AVERAGE
SALARIES FOR BOTH BUSINESS AND LIBERAL ARTS GRADUATES

BW GUIDE TO CAREERS, FEBRUARY/MARCH 1984, PP. 70–72

In one of the most successful marketing campaigns in years, IBM rolled out its long-awaited Personal Computer in 1981. The product had the right mix of technical specifications, software, advertising, customer support, and distribution. Sales exceeded all estimates, and by 1983, IBM was shipping 30,000 computers per month, having risen from nowhere to nearly the top in the personal computer market.

There, in a nutshell, is an indication of how wide the world of marketing is. In a way, marketing can be considered a synonym for business—for everyone, no matter what he or she is selling or producing, must understand and apply marketing principles correctly to achieve a successful product, and to stay in business.

One useful metaphor for understanding what marketing is is to think of a field general during a battle. In order to achieve victory the general must understand the terrain in which he is fighting, the numbers and locations of the enemy, and his resources—tanks, cannon, planes, troops, supply lines. He may use spies or reconnaissance to find soft spots in his enemy's lines and then, with a look to the sky to note the weather, launch his attack. If he is able to maintain the element of surprise, send his troops in the right direction, and support them appropriately, he may be the victor at the end of the day.

Similarly, a marketing manager examines his or her terrain—the mix of products the company and competitors sell. He or she probes for weak spots—"unsatisfied consumer needs"—and seeks to fill them with a new product. He or she consults research and development people for the right ingredients; the distributors for the best way of getting the product to the buyer; the advertising agency for the proper way to publicize the product's existence; the financial people for the correct pricing strategy. All the time, the marketing manager watches over his or her shoulder to see what competitors are doing. The product is launched with a huge advertising campaign, and in a matter of months the marketing manager knows whether the battle is won, or whether to pack up his or her resources to do battle on another field.

Marketing is a huge, diffuse profession, with hundreds of thousands of practitioners involved in figuring out, and then supplying, the goods American consumers are willing to pay for. It is one of the four cornerstones of all business activity—the other three being production, finance, and personnel. Everyone is familiar with consumer goods marketing—groceries, household, and personal-care products and the like—and the companies that tower over these markets—Procter & Gamble, General Foods, Johnson & Johnson, among others. But what is not well known is that marketing continues to be needed in many other businesses. Some of the newest examples are banking and financial services, electronics, and transportation.

Merriam-Webster's dictionary defines marketing as "an aggregate of the functions involved in transferring title and in moving goods from producer to consumer including among others buying, selling, storing, transporting. . ." "Aggregate" is certainly the right word to use in this definition, for there are many different occupations, or responsibilities, that fall within the realm of marketing. (See box, page 181.) It is a field where the generalist, who must be able to deal with many different aspects of the business, is preeminent.

"I love marketing as a career because there are different challenges every day," says Don, a product manager at a Northeastern package-goods company. "One day I'm dealing with choosing models to demonstrate a new line of products; the next day I might be worried about the reproduction quality of our print advertisements; and the day after that with a crisis in our manufacturing plant. Marketing is a 'big-board' game, rather than a race to get from point A to point B."

As befits a generalist's occupation, the training sought for marketing positions is diverse. Most businesspeople speak of the need for a liberal arts education at the bachelor's level as a primary step. But after that, opinions differ widely, and perferences for certain specialties within the marketing umbrella also differ.

"Certainly, going on for an MBA never hurts," says one marketing trade association spokesperson. Conversely, a growing number of schools are offering specialized master's programs for occupations such as direct marketing, advertising creative direction, or package goods design. Some of these can be obtained at the bachelor's level as well.

Then, too, some companies are noted for the heavy training they provide for their personnel. Procter & Gamble, in particular, is renowned for being a "University of Marketing": the entire marketing profession is peopled with ex-P&G workers who went through its intensive training in brand management, and having prior experience from that company on one's resume is a status symbol.

As might be expected, P&G attracts the cream of each graduating class. "We don't really worry about what type of degree our recruits have when we hire them," says Henry Wilson, a brand-manager recruiter at P&G. "Most of them have MBAs, but what we really seek are recruits with the attributes of high motivation, leadership, strong oral and writing skills, and creativity."

Regardless of the specific training one has obtained, or even of the specific marketing job one is seeking, some experience with sales is considered a plus by most recruiters. In its most basic form, marketing and sales are the same thing: finding what a customer wants and then providing it for a mutually acceptable price. In many industries where marketing is important, being a salesperson is the entry-level position that most new hires go through. P&G's Wilson notes that their recruits, who are brought in as brand assistants, go through a couple months of being a trade salesperson before being promoted to assistant brand manager.

And at some companies, sales is practically the only way to get into a marketing slot—the most successful salespeople gradually rise through sales positions, and wind up as product line managers. This is especially true of industrial or business-to-business selling, which requires much more extensive customer-servicing than does consumer goods selling. The level of complexity inherent in installing, equipping, and servicing a large computer, for example, is much greater than that involved in getting a consumer to choose between two brands of soft drinks.

On the other hand, the sophistication involved in the mass marketing of consumer goods is virtually unmatched by any other business activity. Product flavors, smells, and textures are carefully designed; every square inch of packaging is examined; and advertising campaigns costing millions of dollars to film—let alone to air—are rigorously worked out. And all these components are tested and retested before the average consumer sees them.

Because these marketing functions are not seen as extensively in face-to-face selling as in mass marketing, sales experience is not as highly sought in the latter. It doesn't hurt, though; one product manager says that his college summers spent selling exterminating services door-to-door "brought home to me the need to distinguish my product from everyone else's in making a pitch. A salesman who doesn't have unique selling points to describe his product is doomed to fail."

Although there is probably a company and a job for each and every step of the marketing process, certain businesses stand out either in their importance to the marketing function, or the influence they exert in determining what goods are produced and how they are sold. This writer's informal list includes consumer-goods manufacturing, advertising, market research, and consulting.

CONSUMER GOODS MANUFACTURING. Developing a new shampoo, dog food, or cigarette can easily cost $25 million. The person who spends those dollars (with the advice and consent of his or her upper management) is known as a product or brand manager. It is a position to which individuals interested in marketing in its purest, essential form gravitate, and they are rewarded with heavy responsibilities, and hefty salaries—$40,000 to $60,000 after five or more years of experience.

A strong competitive streak is essential to succeeding in this business. Product managers must compete against other companies in the marketplace, and with other product managers within their company. Most consumer-goods companies are set up with centralized research and development, financial, and production departments. All product managers must go to each of these departments to obtain the resources needed to sell the product.

"A truism that I apply to product management is that it is 'management by influence,'" says one such manager. "You have no direct control over these resources, and you have to be able to convince people to go along with your views. It's highly competitive, but it's exhilarating work."

At Procter & Gamble, where the job of brand management was invented in the 1920s, recruits first take positions as assistants to brand managers. Most of their training is on the job, under the guidance of the manager. After a few months in sales, the assistant moves to the slot of assistant brand manager, and in most cases, to

THE 26 MARKETING OCCUPATIONS

A new book is coming out in 1984 that should prove to be an invaluable career guide to marketing students. Entitled *Careers In Marketing,* it is coauthored by David Rosenthal, a professor of marketing at Miami University (Oxford, Ohio), and Michael Powell.

The look is sponsored by the American Marketing Association and the National Council of Physical Distribution Management, a professional organization.

As a result of two years of research and over 200 interviews, the authors developed a list of 26 occupations that they say goes under the umbrella of "Marketing." Here's the list, with paraphrased descriptions of what each job entails:

Product Management

1. Product manager, consumer goods. Develops new products that can cost millions of dollars, with advice and consent of management. A job with great responsibility.
2. Administrative manager. Oversees the organization within a company that transports products to consumers and handles customer service.
3. Operations manager. Supervises warehousing and other physical distribution functions; often directly involved in moving goods on the warehouse floor.
4. Traffic and transportation manager. Evaluates the costs and benefits of different types of transportation.
5. Inventory control manager. Forecasts demand for stockpiled goods, coordinates production with plant managers; keeps track of current levels of shipments to keep customers supplied.
6. Administrative analyst planner. Performs cost analyses of physical distribution systems.
7. Customer service manager. Maintains good relations with customers by coordinating sales staffs, marketing management, and physical distribution management.
8. Physical distribution consultant. Expert in the transportation and distribution of goods.

Advertising

9. Account executive. Maintains contact with clients while coordinating the creative work among artists and copywriters. In full-service ad agencies, account executives are considered partners with the client in promoting the product and aiding in marketing strategy.
10. Media buyer analyst. Deals with media sales representatives in selecting advertising media; analyses the value of media being purchased.
11. Copywriter. Works with art director in conceptualizing advertisements; writes the text of print or radio ads or the storyboards of television ads.

12. Art director. Handles the visual component of advertisements.
13. Sales promotion manager. Designs promotions for consumer products; works at an ad agency or a sales promotion agency.
14. Public relations manager. Develops written or filmed messages for the public; handles contacts with the press.
15. Specialty advertising manager. Develops advertising for the sales staff and customers or distributors.

Retailing

16. Buyer. Selects products a store sells; surveys consumer trends and evaluates the past performance of products and suppliers.
17. Store manager. Oversees the staff and services at a store.

Sales

18. Direct. Door-to-door or other personal selling. Compensation is based mostly on a commission.
19. Sales to channel. Sells to another step in the distribution channel (between the manufacturer and the store or customer). Salesperson's compensation includes salary plus bonus.
20. Industrial/semi-technical. Sells supplies and services to businesses. Compensation is salary plus bonus.
21. Complex/professional. Sells complicated or custom-designed products to business. Requires understanding of the technology of a product. Compensation is salary plus bonus.

Marketing Research

22. Project manager, supplier. Coordinates and oversees the conducting of market studies for a client.
23. Account executive, supplier. Serves as liaison between client and market research firm; similar to an advertising agency account executive.
24. Project director, inhouse. Acts as project manager (see 22) for the market studies conducted by the firm for which one works.
25. Marketing research specialist, advertising agency. Performs or contracts for market studies for agency clients.

Non-Profit

26. Marketing manager, performing arts. Develops and directs mail campaigns, fundraising, and public relations for arts organizations.

Adapted from *Careers in Marketing* by David Rosenthal and Michael Powell to be published by Prentice-Hall Inc., 1984, for the Prentice-Hall-American Management Assn. series in marketing.

brand manager some two to four years after first being hired. "We have 90 brand groups among our divisions, and on average, we try to put a new hire in each group every 15 to 18 months," says P&G's Wilson. "So we might be hiring 50 or 60 people each year."

ADVERTISING. The advertising industry, tireless promoter of everything, certainly doesn't lack for self-promotion. It is a multibillion-dollar business, yet no one thinking of working in this field should forget that most advertising personnel do not work for Madison Avenue agencies, but for manufacturing companies. Often, companies generate their advertising in-house, including everything from artists to film labs.

The counterpart of a product manager at an ad agency is the account executive. His or her job is to maintain contact with the client, while coordinating the creative work going on among artists and copywriters. Often, full-service ad agencies consider their account executives partners with the client in promoting a product and aiding in marketing strategy. Nevertheless, the account executive usually does not have all the financial or strategic information available that the product manager does.

However, the similarity of the two positions leads to many crossovers—agency people changing jobs to work at a manufacturer, and vice versa. Industry sources say going from an agency to a manufacturer is the more difficult transfer, because a product manager needs more comprehensive skills.

MARKET RESEARCH. Many, if not most, of the jobs available in market research are at advertising agencies, which conduct massive surveys of buying habits, TV-viewing habits, and just about anything else, on behalf of their clients. But there are also quite a few companies whose sole business is market research. Probably the best-known, and certainly the biggest, is the A.C. Nielsen Co. (Northbrook, Ill.; 1982 revenues $654 million), renowned for its long experience in monitoring the television-viewing habits of Americans.

Market research can involve fascinatingly complex techniques to find out what consumers' reactions are. Almost everything in consumer-goods marketing—new products, advertising campaigns, buying locations, media—is researched and test-marketed before a full commitment is made. Yet at its most basic—and probably the easiest entry point for new graduates—all that market research involves is talking with consumers, face-to-face in shopping malls, or over the phone.

CONSULTING. Each and every function of the marketing process can be served by a host of specialized consultants in addition to advertising agencies and market research firms. Consulting companies range from one person with the right combination of knowledge and selling skills (in effect, he or she is selling himself or herself to the hiring company), to several hundred executives and their assistants. Generally, consultants are experienced marketing professionals who, having tired of the strictures of corporate life, strike out on their own. But just as there are many management consulting companies that hire graduates fresh out of business school, there is room for new graduates in the marketing consulting field.

One of the hotter areas in consulting is promotion. Promotion has a specific meaning in marketing—it is creating attention for a product through nonadvertising means. One of its commonest forms is couponing—you may have noticed the great increase in the number of coupons being offered on packages and in newspapers during the past few years. Other promotional tools range from toys in cereal boxes to free cars for million-dollar real-estate deals.

Over the past few years, industries where marketing expertise had been a low-level priority are rapidly becoming marketing meccas. One of these is banking. The series of banking deregulation rules that the U.S. government has established have suddenly turned the staid banking business into a veritable bazaar.

At Citibank NA (New York), one of the leading proponents of this trend, marketing training is sought in job candidates. "We're looking for a total relationship with our consumer banking customers, so that they will deal with us not just for a savings account or mortgage, but also pensions, financial planning, etc. Therefore, we carefully design our banking services to nurture that relationship," says Andre Block, vice-president of recruiting services for Citibank. "As a result, we look for some marketing expertise in our job candidates."

However, Block cautions that there is rarely a position like marketing manager into which new hires are dropped. "We have a free flow of people throughout our organization. Job titles are very fluid, and our workers must be able to withstand a fast pace and to have initiative."

Block says that many of the common market research techniques are used at Citibank: it test-markets new financial packages, and advertises heavily. New automated-teller machines, for example, were first tested in a lab that simulated an actual station, and the configuration was changed as a result of the tests. Additionally, the commercial market—banking services for businesses—is also requiring more and more marketing skills, as the financial officers of potential clients are reached through advertising and other media.

Another industry that is creating its own complementary marketing industry is electronics. Personal computers, electronic games, office-automation systems, and telecommunications equipment is changing and growing so quickly that a tremendous demand for market research has developed. It seems that the newer a market research company is in this field, the faster it grows. According to press accounts, Dataquest (San Jose, Calif.), grew from a staff of four in 1971 to 270; The Yankee Group (Boston) grew from four in 1977 to 65; and Future Computing Inc. (Richardson, Tex.) has bloomed from two in 1980 to 50. Such companies serve computer manufacturers by helping to decide what features their products must have to attract customers, as well as the business users of computers, who are having a hard time keeping up with the speed of technological progress in the field.

By Nicholas Basta, a New York-based journalist.

WHEN TO START LOOKING FOR A JOB

DON'T WAIT. START NOW. MOST EXPERTS AGREE IT WILL TAKE AT LEAST SIX MONTHS BEFORE YOU CAN NAIL DOWN THAT FIRST JOB

BW GUIDE TO CAREERS, FEBRUARY 1986, PP. 71–73

When do you start looking for a job? This is an important consideration for the soon-to-be-graduate because it takes at least six months to secure that first position. If you've been procrastinating—don't. The competition is tough out there and, because the process is time-consuming, the best time to begin your job-hunting campaign is now.

"Despite what career counselors, parents, or even professors advise, the majority of students don't begin job hunting until they're ready," says Robert Hopkins, director of the placement service at the University of Pittsburgh. "As a result, many of them miss some terrific opportunities." Many of the opportunities that Hopkins is referring to are interviews or job openings with employers that come through a school's placement service.

Companies in fields such as accounting, financial services, insurance, and retailing often recruit heavily during the fall term because they have management training programs which begin soon after graduation. The winter-spring recruiting schedule, however, is often just as active. It usually begins in February, but at many universities you must sign up for interviews in advance; often there is competition to get on the most popular companies' recruiting schedules.

There's little point in signing up, however, unless you have a fairly good idea of what you're looking for. "Many students underestimate the importance of the first part of the job search process, which is developing career and job awareness," says Nancy Arone Bassett, Associate Director of Career Services and Placement at Simmons College in Boston.

Career awareness means knowing which field or fields are most attractive to you and why. Job awareness involves knowing what fields are best suited to your skills and interests. "Some students arrive at college having already done the research and self-analysis this awareness requires, while some seniors still don't have a clue as to what they're going to do for a living," says Bassett.

Anna Litchfield, a Simmons College graduate, wasn't sure what her career interests were until she took a course on the stock market in the second semester of her junior year. "It got me excited about the possibility of working in the financial services area," says Litchfield, who majored in both economics and finance.

Having worked as a manager of a chocolate-chip cookie store and a bakery during her first two summers in college, Litchfield decided to apply to brokerage firms for summer employment between her junior and senior years. The only jobs she was offered were mail clerk and secretarial positions, which she didn't think would give her access to the people and information she wanted. So she offered her services for free to Dean Witter

Reynolds Inc., a securities firm, on the condition that she could circulate among the various departments.

Her strategy worked: she spent a month in a branch office in her hometown and another month-and-a-half at the firm's headquarters. "It was a great experience and helped me decide that the operations end of a financial services company was definitely for me," says Litchfield. (Operations is the processing area where all transactions are accounted for.)

When she returned to college in the fall, she began interviewing with employers who visited her campus. None of them, however, were quite what she was looking for. She began researching other potential employers on her own. One of the companies she identified, Fidelity Investments, a mutual fund company, posted a job opening for a librarian at her school's placement office. Even though she wasn't interested in that position, she went to visit the company's personnel director to introduce herself and explain what kind of position she'd like to apply for if one opened up.

The company kept her resume on file and contacted her five months later about a management trainee position in its operations division, Fidelity Service Co. Litchfield was one of 15 people being considered for three positions. Three months and 20 interviews later, she was offered one of the spots, just before graduating from Simmons. "Knowing what I wanted and contacting the company on my own initiative definitely helped me get the job," says Litchfield, whose grade-point average in college was "just average."

Students majoring in liberal arts subjects often don't have the exposure in the classroom to work world experiences, as Litchfield did. If you fall into that category, it's even more important that you begin exploring career possibilities through summer or part-time jobs. Working for an employer with whom you might want to get a permanent job upon graduation is an especially good idea.

"More and more companies are hiring students they've gotten to know through previous work experiences," says John Shingleton, director of placement at Michigan State University. "Co-op jobs and internships aren't just for engineering and computer science majors anymore. Retailers, food service, and packaging companies are among those employers who hire students from a variety of majors for summer and part time jobs."

English major Maria Caracciolo was able to determine her career objective—to work in the news media—through four internships she held during summers and winter breaks. Three were with newspapers; the fourth was at Cable News Network (CNN). Caracciolo received a job offer from CNN just as she was ready to graduate and accepted it.

> **Many students underestimate the importance of the first part of the job search process— developing career awareness, says Simmons' Bassett**

After several months, Caracciolo came to the realization that TV news really wasn't for her after all. Feeling somewhat disillusioned because she thought that she had carefully chosen the "right" field, Caracciolo decided to do more extensive research to make sure that her next career move was sound. "I talked to public relations professionals to find out if the pace of their work was as fast as news work, which was one aspect of the field I did like, and whether I could also put my writing and reporting skills to good use," says Caracciolo.

She liked what she found and subsequently sent her resume to public relations directors at banks, colleges, hospitals, and universities. Two months later, Caracciolo got a job offer from the corporate relations department of Manufacturers Hanover Trust. As an account administrator, she deals with clients and shareholders. "The moral of my story is that it pays to be flexible about the kinds of work you're willing to consider," she says.

If you've missed out on the opportunity to explore career options through summer work experiences or part-time jobs during the school year, you can do what Caracciolo did—set up informational interviews with people who are working in fields that appeal to you.

Spring break is a good time to arrange such interviews. Check with your placement or alumni office for the names of graduates in the field or fields that interest you. You'll get a better idea of what entry-level jobs involve if you talk to people who have only been out in the work world for a few years. It's also easier to arrange appointments with them than with higher-level people whose schedules are more hectic.

In addition to finding out what they do in their jobs, what they like and dislike about their work, ask how they got into the field and/or particular job. Be sure to send the people you interview for information a thank-you note. Good manners aside, you'll want to get back in touch with those contacts who were particularly helpful a few months down the road when you've developed a better handle on what job area you're going to direct your job-hunting efforts toward. They should be able to give you "inside information" about companies in the field that are hiring entry-level job hunters and the names of specific people to contact.

Targeting a cover letter/resume campaign to a carefully researched list of employers who you know hire job candidates with skills like yours is much more effective than a blitz approach to a wide variety of companies. "If you're graduating in May or June, it doesn't hurt to get in touch with employers you hope to interview with in March or April," says Don DeCamp, vice-president of operations for Snelling & Snelling, which has 500 placement offices in the U.S. "An increasing number of employers, including small-and medium-size companies, are able to project what their personnel needs will be months in advance partly as a result of the growing use of computers, which allows them to do long-range planning."

Your chances of getting an interview are much higher if you take the time to write an individualized cover letter to each company explaining why working there interests you, what kind of job you're interested in and why it's worth that employer's while to see you.

A follow-up phone call is smart because many people don't respond unless you're writing at the recommendation of a friend or colleague. Find out if there's a possibility of arranging a preliminary interview during spring break. If the employer isn't interested in interviewing you until you're available for employment, say that you'll be in touch to arrange an interview shortly after you graduate.

In some industries, including the media, advertising, and public relations, employers usually don't extend job offers in advance of specific positions opening up. That's why Michael Brooks (pseudonym) waited until the time of his graduation from the University of Massachusetts at Amherst to contact advertising agencies in New York City. He received only two interview offers in response to the 40 resumes he sent out. Neither of those resulted in a job, so Brooks began exploring options in related media fields, including technical and newspaper writing and public relations work.

After two months of living on his savings and having no luck landing a job, Brooks resigned himself to doing temporary work while continuing his job search. Over the next 10 months he worked as a housepainter, a shoe salesman, and a clerk-typist.

Although he had a strong gradepoint average, Brooks had spent most of his summers working in resorts and hadn't developed contacts in his chosen field. "It wasn't until I couldn't even set up interviews that I realized the importance of having contacts who were familiar with my work or willing to give me a chance," says Brooks.

It was with the help of a friend that Brooks eventually landed a job as a news assistant for a major business publication. The friend kept him posted on hiring activity and suggested the name of the person he should contact.

Although he enjoys his job and believes that there are good possibilities for advancement, Brooks hasn't given up his original goal to work in advertising. In his free time, he has been promoting a line of clothes for a small company in exchange for a percentage of the sales.

Although it was a year after graduating before Brooks found his first professional job, career placement professionals and employers say that waiting until you graduate to begin your job search doesn't necessarily preclude your getting a good job sooner.

"Job hunting requires a certain amount of momentum that many students don't have until they're faced with the reality of having no more classes to attend," says University of Pittsburgh's Hopkins. "Without momentum, it's hard to withstand the inevitable setbacks that are part of looking for a job," he says.

Most experts agree that you will need to spend a minimum of six months looking for your first job. That means keeping yourself informed on a regular basis of potential interview possibilities through your school's placement office, the help-wanted ads in the newspaper of the city where you're planning to work, and through contacts (alumni, professors, former employers). Following up with letters and phone calls to arrange interviews is a must.

There's no reason to be discouraged if you're an average student or don't have summer or part-time experiences related to the kind of job you're looking for. "If you can articulate what it is you'd like to do, even if it's a long-term objective such as being a manager in a business environment, and let an employer know that you're committed to finding a job that will help you reach that goal, you stand a good chance of getting hired," says DeCamp. "Enthusiasm and the willingness to learn by working hard are prized qualities among today's productivity-conscious employers."

By Peggy Schmidt, whose latest book is Making It Big in the City *(McGraw-Hill)*

THE HIRING PROCESS – HOW IT WORKS

YOUR OPTIMAL JOB SEARCH STRATEGIES MUST INCORPORATE ALL FACTORS IN THE HIRING EQUATIONS COMPANIES USE

BW GUIDE TO CAREERS, SPECIAL EDITION, PP. 29–32

Company A has figured out that it needs 100 trainees each year to feed the pipeline that leads from assistant manager to group vice president in its retailing operation. It interviews 2,250 seniors on 150 campuses, invites 1,200 for second interviews with district managers, and makes offers to 300 finalists in order to reach its 100 recruit goal.

To attract the right college seniors to its interview schedule, it:

■ holds information meetings prior to the announced interview date;

■ advertises in campus publications and newspapers;

■ contacts faculty members, coaches, and other advisors who have heavy student contact;

■ disseminates recruiting brochures that describe the company and the type of student it seeks.

Company B, a statewide commercial bank, is planning to open 10 branches next year. It plans to hire 50 new entry-level tellers and customer service reps through ads in the local newspapers and by word-of-mouth referrals.

The owner of Company C, a small advertising agency, needs someone to call on prospective accounts, a job he used to do himself but now has no time for. He may rely on an employment agency to do the screening and send him only candidates that meet his specifications. He also places a blind ad in the paper so that he doesn't have to reply to unsuitable applicants or receive a blizzard of phone inquiries. He calls a few of the area colleges asking placement directors to let any "bright young people willing to work hard and learn the business" know of his opening. Despite his attempts to recruit, he may wind up hiring the daughter of his tennis partner just because he knows her and she's available.

Companies A, B, and C may all be offering positions that *you* could qualify for. How do you find out about them, position yourself for that all-important interview, and receive the prize—a job offer? An understanding of the various ways that companies hire college graduates can help you develop job search strategies that will start you on the road to getting hired.

ON-CAMPUS RECRUITMENT. Many national and regional companies recruit on campus for graduates to fill their entry-level management positions in either a formal training program or a trainee position in a particular department. Although methods vary from company to company, the basic procedures are pretty much the same. Campus recruitment is essentially a screening process to identify those with the basic qualifications the company has identified as desirable in its managers. Some companies even institute a screening process before the campus interview by "prescreening" resumes that are submitted to them through the placement office and then specifying who will be allowed to sign up for an interview.

The campus interviewer may be a member of the personnel department or a line manager in an area the company is recruiting for. During a typical 30-minute session, the interviewer will make a preliminary assessment of your qualifications, background, and career goals. He or she will pay attention to your interpersonal skills, ability to communicate, professional attitude and dress, ease in social situations, and other variables that cannot be assessed through a resume or transcript. You will also have an opportunity to ask questions about the company. Asking knowledgeable questions that demonstrate an awareness of products, services, and company goals gleaned from the annual report and recruiting brochure shows that you are interested in the company and know how to do research.

At the close, be sure the interviewer indicates what the next steps in the process will be and when you may expect a response from the company. If you do not hear by the specified date, it's appropriate to call. It is a good idea to make a note of the interviewer's name, title, and address for follow-up correspondence. A thank-you note is proper.

> Be sure the interviewer
> indicates what the next steps
> of the process are
> and also when you can expect
> a response

APPLYING DIRECTLY. On-campus recruiting is a very efficient way for you to make contact with a wide range of companies. But how do you reach Company B, which advertises only in its local area, or Company C, which is truly in the hidden job market, requiring special techniques?

"Most students don't start out early enough," says Jack Erdlen, head of the Employment Management Association. "You need to understand the jobs you're qualified for. At least a month's preparation is required before you start going into companies. Get help from people, get help from the library, start with your friends. Read newspapers for news of companies moving into town, who's getting a government contract, reports of promotions and new appointments." Bob Green, a recent graduate in communications from Syracuse University, used this last tactic to get his entry job in television. After reading about the start-up of a statewide TV network, he kept calling the director to tell him of his interest. Three months later, when the director was ready to hire an assistant, he immediately thought of Bob.

Concentrating on one local area is another way to tackle the job market. "Geographical targeting maximizes the amount of activity and contacts a job hunter can generate," advises Dr. Howard Figler, director of the career center at the University of Texas at Austin. "Use the phone to find out who's hiring; it's a more efficient use of your time than writing letters or pounding the pavement."

Networking is a technique recommended by most employment experts as a way of finding out where openings can be found and what it takes to get hired. Many colleges ask their alumni to serve as mentors and will give their names to new graduates. The best way to network is to start with people you know—friends, relatives, neighbors, faculty members, former teachers and employers. Attend meetings of the local chapters of trade and professional associations; visit trade shows, career fairs, and open houses. You will be meeting people in the field you are interested in, often people at high levels who may be approached directly for advice and information in these more informal situations.

The library is also an excellent resource for finding directories to every industry from advertising to tourism with names of companies and individuals to write or call. In some cases, directories may be the only way to find out about companies in your field of interest. American Airlines, for example, does not advertise its openings, yet it filled 250 entry-level slots in the Chicago area alone last year through job-hunters who applied on their own.

Don't overlook the want ads. A recent Employment Management Association survey reports that of 291 employers who responded, 31% got their new hires through recruitment advertising. Other major sources were: employee referrals (27%), employment agencies (24%) and direct contacts (8%).

The high rate of hiring through employee referrals "emphasizes the importance of contacting friends and acquaintances when you are looking for a job," notes Jack Erdlen of the EMA. Referrals from members of the community also influence hiring managers, as do those from faculty members and placement officers. Kathy Beechem, director of employment and recruiting at First National Bank of Cincinnati, advises students to make themselves known to their college placement staff members because they are often asked to suggest qualified students.

Many students wonder whether they should use employment agencies. Experts caution that agencies will not take care of your job hunt for you. They rarely seek new college graduates unless they have office skills or directly related experience. Temporary agencies may be better bets because they offer the opportunities to get work experience in your field in a variety of settings; once you get exposure as a "temp," there is a chance of a permanent offer.

The direct contact—sending a letter and resume

WHAT INTERVIEWERS FOCUS ON DURING THE INTERVIEW

First impressions. Firm handshake; don't just offer your fingers! Conventional business attire; suits for men and women. Eye contact maintained briefly from time to time. Relaxed but poised demeanor; good manners.

Information about you. Academic record; creative and intellectual capabilities. Extracurricular activities; how you use discretionary time. Work experience (summer jobs, internships, volunteer work). Character and personality, e.g. maturity, initiative, energy level, alertness, sense of humor, confidence, integrity. Ability to work well with others; leadership and teamwork. Articulateness; how well you express your ideas. Career plans and goals; do you have a sense of direction? Knowledge of and interest in the industry and company; how motivated are you in pursuing your goals?

Information about the company. Presentation by interviewer of company structure, goals, products and services and specifics of the position to be filled. Opportunity for you to ask informed questions and display your interest and seriousness of purpose.

Conclusion. Review of next steps you should take, e.g. complete application form, supply references. Procedure company will follow in the hiring process and when you may expect a decision or indication of further interest.

"cold" to a company without knowing about their needs is popular among college students because it's the "least ego-taxing way of seeking employment," says Bill Corwin, assistant director of career services at Princeton University. "They can say, 'See, Mom, I'm looking for a job.'" But it's less effective, as the EMA study shows, accounting for less than 8% of hires. "A standard cover letter saying that you're graduating from X College and are looking for a job, and here's my resume, and I'll call you next week to set up an appointment, is just not going to do it," continues Corwin. "Your message must stand out, be different from the mass." Corwin recalled a letter he received when he was college relations officer at Bankers Trust. "Here was a guy from a second tier state school whose only work experience was as a special education teacher but whose letter outlining his skills and motivation for banking persuaded us to interview and hire him."

ADVICE ON LETTERS AND RESUMES. Jack Erdlen of the EMA concurs on the importance of good letters and resumes. "Your letter and resume must be tailored to the industry. Write a special resume for each type of job you're applying for. Think of your skills in terms of job requirements," he urges.

Other personnel officers echo this advice. They want to see evidence in your resume that you have some interest and commitment to the industry, even if you are a liberal arts major who has not yet worked in the field. For example:

■ Stanley Mason, manager of college relations and equal employment for J.C. Penney, looks for work or extracurricular experience related to retailing or sales.

■ For Burston-Marsteller, one of the largest public relations firms in the world, recruiter Alan Gaynor hopes to find graduates with some writing experience and courses in journalism and communications.

■ "Hoteling is a general skill," according to Steve Trombetti, media relations manager for the American Hotel and Motel Association. Hotel managers seek sales ability, general business awareness, and good interpersonal skills.

■ For the financial field, evidence of quantitative and analytical skills and an interest in finance from coursework or job exposure is what counts with Allan Wechsler, vice president at Thomson McKinnon Securities, Inc., one of the largest privately held investment firms.

The importance of written communications tailored to the specific industry cannot be overstressed. The time, effort, and research you put into preparing them will help you in both getting the interview and making a good impression.

THE HIRING INTERVIEW. Your first formal interview with a company will probably be with the personnel office. You may be asked to fill out an application blank. Do this willingly and carefully even though much of the information requested is on your resume. The personnel representative may ask you a few routine questions before sending you to the hiring manager. Or personnel may conduct a thorough screening interview similar to those done on campus, and send on only a few selected applicants for the hiring manager's consideration. Small companies (under 300 employees) usually do not have a personnel department. The department manager or the owner will probably conduct the interview.

The kinds of questions likely to be asked at hiring interviews are substantially the same as those mentioned in connection with the campus screening interview. Academic record, work and extracurricular activities, career goals as well as communications and interpersonal skills are the factors most often evaluated. Most interviewers want you to be comfortable and will try to help establish a relaxed atmosphere before getting down to business. "Students think there is some kind of mystique to the interview, but there really isn't," says Larry McKinley, director of executive and professional

---

> Most significant in the final decision are interpersonal skills, leadership, and a commitment to the industry

---

recruiting at NCR Corp. "Interviewers are trying to make the best match, not give anyone a hard time. They want to give you the chance to express your accomplishments, your record of success." Stanley Haude, personnel supervisor for advertising at Procter & Gamble, encourages students to use the interview to their advantage. "Even the top students we see do not have enough self-confidence and are reluctant to merchandise their background during the interview."

Companies that hire college graduates for management training programs tend to make the hiring interview an all-day affair, scheduling interviews with several different managers and perhaps a lunch with some recent graduates who are currently in the program. The hiring decision is usually made by a consensus of the interviewers with the input of the campus recruiter.

When you are being hired directly into a specific position, the manager you will be working for typically conducts the interview and makes the hiring decision, sometimes consulting others who met you.

References from former supervisors and faculty members are usually checked before the decision is finalized, as is a routine check with your college's registrar to make sure you are a bona fide graduate.

FACTORS IN THE HIRING DECISION. The decision to select one from among many well-qualified candidates is based on subtle factors beyond having the stated credentials for the job. There seems to be unanimous agreement among personnel and placement professionals that the most significant factors in the final hiring decision are interpersonal skills, leadership ability, and a commitment to working in that industry.

Many of the industries open to liberal arts and business graduates—finance, retailing, hospitality, sales, marketing—are in the service sector, where the ability

---

A PRO'S ADVICE ON GETTING HIRED

"The student who is well prepared is the student who is hired. Having a warm and winning personaility is very helpful, but the less attractive, less ebullient student can still stand out by knowing something about the industry and the company." Patricia Rose, director of career planning and placement, University of Pennsylvania.

"It's a mistake to try to be something you're not. Don't be misled by the mystique of what it supposedly takes to get a job." Larry McKinley, director of executive and professional recruiting, NCR Corp.

"Persistence and determination; with those, you can make 100 mistakes but you'll get hired by someone." Dr. Howard Figler, director of the career center, University of Texas at Austin.

"Saying 'I love working with people' doesn't do the trick." Barbara Hopkins, manager of personnel services, Chicago office, American Airlines.

"No magic formula; be yourself and know the industry." Kirk Miklavic, corporate personnel, The Sheraton Corporation.

"Creative, innovative, problem-solving skills—the ability to tackle a problem and come up with a solution—are key in the consumer goods industry." Stanley Haude, personnel supervisor, advertising department, Procter & Gamble.

"Read between the lines, don't look only at the obvious stuff. Who does the company really hire? What are their values?" Bill Corwin, assistant director of career services, Princeton University.

"The biggest turnoff for me is dishonesty. Don't say what you think the interviewer wants to hear if you don't believe it yourself." Richard Plaza, national staffing manager, Webber Consumer Markets.

"The ability to establish interpersonal rapport quickly, since customer relations are extremely important in almost every position in banking." Kathy Beechem, director of employment and recruiting, First National Bank of Cincinnati.

"There is no typical way to get hired. Decisions are often made by stumbling and fumbling. Jobs open up overnight in companies." Jack Erdlen, executive director, Employment Management Association.

to relate to customers is crucial. This skill is singled out through such comments as:

"Well-spoken; articulate."

"Present themselves in a professional way yet stay relaxed."

"Can communicate with all levels of management."

Sending a letter and resume cold is popular, but studies show it accounts for only 8% of hires

---

"Dynamic, confident; someone with a sense of presence."

Several experts consider communications skills so important that they urge students to take a course in writing or public speaking.

Leadership is another quality highly prized in the selection process as it demonstrates qualities of initiative and accomplishment—what one does without being required to. Comments such as:

"Solid record of achievement in extracurricular activities."

"Someone who can originate action—self-starter."

"Someone who has taken a project from beginning to end."

"We hired someone who started his own business before he went for his degree."

Although companies value academic achievement, and expect a "solid" academic record, they prefer a 3.0 student who headed the debate team to a 4.0 shrinking violet. GPAs below 3.0 can be compensated for by outside activities, but for some competitive training programs, employers insist on excellence.

Commitment to the industry is the third most frequently mentioned criterion for job-getting success. As Richard Plaza, national staffing manager for Paine Webber Consumer Markets puts it: "The student who comes to me saying 'I'm thinking of working for Procter & Gamble, and I'm thinking of going to graduate school, and I'm thinking of working for Paine Webber' is not going to have as good a chance as the young person who says, 'I want to work in the financial services industry and I'm looking only at the financial services industry.'" This, of course, requires students to do some self-analysis and research to identify the industry in which they want to use their skills and talents. Companies want to see that applicants have done their homework and have a realistic idea of the industry.

There is substantial agreement among hiring authorities about what it takes to get hired. The most important job-hunting skills can be learned. Even the lack of an exemplary college record can be compensated for by diligent preparation in the job campaign. Start now! Use the facilities of your placement office and the other resources and contacts that you already have. Take a few initial steps, and you'll find that the process is one that you can master and even enjoy.

Sandra Grundfest, Ed. D., has a private career and educational consulting practice in Princeton, New Jersey. She was formerly assistant director of career services at Princeton University and careers editor at Peterson's Guides.